Universal Access to
Outdoor Recreation:
A Design Guide

a design guide

universal
access
to outdoor
recreation

PLAE, Inc.
in conjunction
with other public and
private partners

*with special thanks to
the USDA Forest Service
and Sea Reach, Ltd.*

PLAE inc.

Berkeley, CA

This book is a publication of PLAE, Inc. of Berkeley, California.
It is available exclusively from MIG Communications, 1802 Fifth Street, Berkeley, CA 94710 USA
(510) 845-0953; fax (510) 845-8750

Managing Editor: David Driskell
Assistant Editor: Steve Wohlford
Illustrator: Nana Kirk
Art Director: Anne Endrusick
Production Assistant: Christopher Hamilton
Copyeditor: Mi-Yung Rhee
Indexer: Nancy Freedom

Library of Congress Catalog Number: 93-092806

ISBN 0-944661-25-4

Limits of Liability. The authors, editors, publishers, contributors, and others involved in the preparation of this document assume no risk or liability arising from the application of this information in any way whatsoever. The guidelines contained in this document are not standards and have not been adopted by any agency or jurisdiction of the federal government. The document should not be construed as a substitute for the ADA Guidelines, the Uniform Federal Accessibility Standards, or the applicable accessibility codes or standards of the state or jurisdiction in which the document is used. In addition, these guidelines do not incorporate fire codes, plumbing codes, building codes, electrical codes, structural code requirements, or life safety standards.

Those who make use of these guidelines in the planning, design, and management of outdoor recreation settings are responsible for the accessibility and the safety of the environments they plan, design, and manage. The material contained in this book is intended for use by organizations and communitites in the process of developing their own guidelines which, ultimately, must be adapted to local conditions.

contents

foreword

Project Play and Learning in Adaptable Environments, Inc. (PLAE), a nonprofit, multi-disciplinary organization, is pleased to present *Universal Access to Outdoor Recreation: A Design Guide*. This book, developed through a public/private partnership between PLAE and the USDA Forest Service, presents a unique approach for incorporating universal designs into the outdoor recreation environment based on customer expectations and related levels of accessibility.

In the mid-1980s, as a result of a Presidential Panel on Outdoor Recreation, the Forest Service challenged its Federal partners in public land stewardship, its customers, and corporate America to embark on a National Recreation Strategy—a strategy to meet the overwhelming demand for recreation and leisure activities across our country. Three guiding principles were developed to help focus the effort—Create Customer Satisfaction; Forge Partnerships; and Pursue Excellence. PLAE's development of this design guide is a direct outgrowth of the National Recreation Strategy.

People are drawn to outdoor recreation for different reasons. Some seek the solitude of the primitive backcountry, others a rustic campsite nestled in the woods, while others look for a social setting with convenient facilities. No matter the reason or the setting, they all seek to enjoy an outdoor experience.

Yet, for a large and growing segment of our country's population, the vast majority of public land recreation sites are not accessible. Historically, recreation facilities and programs were designed for the "average" person, which generally excluded people with disabilities. When you consider their family and friends, choices for a desirable recreation experience are limited for far more than 100 million people, nearly half of the U.S. population.

In response, the USDA Forest Service has been instrumental in developing design guidelines which integrate the principles of universal design across a spectrum of recreation settings—designs which are responsive to a diversity of ages, abilities, and cultures. These principles bring together customer choices in a variety of landscapes, from urban, highly developed areas to wild, primitive settings, fostering a sense of dignity, independence, and social integration. When we design and build campgrounds, restrooms, trails, and other visitor facilities and programs to accommodate the needs of all individuals, we improve the experience and comfort for everyone. Universal design just makes good business sense!

With majestic mountains, deep rugged canyons, high pristine lakes, wild rivers, immense forests, and open meadows, America's public lands offer countless adventures for outdoor recreation. This partnership embraces the comprehensive knowledge and experience of the USDA Forest Service and other leaders in the field. I urge you to join the efforts of the many public and private partners involved in the development of this design guide. Through universal design, integration, and a positive attitude, we can ensure that everyone has access to America's Great Outdoors.

Susan Goltsman, Director
PLAE, Inc.

preface　The Americans with Disabilities Act (ADA) was signed on July 26, 1990. This marked the end of a long struggle as well as a new beginning—a beginning for Americans with disabilities to enjoy basic human rights with dignity and a beginning for all Americans to take responsibility.

Passage of the ADA signified the world's first comprehensive declaration of equality for people with disabilities and made this country an international leader on this basic human rights issue. The world is now watching to see how we use this act, and how we will remove the physical and social barriers that exist throughout our society. Our success or failure in keeping the promise of the ADA will affect the lives of the more than half billion individuals with disabilities throughout the world.

The ADA does more than make the American dream of equality a reality for Americans with disabilities; it offers fresh testimony to our nation's greatness. It demonstrates how we can advance the cause of civil rights.

The country has made tremendous advances since the ADA was passed, and changes have been introduced that will transform people's lives. Federal departments and agencies have been charged with taking a leadership role in implementing the various directives of the ADA relating to employment, transportation, communications, and public accommodations. This design guide is a response to that charge.

Establishing guidelines for universal design in outdoor recreation environments has been a challenge. While many guidelines have been developed for the "built" or city environment, there has been little information available regarding universal design in outdoor park and recreation settings. The guidelines presented here are among the first to comprehensively address this frontier.

The project's scope required the working partnership of many people, including park and recreation managers, consumers, and service providers. Their collective knowledge, expertise, design philosophy, and efforts have contributed to a document that is both thorough and dynamic. In particular, acknowledgment and thanks are owed to the following organizations and individuals:

■ In the **USDA Forest Service**: Joe Meade, leader of the National Accessibility Program; Chuck Frayer, Mobility Technical Specialist and Pacific Northwest (PNW) Accessibility Manager; and Ruth Doyle, Landscape Architect, for their leadership in developing the guide. Many of the agency's 350 landscape architects as well as architects and engineers were involved in various dimensions of the project. Of special note: Robert Ross, Chief Landscape Architect; Brian Kermeen, Landscape Architect (LA); Ken Kunert, LA; Nancy Ruthenbeck, Recreation Staff Officer and LA; Glen France, LA; Warren Bacon, Regional LA; Stan Specht, Regional Access Specialist and LA; Carolyn Holbrook, Assistant Director of Recreation—Planning and Design; Janet Zeller, Regional Access Specialist and educator; and Al Seltzer and Jane Leche, writers/editors.

■ At **Sea Reach, Ltd.**, Brian O'Callaghan, writer and researcher, and business partner Susan Jurasz.

■ At **Wilderness Inquiry**, Director Greg Lais, and at **Beneficial Designs**, Director Peter Axelson, for their reviews and valuable input. Dr. Ed Hamilton, Director of Research at the **National Center on Accessibility, Indiana University at Bloomington**, was of great assistance, while the **Paralyzed Veterans of America** and many of its chapters nationwide provided valuable assistance in gaining broad consumer participation.

■ In the **USDI National Park Service**, Dave Park, Chief of the Special Programs and Populations Branch.

■ In the **USDI Bureau of Reclamation**, Karen Megorden, Manager of the PNW Region's Accessibility Program and LA.

■ Staff members of the **Architectural and Transportation Barriers Compliance Board** for their valuable technical assistance. The **Bureau of Land Management**, the **Army Corps of Engineers, Recreation Division**, and the many state and local park and recreation entities for their review of this project.

■ And finally, the staff at **Moore Iacofano Goltsman** and **PLAE, Inc.**, for carrying this project through to final editing, design, and production: David Driskell, Managing Editor; Steve Wohlford, Assistant Editor; Nana Kirk, Illustrator; Anne Endrusick, Art Director; Christopher Hamilton, Production Assistant; and Mi-Yung Rhee, Copyeditor. Thanks also to indexer Nancy Freedom.

introduction and general concepts

I

purpose and organization

Since the barrier-free design movement began in 1959, there has been considerable progress in the design and construction of accessible buildings and facilities. However, this progress has been primarily in the highly developed built environment. Many aspects of the outdoor recreation environment remain inaccessible to people with disabilities.

One of the reasons outdoor recreation environments have lagged in providing accessibility to people of all abilities has been the lack of technical specifications on how to design accessible facilities in outdoor settings. Although some specifications have been developed for outdoor facilities such as campgrounds, picnic areas, and trails, they have been limited in scope. In addition, there has been no consistent method for applying such specifications in recreation settings, where site characteristics and recreation needs can vary widely.

Universal Access to Outdoor Recreation provides a single, comprehensive source for accessibility specifications related to outdoor recreation environments. It also seeks to provide a logical, consistent framework for the application of such specifications in diverse recreation settings. It has been developed through a working partnership of designers, engineers, architects, and researchers with and without disabilities. These individuals and their associated organizations represent the country's key players in the provision and management of outdoor recreation settings and in the design of accessible outdoor environments. Their combined expertise has resulted in a document that will help designers and managers of outdoor environments ensure a spectrum of recreation opportunities that can be enjoyed by people of all abilities.

Addressing Accessibility Issues: an Ongoing Process

Providing accessibility in outdoor recreation settings is extremely complex. *Universal Access to Outdoor Recreation* seeks to address the full spectrum of recreation needs by encouraging environmental designs that provide a diversity of recreation opportunities. In doing so, the book focuses on issues of physical access. However, issues of program access are equally important for ensuring that recreation opportunities are accessible to everyone. These issues will be addressed through the continuing process of addressing accessibility concerns in the outdoor environment.

This document is an important milestone in that process. However, the guidelines presented here are subject to change as new information becomes available and the process of dialogue and education continues. They provide information for consideration when designing outdoor recreation facilities for use by all members of the community, irrespective of age or ability (mental, physical, or sensory). *They are not standards.* Rather, they are suggested guidelines for use by administrators, architects, landscape architects, engineers, recreation planners, interpreters, individuals, and organizations interested in access to outdoor recreation facilities.

In preparing this document, a wide range of empirical research, approved technical provisions, and other relevant design manuals were examined. In addition, earlier draft versions of the document have undergone a broad and extensive public review. Copies were distributed to over 300 advocacy groups and park and recreation agencies at the municipal, state, and Federal levels.

Document Structure

Universal Access to Outdoor Recreation is presented in four chapters:

I.   **Introduction and General Concepts** provides an overview of accessibility concepts and definitions that will help the reader understand and apply the information presented in Chapters II, III, and IV.

II.   **The Outdoor Recreation Environment** discusses the differences between the built environment and the outdoor recreation environment and introduces the Recreation Opportunity Spectrum (ROS) as a land management tool for answering questions about when accessibility is expected, where it is expected, and at what level of accommodation it is expected.

III.   **Applying the Guidelines** discusses issues related to site planning and design, and illustrates the application of the design guidelines (presented in Chapter IV) in recreation settings with different ROS classifications.

IV.   **Design Guidelines** presents technical specifications for the various components of outdoor recreation sites that should be applied to achieve the desired level of accessibility. These guidelines are based on the ADA Accessibility Guidelines (ADAAG) and empirical research related to access in outdoor environments.

The final sections of the book include a discussion of **How To Measure Slopes**, a **Slope Conversion Table**, an **ADA Comparison Table** that provides a quick reference for comparing the design guidelines of this book against ADAAG; a **Glossary** of key terms; a list of **References**; and an **Index**.

people with disabilities

(adapted from Institute of Medicine 1991)

Disability is an issue that affects every individual, community, neighborhood, and family in the United States. It is more than a medical issue; it is a costly social, public health, and moral issue.

- About 43 million Americans (one in every five) have disabling conditions that interfere with their life activities.

- More than 9 million people have physical or mental conditions that keep them from being able to work, attend school, or maintain a household.

- More than half of the 4-year increase in life expectancy between 1970 and 1987 is accounted for by time spent with activity limitations.

- Disabilities are disproportionately represented among minorities, the elderly, and lower socioeconomic populations.

- Of the current 75-year life expectancy, a newborn can be expected to experience an average of 13 years with an activity limitation.

- Annual disability-related costs to the nation total more than $170 billion.

Disability is the expression of a physical or mental limitation in a social context— the gap between a person's capabilities and the demands of the environment. People with such functional limitations are not inherently disabled, (i.e., incapable of carrying out their personal, familial, and social responsibilities). It is the interaction of their physical or mental limitations with social and environmental factors that determines whether they have a disability.

The pattern of conditions that cause disability is complex and difficult to summarize. For young adults, mobility limitations such as those caused by spinal cord injuries, orthopedic impairments, and paralysis are the most common causes. For middle-aged and older adults, chronic diseases, especially heart and circulatory problems, predominate as causes of limitation. Figure 1 shows the prevalence of the main causes of activity limitation for different age groups.

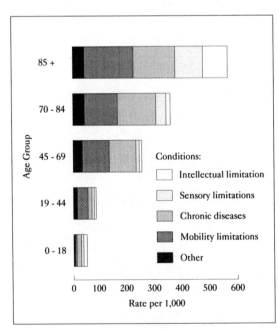

Figure 1. *Prevalence of main causes of activity limitation, by age, 1983-1985. (Source: Institute of Medicine 1991.)*

Understanding "Disability"

There are two major conceptual frameworks in the field of disability: the International Classification of Impairments, Disabilities, and Handicaps (ICIDH), and the "functional limitation," or Nagi, framework, which is not accompanied by a classification system. Both frameworks are used widely and both have four basic concepts. The Nagi framework is presented in this document because of its conceptual clarity and terminology.

The Nagi framework describes what is called "the disabling process." The four concepts or stages of that process are pathology, impairment, functional limitation, and disability. Figure 2 summarizes the four stages of the Nagi framework.

Pathology ▶	Impairment ▶	Functional Limitation ▶	Disability
Interruption or interference of normal bodily processes or structures.	Loss and/or abnormality of mental, emotional, physiological, or anatomical structure or function; includes all losses or abnormalities, not just those attributable to active patholgy; also includes pain.	Restriction or lack of ability to perform an action or activity in the manner or within the range considered normal that results from impairment.	Inability or limitation in performing socially defined activities and roles expected of individuals within a social and physical environment.
Level of Reference	*Level of Reference*	*Level of Reference*	*Level of Reference*
Cells and tissues.	Organs and organ systems.	Organism — action or activity performance (consistent with the purpose or function of the organ or organ system)	Society — task performance within the social and cultural context
Example	*Example*	*Example*	*Example*
Denervated muscle in arm due to trauma.	Atrophy of muscle.	Cannot pull with arm.	Change of job; can no longer swim recreationally.

Figure 2. *An overview of the Nagi model: pathology, impairment, functional limitation, and disability. (Source: Institute of Medicine 1991)*

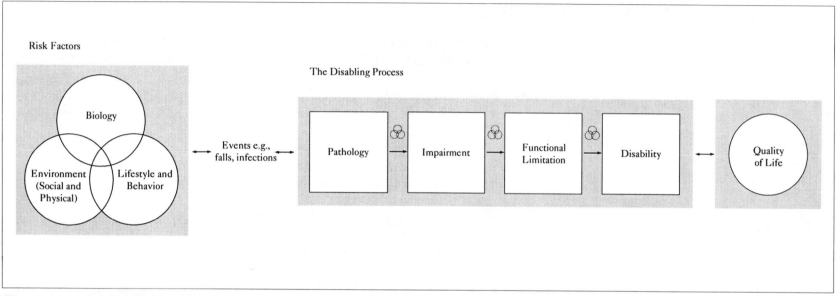

Figure 3. *Model of disability, showing the interaction of the disabling process, quality of life, and risk factors. (Source: Institute of Medicine 1991)*

The Committee on a National Agenda for the Prevention of Disabilities developed a model for understanding disability by building on the conceptual framework of the Nagi model as well as that of the ICIDH, placing them within the appropriate context of health and social issues. Summarized in Figure 3, this model depicts the interactive effects of biological, environmental (physical and social), and lifestyle and behavioral risk factors that influence each stage of the disabling process; the relationship of the disabling process to the quality of life; and the stages of the disabling process that often precede disability.

■ **Risk Factors.** Risk factors are biological, environmental (social and physical), and lifestyle or behavioral characteristics that are causally associated with health-related conditions. These factors have significant implications for the disabling process.

■ **Quality of Life.** The quality of life concept subsumes many aspects of personal well-being that are not directly related to health. As depicted in Figure 3, quality of life affects and is affected by the outcomes of each stage of the disabling process.

Research indicates that a person's perception of quality of life influences his or her responses to potentially disabling conditions and, therefore, outcomes. In turn, each successive stage in the disabling process poses an increasing threat of diminished quality of life. Measures that reduce this threat—for example, providing assistive technology that enables an individual to remain autonomous in at least some roles or modifying the work site to accommodate a person's limitations—can be effective interventions for preventing disability.

■ **The Disabling Process.** At the center of the model in Figure 3 is the disabling process. A variety of personal, societal, and environmental factors can influence the progression of a disabling condition from pathology to disability. They can also affect the degree of limitation or disability a person experiences and the occurrence of secondary conditions. A few of these factors are health status, psychological state, socioeconomic status, educational attainment and vocational training, climate, and the presence of multiple conditions and disabilities.

Although the model seems to indicate a unidirectional progression from pathology to impairment to functional limitation to disability, and although such progressions often occur, progression from one stage to another is not always the case. An individual with a disabling condition might skip over components of the model, for example, when the public's attitude toward a disfiguring impairment causes no functional limitation but imposes a disability by affecting social interaction. Also, the effects of specific stages in the model can be moderated by such interventions as assistive devices. Similarly, environmental modification (e.g., elimination of physical obstacles and barriers) is an important form of disability prevention.

Disability is the product of a complex interactive process involving biological, behavioral, and environmental (social and physical) risk factors, and quality of life. Although disability always begins with a pathological condition, it is not inevitable—even for people with incurable diseases or injury-related conditions that carry the highest risks. There are usually, if not always, many points in the progression to disability at which to intervene and improve the quality of life for people with potentially disabling conditions.

accessibility: the movement and the law

1919

Congress authorizes a vocational rehabilitation program for veterans disabled during World War I.

1920

Congress extends coverage of the 1919 vocational rehabilitation program for veterans to include the general public.

1959

Birth of barrier-free design: publication of *Tentative Guide—Facilities in Public Buildings for Persons with Ambulatory Impairments* by Dr. Dwight York.

1961

ANSI publishes ANSI A117.1, *Making Buildings Accessible to and Usable by the Physically Handicapped.*

1964

Congress passes the Civil Rights Act (P.L.-88 352).

1965

Congress passes the Vocational Rehabilitation Amendment Act (PL 89-333).

continued

Figure 4. *Important developments in accessibility legislation and guidelines, 1919-1992.*

The word "accessible," when used in reference to people with disabilities, means different things to different people. It is also frequently misunderstood and misinterpreted (Park 1989). However, with the evolution of national standards that specify the ways in which accessibility must be provided, the term has acquired a very specific legal meaning.

The Uniform Federal Accessibility Standards (UFAS) defines a facility or site as being accessible if it "complies with *these standards* and . . . can be approached, entered, and used by physically disabled people" (ATBCB 1988a). This definition is important because it defines a facility or site as being accessible only if it meets both of these criteria: conformance with standards *and* usability (Park 1989). Simply providing physical access up to a required standard is not enough; people must be able to use the facility once physical access has been achieved. To be truly accessible, programs and facilities must offer the person with a disability an opportunity to achieve experiences similar to those offered to others.

The Movement Begins: 1919-1959

Accessibility as an issue of national concern is not new. It was first raised by the Congress in 1919 when it authorized a vocational rehabilitation program for veterans disabled during World War I. The program was extended the following year to include all disabled Americans (Kerpen et al. 1980).

In a similar manner, the post-World War II era was an important period for the development of accessibility rights and standards, providing the beginnings for the accessibility movement as we know it today. In the late 1940s and 1950s, the population of people with disabilities swelled due to the large numbers of severely injured and disabled veterans and the more than 400,000 victims of the great polio epidemics. This increase, coupled with advancements in medical care, rehabilitation, and expanding opportunities for educational and vocational training, led to growing numbers of people with disabilities ready to join the work force and society (Lusher 1989). This in turn led to a general increase in the demand for building standards, laws, and codes to provide a more accommodating environment for people with disabilities.

1968

Congress passes the Architectural Barriers Act (ABA) (P.L. 90-480).

1973

Congress passes the Rehabilitation Act (P.L. 93-112).

1978

Sections 502 and 504 of the Rehabilitation Act of 1973 (P.L. 93-112) are amended.

1982

ATBCB publishes *Minimum Guidelines and Requirements for Accessible Design* (MGRAD).

1984

ATBCB publishes *Uniform Federal Accessibility Standards* (UFAS).

1986

ANSI publishes revised version of ANSI A117.1 designated ANSI A117.7–1980.

1990

Congress passes the Americans with Disabilities Act (ADA) (P.L. 101-336)

1991

ATBCB publishes *Americans with Disabilities Act Accessibility Guidelines for Buildings and Facilities* (ADAAG).

Figure 4, continued. *Important developments in accessibility legislation and guidelines, 1919-1992.*

The First National Standard: ANSI A117.1

In 1959, the President's Committee on Employment of the Handicapped, the National Society for Crippled Children, and the American Standards Institute sponsored a project to develop the first national standards for accessibility.[1] This project culminated with the publication of a draft document in 1961 entitled *Making Buildings Accessible to and Usable by the Physically Handicapped*, also known as ANSI A117.1.[2]

Publication of ANSI A117.1 was concurrent with a national education campaign aimed at ensuring the adoption of accessibility specifications by state bodies. In 1965, through the concerted efforts of various public and private agencies, twenty-four states had taken some type of action towards implementing ANSI standards through legislation or adoption into local building codes (ATBCB 1974, in Steinfeld et al. 1978). This effort was ultimately frustrated, however, by the fact that legislation in the various states was not comprehensive, and sanctions to ensure compliance were never developed (Steinfeld et al. 1978).

ANSI A117.1 was adopted and published in final form in 1971, detailing the minimum requirements for removal of physical barriers to people using public buildings and facilities. ANSI A117.1 subsequently formed the technical basis for the first accessibility standards adopted by the Federal government and most state governments (ATBCB 1988a). The ANSI standards were revised based on extensive research that began in 1980. They were then presented in a document that was circulated in draft form until it was officially adopted and published in 1986. This current edition of the ANSI standard (redesignated ANSI 117.1–1980) "has generally been accepted by the private sector and has been recommended for use by the Council of American Building Officials" (ATBCB 1988a).

1.   The President's Committee on Employment of the Handicapped, the National Society for Crippled Children, and the American Standards Institute are known today, respectively, as the President's Committee on Employment of People with Disabilities, National Easter Seal Society, and American National Standards Institute (ANSI).
2.   ANSI is a nongovernmental, national organization that publishes a wide variety of voluntary standards. ANSI's standards for barrier-free design are developed through a consensus process by a committee made up of 52 organizations representing people with disabilities, rehabilitation professionals, design professionals, builders, and manufacturers.

The Sixties and the Civil Rights Movement

In 1964, the historic Civil Rights Act (Public Law 88-352) became law. Unfortunately, the provisions of the act and subsequent legislation addressing civil rights issues were not extended to include people with disabilities. However, partially in response to these exclusions, Congress did pass the Vocational Rehabilitation Amendment Act of 1965 and the Architectural Barriers Act of 1968 (Steinfeld et al. 1978).

The Vocational Rehabilitation Amendment Act of 1965 (Public Law 89-333) was the first piece of Federal legislation to directly address accessibility. Section 15 of the act authorized formation of the National Commission on Architectural Barriers to Rehabilitation of the Handicapped. The Commission's duties were to:

1) Determine how and to what extent architectural barriers impede access to or use of facilities in buildings of all types by people with disabilities.

2) Determine what is being done by relevant public and nonprofit agencies to eliminate barriers from existing buildings and to prevent them in future construction.

3) Prepare proposals and plans for further action as necessary to ensure ready access and full use of facilities in buildings of all types by the handicapped, including proposals for bringing together groups already working toward such goals and groups whose cooperation is essential to effective and comprehensive action (U.S. Statutes 1965, in Steinfeld et al. 1978).

The National Commission on Architectural Barriers to Rehabilitation of the Handicapped studied these issues for two years. In 1968, it published its findings in a document entitled *Design For All Americans*. The Commission found, among other things, that architects, manufacturers, suppliers of building materials, and the public at large were generally ignorant of accessibility issues and, in particular, the ANSI A117.1 recommendations. Furthermore, it found that voluntary compliance was not enough. In response, the Commission recommended enactment of Federal legislation to require that all new buildings and facilities be designed to accommodate the elderly and people with disabilities (Steinfeld et al. 1978).

The Architectural Barriers Act of 1968 (ABA; Public Law 90-480) was passed by Congress in response to the Commission's report. The ABA required physical accessibility in all new buildings or renovations funded in whole or in part by the Federal government. To implement this requirement, the ABA designated the General Services Administration (GSA), Department of Defense (DOD), Department of Housing and Urban Development (HUD), and U.S. Postal Service (USPS) as the four Federal agencies responsible for setting standards on accessibility:

> ". . . GSA prescribes standards for all buildings subject to the ABA that are not covered by the other three standard-setting agencies; DOD prescribes standards for DOD installations; HUD prescribes standards for residential structures covered by the ABA, except those funded or constructed by DOD; and the USPS prescribes standards for postal facilities." (ATBCB 1988a)

To meet their charge, each agency in turn established and published its own set of technical provisions that reflected its individual needs. The promulgation of four separate sets of requirements and the overlapping authority of these agencies led to considerable confusion regarding Federal accessibility standards.

Codifying the Law: the Seventies and Eighties

In 1973, the Rehabilitation Act (Public Law 93-112) became law, establishing the Architectural and Transportation Barriers Compliance Board (ATBCB) as an independent regulatory agency with authority to enforce the 1968 ABA. The ATBCB is composed of representatives of 11 Federal agencies and 12 members appointed by the President from the general public.[3]

In a 1978 amendment to Section 502 of the Rehabilitation Act, the ATBCB was given the responsibility for organizing and codifying all of the existing Federal accessibility specifications for the purpose of issuing minimum guidelines and requirements for use by the four standard-setting agencies. In 1982, the ATBCB published *Minimum Guidelines and*

---

3.   The Departments of Education, Health and Human Services, the Interior, Justice, Labor, Transportation, and Veteran Affairs joined GSA, DOD, HUD, and USPS in the determination of accessibility standards under the ABA.

Requirements for Accessible Design (MGRAD), based on the publications of ANSI, ATBCB-sponsored research, and the existing agency standards.

In 1984, the ATBCB updated MGRAD and published another document, the *Uniform Federal Accessibility Standards* (UFAS). UFAS was adopted by the standard-setting agencies and became the standard set of accessibility specifications for all buildings or renovations funded in whole or in part by the Federal government.[4]

Section 504 of the Rehabilitation Act of 1973 was also amended in 1978, in conjunction with the amendment to Section 502. This amendment required programmatic accessibility in addition to physical accessibility in all facilities and programs funded by the Federal government. In 1973, Section 504 covered federally *assisted* facilities. As amended, all facilities and programs *assisted or conducted* by the Federal government were prohibited from discriminating against people with disabilities. The amendment was very brief, stating:

> "No otherwise qualified handicapped individual in the United States shall, solely by reason of his handicap, be excluded from the participation in, be denied the benefits of, or be subjected to discrimination under any program or activity conducted by Federal financial assistance or by any Executive Agency" (U.S. Code 1978).

In essence, Section 504 requires that "programs and facilities be, to the highest degree feasible, readily accessible to and usable by all persons who have a disability, including mobility, visual, hearing, or mental impairments" (BOR n.d.).

Under the prescripts of Section 504, all Federal agencies subject to the law must develop and implement accessibility regulations for the federally assisted or conducted programs under their auspices. The Department of Agriculture, for example, adopted regulations for nondiscrimination on the basis of disability in its programs and activities. Regulations for federally assisted programs were established in 1982 as 7 CFR part 15b. In 1993, the USDA published its final rule for federally conducted programs, 7 CFR part 15e.

---

4.   GSA adopted UFAS in 41 CFR 101-19.6, Aug. 7, 1984; HUD in 24 CFR part 40, Oct. 4, 1984; DOD by revising Chapter 18 of DOD 4270.1-M, "Construction Criteria" in a memo dated May 8, 1985; USPS in handbook RE-4, "Standards for Facility Accessibility by the Physically Handicapped," Nov. 15, 1984 (ATBCB 1988a).

Broadening the Law: the Americans with Disabilities Act

On July 26, 1990, the Americans with Disabilities Act (ADA; PL 101-336) became law. The ADA addresses discrimination against individuals with disabilities in employment, public services, public accommodations, and telecommunications. The ADA extends the principles of Section 504 of the Rehabilitation Act, as amended, to protect persons with disabilities in all public facilities and programs irrespective of the funding source. The ADA also extends coverage to many privately owned commercial facilities, confirming and reinforcing earlier legislation concerning accessibility.

In 1991, the ADA's accessibility guidelines (ADAAG) were published. Based on the ANSI technical provisions and other established standards, ADAAG sets forth accessibility standards for all public accommodations, including those constructed and operated by the private sector. While UFAS still applies directly to many Federal agencies, the Departments of Justice (DOJ) and Transportation (DOT) have already adopted ADAAG as their standard. Since DOJ and DOT are vested with the authority to enforce accessibility laws, it is likely that ADAAG will soon replace UFAS as the nation's sole accessibility standard.

In summary:

- ANSI, MGRAD, UFAS, and ADAAG are all acronyms for accessibility specifications and guidelines.

- The standards presented in ANSI A117.1–1980 are voluntary unless they have been officially adopted or referenced in legislation or regulations that have jurisdiction over the design and construction of facilities.

- MGRAD is an amalgamation of the four disparate sets of accessibility standards produced by Federal agencies under the ABA.

- UFAS was created in 1984 through a combination of MGRAD and aspects of ANSI A117.1–1980. The accessibility standards presented in UFAS apply to all Federal and federally funded buildings and facilities.

■   ADAAG, published under the auspices of ADA in 1991, is based on UFAS and ANSI A117.1–1980. It delineates accessibility guidelines for the private sector and other entities covered under ADA.

Implementing the Law: the Challenge of the Nineties and Beyond

The passage of ADA and the development of ADAAG do not conclude the history of the accessibility movement. They mark a new beginning. While tremendous progress has been made to date, most of this progress has been legislative. Effective compliance mechanisms are needed to remove the many barriers that handicap millions of people on a daily basis. Given the various legislative mandates, the challenge now is to educate both professionals and the general public, and to develop an adequate design philosophy—along with systematic implementation procedures—that will ensure accessibility for all.

universal design

Historically, the design of buildings and facilities has emphasized the needs and ability levels of the "average" human being. The widths of doors, heights of counters, and placement of electrical outlets, for example, were designed to cater to the average man and woman.

Unfortunately, this design approach is based on a myth that ignores most of the population. There is no such thing as an average human being. Some people are tall, others are short; some are ambulatory, others use wheelchairs; many individuals have perfect vision, others are blind or otherwise visually impaired; some individuals hear clearly and speak distinctly, others require assistance. The range of human abilities and needs is truly vast.

The myth of the average human being, and the predominant design paradigm that is based upon it, have led to the development of physical environments that are inaccessible and often hostile to many people (Kidd and Clark 1982).

Challenging Assumptions: the Barrier-Free Design Movement

The first serious challenge to traditional design was the 1959 publication of a document by the President's Committee on Employment of the Physically Handicapped, *Tentative Guide: Facilities in Public Buildings for Persons with Ambulatory Impairments*. As a result of this guide, the Public Building Administration issued a directive to its field offices throughout the country stating: "All new Federal buildings shall provide easy access of wheelchairs to the first floor entrance lobby. Where entrance steps are unavoidable, ramps and handrails must be provided" (President's Committee 1959, in Steinfeld et al. 1978). The *Tentative Guide*, together with the 1961 publication of the first ANSI standard, *Making Buildings and Facilities Accessible to and Usable by the Physically Handicapped* (ANSI A117.1), marked the beginning of the barrier-free design movement.

"Barrier-free design" promotes the elimination of physical barriers to access in the design and construction of buildings and sites. In doing so, it focuses on the anthropometrics and spatial needs of the two major categories of people with disabilities: those who have a disability but are ambulatory, and those who must use wheelchairs.

The majority of people with disabilities are ambulatory. Their disability may be related to one or more impairments resulting from temporary illness; accident; degenerative, hereditary, or congenital condition; disease; or damage to the nervous system (see discussion of people with disabilities on pages 6-9). The most common impairments are heart and respiratory problems, arthritis, paralysis of various parts of the body due to stroke or disease, and the effects of aging. Each impairment or combination of impairments presents the individual with a particular disability or set of disabilities. Each individual, in turn, develops a unique ability to cope and adapt.

Wheelchair users are a distinct minority among the population of people with disabilities. But as is the case with people who are disabled but ambulatory, people who use wheelchairs may also experience more than one impairment. In some instances, wheelchair users may actually be less severely disabled than many people who are disabled but ambulatory. For example, those with intact arms and sufficient upper body strength may be extremely mobile and capable of independently propelling themselves over great distances. However, many wheelchair users are severely disabled, elderly, or young, and require electric wheelchairs or regular assistance.

Anthropometric and spatial requirements vary by individual. People who are disabled but ambulatory often use walking aids that become functional parts of their bodies. These aids present specific anthropometric and spatial requirements, especially where stairs, curbs, ground surfaces, and slopes are concerned. Likewise, wheelchairs pose a specific set of requirements. Their narrow wheels and short wheelbases make wheelchairs usable only on relatively smooth surfaces. Small changes in elevation or cross slopes that may be negotiable by a person using a walking aid can be difficult, if not impossible, for a person in a wheelchair. Uneven, soft, or muddy ground, and steps, narrow entrances, or steep gradients can also present insurmountable barriers to a person in a wheelchair.

Although barrier-free design considers the needs of both people who have disabilities but are ambulatory and people who use wheelchairs, the needs and abilities of each group are not emphasized equally. Because of its dimensions and the unique physical limitations it imposes, the wheelchair is viewed as the common denominator for barrier-free access. Barrier-free designs assume that sites, buildings, and facilities that are accessible to wheelchairs will also be accessible for people with other disabilities.

This assumption has guided the development of numerous accessibility specifications, from ANSI A117.1 to ADAAG, resulting in the removal of many barriers to accessibility. However, the assumption does not always hold. People with other disabilities have many needs that are not satisfied by designs that accommodate wheelchair users alone (Steinfeld et al. 1978). Furthermore, some barrier-free features, if designed solely for accessibility by wheelchair users, can be hazardous or unusable by others. For example, the elimination of curbs may remove a positive cue for people with visual impairments (Kidd and Clark 1982).

Broadening the Paradigm: Percentile Distribution and The Enabler Model

To mitigate the reductionist view of disability posed by "the wheelchair paradigm," designers began to look for an approach to accessible design that would serve a larger portion of the population. One method suggested in the late 1960s was based on the statistical technique of percentile distribution (Goldsmith 1967). Using the full anthropometric range as the starting point, it was argued that design decisions should be made to accommodate the 5th or the 95th percentile of that range (depending on the nature of the design problem). The resulting design would theoretically accommodate 90 percent of the population (Panero and Zelnick 1979).

The problem with the percentile distribution approach is that human beings are not normally distributed in all body dimensions or ability levels. For example, a person with a 50th percentile height and a 12th grade reading level may have a 60th percentile side arm reach and be blind, or a 35th percentile knee height and use a wheelchair. While a design decision based on percentile distribution may accommodate 90 percent of a given population in theory, in reality it may still not accommodate the majority of people.

A further attempt to mitigate the shortcomings of barrier-free design was made in 1978, when it was suggested that an alternate image of people with disabilities was required:

> ". . . this image must be easy to conceptualize in terms of building design and must integrate all the relevant disabilities in a simplified way. All relevant disabilities must

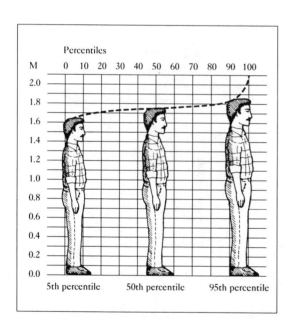

Figure 5. Male Height Percentile Distribution.

be easily visualized so that a designer, researcher, or building evaluator can picture, in their mind, who it is that accessibility is meant to help" (Steinfeld et al. 1978).

This new conceptual image was presented in the form of an ideogram called "The Enabler Model." The Enabler Model considers 15 different disability concerns, categorized in terms of mental functions, the senses, and motor impairment. The model also considers "invisible" disabilities like the lack of stamina and other disabilities that are often overlooked, such as extremes of size and weight.

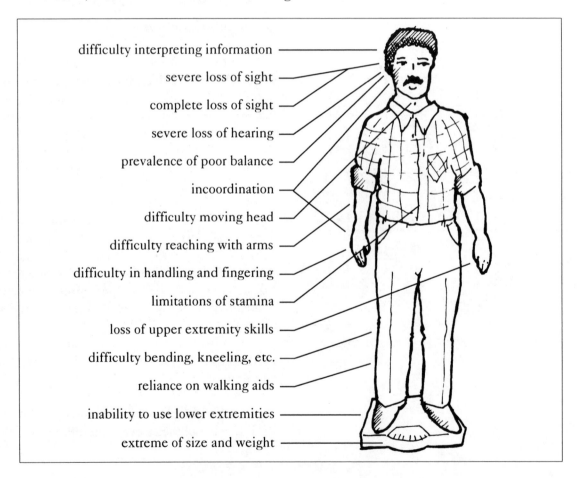

difficulty interpreting information

severe loss of sight

complete loss of sight

severe loss of hearing

prevalence of poor balance

incoordination

difficulty moving head

difficulty reaching with arms

difficulty in handling and fingering

limitations of stamina

loss of upper extremity skills

difficulty bending, kneeling, etc.

reliance on walking aids

inability to use lower extremities

extreme of size and weight

Figure 6. *The Enabler Model.*

In light of the argument that disability is the typical human condition, the Enabler is a more accurate human paradigm than either the "average human being" (traditional design) or the "wheelchair user" (barrier-free design). It serves as a conceptualization aid that helps designers empathize with the people who will actually be using a site, building, or facility, and encourages a more comprehensive and integrated view of people with and without disabilities. As such, it has formed the basis for a design philosophy that today is becoming known as "universal design."

Building the Universal Design Paradigm

Universal design is still in its infancy. It provides a philosophical approach to accessible design that combines the basic principle of barrier-free design (elimination of barriers to access) with the more comprehensive view of the human being as suggested by The Enabler Model. Universal design attempts to consider (or at least increase designers' sensitivity to) all degrees of sensory awareness, all types of locomotion, and all levels of physical and intellectual function. It does so by accommodating the broadest possible spectrum of people through a single, all-encompassing design, rather than the provision of multiple elements specially designed for use only by discrete groups.

In principle, universal design considers the anthropometrics, spatial requirements, and other needs of people with disabilities as suggested by The Enabler Model. It then attempts to accommodate these needs in a fashion that also addresses the abilities and needs of the able-bodied population, incorporating features designed to accommodate both groups. Two examples of universal design are the accessible picnic table and the common

accessible ramp used in conjunction with stairs. Both are accessible to and usable by most people irrespective of ability.

Universal design recognizes the value of the scoping provisions and technical specifications delineated by existing standards such as UFAS and ADAAG. But it also recognizes that adherence to these standards, while perhaps ensuring compliance with the law (see preceding discussion of accessibility laws), may not ensure accessibility or use for all people.

Universal design is not yet an established or systematic design methodology with well-defined parameters, technical specifications, or implementation procedures. The development of universal design from a philosophical concept into a concrete, applicable design methodology awaits the interest and attention of design professionals. The attempt to combine the fundamentals of barrier-free design with the Enabler paradigm presents one of the greatest challenges ever faced by the design profession.

the outdoor recreation environment

II

the recreation opportunity spectrum

The great outdoors presents a tremendous diversity of recreational opportunities. Likewise, the recreating public represents a tremendous diversity of recreational interests and needs. From city parks to pristine wilderness, people look to the outdoors to satisfy their recreational needs. In doing so, they attempt to match their desires, abilities, and expectations to a particular activity and setting. Recreation researchers have long recognized the importance of this relationship between expectations and settings. Many have suggested that recreation managers should provide a range or continuum of opportunities to best serve the diversity of public tastes for recreation (Clark and Stankey 1979).

The recreation management approach used by the USDA Forest Service is called the "Recreation Opportunity Spectrum" (ROS).[5] The ROS provides a framework for stratifying and defining classes of outdoor recreation environments. It can be applied to all lands regardless of ownership or jurisdiction (USDA Forest Service 1982). What is more, the ROS framework systematically and explicitly recognizes and organizes accessibility as a primary recreation expectation for all people, irrespective of ability.

The ROS framework is based on a continuum of possible combinations of recreation settings, activities, and experiential opportunities, as well as the resulting benefits that can accrue to the individual (by improving physical and mental well-being) and society (Driver and Brown 1978). The primary structure of the ROS is based on the continuum of possible recreation settings. While this continuum can be defined in many ways (Stankey et al. 1977), the ROS continuum is defined primarily in terms of perceivable modifications to the natural environment, e.g., the presence of roads and trails or the existence of buildings, facilities, and conveniences (Marshall 1933, Wagner 1966, Driver and Brown 1978, Clark and Stankey 1979). These definitions are based on researcher preferences rather than conceptual differences, and are described in greater detail in the *ROS Primer Field Guide* (USDA Forest Service 1990).

5. The ROS was adopted by the USDA Forest Service as the basic framework for inventorying, planning, and managing recreation resources in accordance with the Forest and Rangeland Renewable Resources Planning Act of 1974 (PL 93-378), as amended by the National Forest Management Act of 1976 (PL 94-588).

The current ROS of the USDA Forest Service divides recreation settings into six very broad and sometimes overlapping categories: urban; rural; roaded natural; semi-primitive motorized; semi-primitive nonmotorized; and primitive. *Universal Access to Outdoor Recreation* subscribes to the same ROS, but in the interest of simplicity it combines recreation setting classifications to yield four basic categories: **urban/rural**; **roaded natural**; **semi-primitive**; and **primitive**.

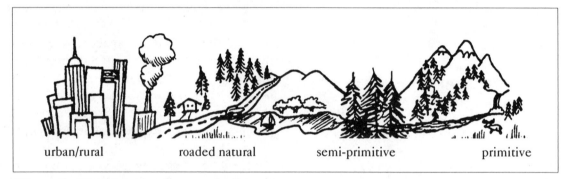

urban/rural   roaded natural   semi-primitive   primitive

Figure 7. *The Recreation Opportunity Spectrum*

An ROS classification is assigned to a particular setting based on the setting's physical characteristics and on the recreation activities and experience opportunities that are expected there. Figures 8, 9, and 10 on pages 28 through 31 summarize the activities, settings, and experiences associated with each ROS classification.

Philosophically, the ROS is based upon several premises:

■   People purposefully choose settings for their recreation activities.

■   Choices are made with the expectation of achieving particular recreation experiences.

■   It is desirable, from a macro-planning perspective, to present a diverse spectrum of activity and recreation setting opportunities, ranging from highly developed to primitive, from which people may choose.

ROS classifications are assigned to recreation settings based on a number of criteria. First, the site is inventoried for a broad range of physical, social, and managerial components and characteristics, such as remoteness, size, evidence of human activity, social encounters, and managerial presence. Then, through land management planning that includes public involvement, the inventory results are evaluated in combination with public expectations regarding recreational activities and experience opportunities. Based on this thorough evaluation, a final ROS classification is made.

Within the ROS framework, recreation areas are planned and managed to maximize the potential level of recreation satisfaction achievable given a setting's ability to meet expectations. Urban/rural recreation settings are generally managed to maximize the potential for satisfying typical urban/rural recreation expectations, whereas wilderness settings are often managed to preserve typical primitive recreation opportunities.

It is not necessary or desirable to develop all recreation settings equally. Many people enjoy being in settings that are completely undeveloped; therefore, remote countryside or wilderness should not always be developed or modified to meet expectations that may be satisfied elsewhere. From the ROS perspective, each site should be developed or modified in a manner that achieves harmony between recreation expectations and the environment. Development must be tailored to complement the setting. As a result, highly developed visitor centers with paved parking lots and nature trails are generally not found in primitive settings; nor are rustic outhouses normally found in urban/rural settings.

The classification assigned to a particular setting is a generalization of what may be expected within that area. It should also be expected that variations will exist within each setting and that classifications may change with time. Recreation areas may become more developed or modified because of demonstrated use or popularity. For example, a hiking trail in a semi-primitive setting may become so popular that its use approximates that expected only in urban/rural areas, or an urban park may be so pristine as to offer experiences expected only at semi-primitive or primitive sites.

When a setting's use is inconsistent with its ROS classification, the original survey of the setting should be reevaluated to expose possible errors or the inconsistency should be evaluated against the other criteria of the classification through a statistical weighted

| urban/rural | roaded natural | semi-primitive | primitive |

Land Based Activities

Viewing scenery	Viewing scenery		Viewing scenery
Viewing activities			
Viewing works of humanity			
Automobile use, including off-road use	Automobile use, including off-road use		
Motorcycle and scooter use	Motorcycle and scooter use		
Train and bus touring			
Aircraft use	Aircraft use		
Aerial tram and lift use			
Hiking and walking	Hiking and mountain climbing		Hiking and mountain climbing
Bicycling			
Horseback riding	Horseback riding		Horseback riding
Camping	Camping		Tent camping
Picnicking			
Resort and commercial services use			
Resort lodging			
Recreation cabin use			
Hunting	Hunting		Hunting
Nature studies	Nature studies		Nature studies
Gathering forest products			
Interpretive services			
Team sports participation			
Individual sports participation			
Games and play participation			

Figure 8. *Recreation Activities by ROS Classification (Source: USDA Forest Service 1982).*

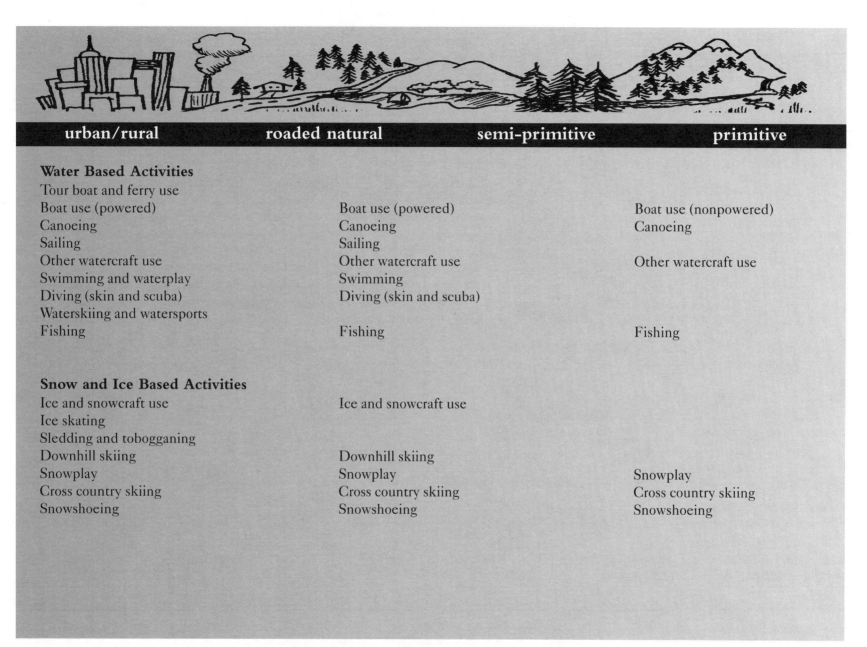

urban/rural	roaded natural	semi-primitive	primitive

Water Based Activities

Tour boat and ferry use			
Boat use (powered)	Boat use (powered)		Boat use (nonpowered)
Canoeing	Canoeing		Canoeing
Sailing	Sailing		
Other watercraft use	Other watercraft use		Other watercraft use
Swimming and waterplay	Swimming		
Diving (skin and scuba)	Diving (skin and scuba)		
Waterskiing and watersports			
Fishing	Fishing		Fishing

Snow and Ice Based Activities

Ice and snowcraft use	Ice and snowcraft use		
Ice skating			
Sledding and tobogganing			
Downhill skiing	Downhill skiing		
Snowplay	Snowplay		Snowplay
Cross country skiing	Cross country skiing		Cross country skiing
Snowshoeing	Snowshoeing		Snowshoeing

Figure 8. **(continued)** *Recreation Activities by ROS Classification (Source: USDA Forest Service 1982).*

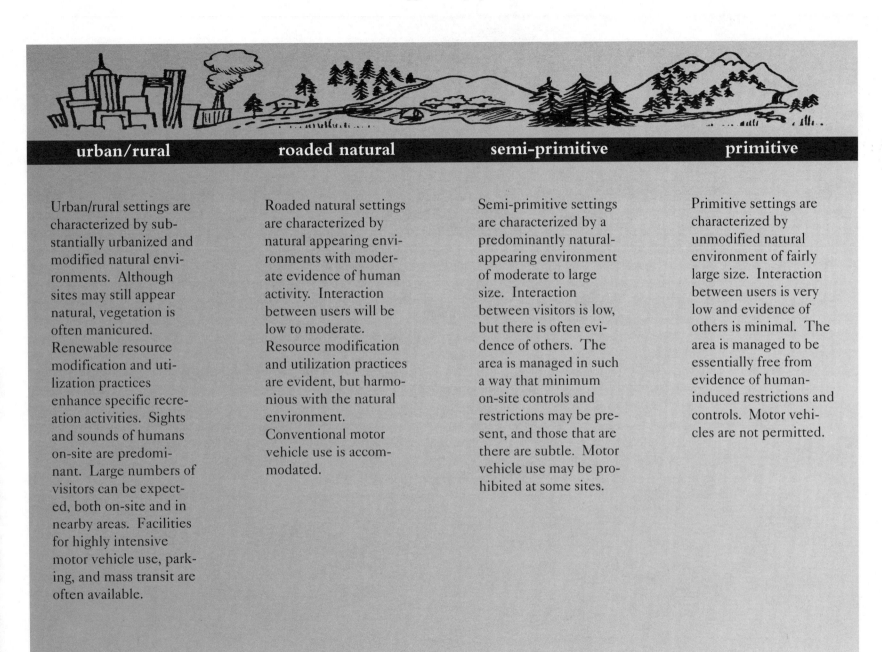

urban/rural	roaded natural	semi-primitive	primitive
Urban/rural settings are characterized by substantially urbanized and modified natural environments. Although sites may still appear natural, vegetation is often manicured. Renewable resource modification and utilization practices enhance specific recreation activities. Sights and sounds of humans on-site are predominant. Large numbers of visitors can be expected, both on-site and in nearby areas. Facilities for highly intensive motor vehicle use, parking, and mass transit are often available.	Roaded natural settings are characterized by natural appearing environments with moderate evidence of human activity. Interaction between users will be low to moderate. Resource modification and utilization practices are evident, but harmonious with the natural environment. Conventional motor vehicle use is accommodated.	Semi-primitive settings are characterized by a predominantly natural-appearing environment of moderate to large size. Interaction between visitors is low, but there is often evidence of others. The area is managed in such a way that minimum on-site controls and restrictions may be present, and those that are there are subtle. Motor vehicle use may be prohibited at some sites.	Primitive settings are characterized by unmodified natural environment of fairly large size. Interaction between users is very low and evidence of others is minimal. The area is managed to be essentially free from evidence of human-induced restrictions and controls. Motor vehicles are not permitted.

Figure 9. *Setting Characteristics by ROS Classification (Source: USDA Forest Service 1982).*

(left margin, vertical text) 11   the outdoor recreation environment

urban/rural	roaded natural	semi-primitive	primitive
Recreation sites and opportunities are convenient, and there is high probability of experiencing affiliation with individuals and groups. Experiencing natural environments, having challenges and risks afforded by the natural environment, and using outdoor skills are relatively unimportant. Opportunities for competitive and spectator sports and for passive use of highly human-influenced parks and open spaces are common.	Approximately equal probability of experiencing affiliation with other user groups and experiencing isolation from the sights and sounds of humans. Opportunities for a high degree of interaction with the environment are common. The challenge and risk opportunites associated with more primitive types of recreation are not very important. Practice and testing of outdoor skills may be important.	Moderately high probability of experiencing isolation from the sights and sounds of humans. Opportunities for independence, closeness to nature, tranquility, and self-reliance through the application of outdoor skills in an environment that offers a high degree of interaction with the natural environment.	Extremely high probability of experiencing isolation from the sights and sounds of humans. Opportunities for independence, closeness to nature, tranquility, and self-reliance through the application of outdoor skills. Recreation opportunities often present high degrees of challenge and risk.

Figure 10. *Recreation Experiences by ROS Classification (Source: USDA Forest Service 1982).*

11   the outdoor recreation environment

comparison. In this manner, inconsistencies can be determined to be acceptable; eliminated by changing the setting's classification; resolved because they are not statistically significant; or determined to be unacceptable. Unacceptable inconsistencies may be subject to managerial action. For example, to address the problem of high-density use in a primitive setting, certain roads might be closed, facilities eliminated, or other on-site modifications instituted (Clark and Stankey 1979).

To summarize, the ROS is based on the assumption that quality outdoor recreation is best provided through a diversity of opportunities (Clark and Stankey 1979). It is also based on the axiom that recreation settings present certain innate recreation opportunities. Primitive recreation settings, for example, are expected to present different opportunities than semi-primitive, roaded natural, or urban/rural settings. Lastly, the ROS assumes that people will intelligently choose recreation settings to best suit their recreation expectations and needs. As a result, people who desire a primitive wilderness experience will not pursue their recreation activities in urban/rural settings.

expectations of accessibility

People choose recreation settings based on their expectations about the nature of the potential recreation experience. Expectations regarding accessibility are often central to the choice that is ultimately made by many individuals.

Expectations of accessibility are evoked by characteristics inherent to a setting's location along the spectrum of possible recreation settings. In general, urban/rural settings are expected to have the most development and modification of the environment and primitive settings the least. As the level of development and modification decreases along the spectrum from urban/rural to primitive, expectations of comfort, security, and accommodation for accessibility are also expected to diminish, while expectations of rusticity, challenge, and risk increase.

Each recreation setting classification has an associated expectation regarding the level of accessibility. These expected levels of accessibility evoke adjectives that suggest degrees of difficulty:

- Urban areas, because they are highly developed, evoke expectations of *easy* accessibility.

- Roaded natural settings are farther along the spectrum; they are less developed than urban areas, but more developed than semi-primitive, and thus evoke expectations of *moderate* accessibility.

- Semi-primitive areas are rarely developed, so expectations of *difficult* accessibility prevail.

- Primitive areas are primarily undeveloped and have few, if any, environmental modifications; these settings evoke expectations of the *most difficult* accessibility.

The classification assigned to a recreation setting is a generalization. It is almost always possible to find aspects of one recreation setting in another. For example, environmental conditions and recreation opportunities that are normally expected within a roaded natural setting may also be found in an urban/rural environment. Likewise, some environmental features and recreation opportunities, although possible, are generally unexpected or inconsistent within an ROS setting. For example, undisturbed natural areas, although possible, are generally not found in urban settings.

Nonetheless, because accessibility is an important recreation expectation, every site should be developed to provide the level of accessibility that would normally be expected within its recreation setting classification. This will maximize recreation satisfaction and better serve public needs. Recreation planners, designers, and managers must evaluate both new and existing facilities in light of the expected levels of accessibility to ensure that their sites and facilities are harmonious with both the environment and visitor expectations.[6]

Description	Urban/ Rural	Roaded Natural	Semi- Primitive	Primitive
Easy	**Norm**	Possibility	Inconsistent	Inconsistent
Moderate	Possibility	**Norm**	Inconsistent	Inconsistent
Difficult	Inconsistent	Possibility	**Norm**	Inconsistent
Most Difficult	Inconsistent	Inconsistent	Possibility	**Norm**

Figure 11. Expectations of Accessibility by ROS Classification (Source: USDA Forest Service).

6. Researchers have long recognized that recreation settings and sites present inherent levels of difficulty or challenge, and many classification systems have been developed. In 1979, the Minnesota Department of Natural Resources introduced a graduated level of difficulty classification system for trails in their booklet, *Access For All: A Workbook for Outdoor Accessibility* (ATBCB 1979). This concept was subsequently incorporated into numerous other publications, most notably in *Outdoor Access Standards* (Harris and Fishbeck n.d.) and *Accessible Fishing: A Planning Handbook* (Nordhaus et al. 1984).

the outdoor recreation site

The built environment and the outdoor recreation environment are fundamentally different. The built environment creates an environment to suit human needs at home and at work. It is an environment of fixed elevations and well-defined parameters intended to accommodate the ordinary but necessary activities of everyday life. The outdoor recreation environment is the domain of leisure and extraordinary activities. It is an environment that offers dynamic and challenging opportunities on land, water, and even in the air. Although aspects of the outdoor recreation environment are sometimes constructed, modifying the natural environment, this generally is done only to provide access or to ensure safety. Nature trails, for example, are provided to allow people access to nature. Sidewalks, on the other hand, are provided to ensure safety in, and access to, various aspects of the already highly developed built environment.

Outdoor recreation sites, like the buildings and other features of the built environment, have two primary components: discrete features or elements, and the areas or spaces in which those elements are placed or found. These elements and spaces can be defined as follows:

- **Element.** An architectural or mechanical component of a building, facility, space, or site, e.g., telephone, curb ramp, door, drinking fountain, seating, or water closet.

- **Space.** A definable area, e.g., room, toilet room, hall assembly area, entrance, storage room, alcove, courtyard, or lobby (ATBCB 1991).

The elements and spaces of outdoor recreation sites serve to support or facilitate the pursuit of recreation activities. From parking lots to visitor centers to remote campsites, no structure or other modification to the natural environment should be made unless it is necessary to the provision of opportunities for recreation experiences.

Accessing Recreation Elements and Spaces

One of the most critical aspects of accessibility in outdoor sites is the system of paths that connects the various recreation elements and spaces. *Universal Access to Outdoor Recreation* identifies two types of paths in outdoor recreation sites and provides a separate set of accessibility guidelines for each:

- **Outdoor Recreation Access Routes**: paths that provide access to the site's primary developed recreation activities and elements; and

- **Recreation Trails**: paths that provide access to the site's other, lesser-developed recreation activities and elements.

The guidelines for outdoor recreation access routes are applicable in urban/rural settings, roaded natural settings, and semi-primitive settings where visitors will expect the basic support services and primary activities of the site to be accessible at an easy or moderate level of accessibility. Recreation trails, typically 1/4-mile or more in length, provide access to lesser-developed areas of a site, where natural features are emphasized along with customer expectations and the level of development when determining accessibility modifications. The guidelines for accessible recreation trails should be considered in urban/rural, roaded natural, and semi-primitive sites. They are less stringent than the guidelines for outdoor recreation access routes.

Designers and managers must carefully identify the primary activities and elements of each developed recreation site and ensure that there is a comprehensive system of outdoor recreation access routes that connects all primary activities and elements with each other and with accessible parking spaces and facility entrances.

Development of Sites Across the ROS Spectrum

The extent to which developed elements and spaces are provided will vary depending on the ROS classification. Urban/rural sites will have developed facilities such as flush toilets and telephones that may be less abundant or absent at sites in roaded natural, semi-primitive, or primitive settings. Likewise, the manner in which developed facilities are presented may be expected to vary. Toilet facilities will generally be presented in elaborate structures at urban/rural sites but may resemble rustic outhouses farther down the spectrum. In primitive settings, pre-existing trails may be absent altogether. In these settings, modifications are provided only to ensure protection of the environment, in accordance with the Wilderness Act of 1964 (16 USC 1131).

scope information and technical information

Accessibility standards such as UFAS and ADAAG present two types of information:

- **Scope information**, which describes *where* accessibility is appropriate, *when* it is required, and *how many* aspects of a building, facility, or site must be accessible to comply with legal requirements.

- **Technical information**, which delineates *what* aspects of a building, facility, or site should be accessible, and *how* these features should be designed and installed to ensure accessibility (Barrier Free Environments 1991).

Scope Information

Scope requirements have traditionally been determined by consensus or fiat, and have emphasized accommodation of the percentage of the population considered disabled at any given time. For example, a scope requirement might state that a certain percentage of parking spaces in a shopping center's parking lot must be accessible given that a certain percentage of the total population requires such accommodation.

In the outdoor recreation environment, scope requirements should be structured to ensure that accessibility is provided where and when it is expected, and at the level of accommodation expected given a recreation site's ROS classification. Urban/rural sites should provide easy accessibility; roaded natural sites should ensure a moderate level of accessibility; semi-primitive recreation sites might present a difficult level of accessibility; and primitive sites might present the most difficult accessibility for all people irrespective of ability.

In the built environment, all aspects of a site or facility should be accessible, accommodating the broadest possible range of human abilities. In the outdoor recreation environment, accessibility may in some instances be impracticable due to site characteristics such as steep slopes or dense vegetation. For example, a hiking trail that steeply ascends a sheer rock cliff in a very short distance may be impossible to grade or pave. Even when practicable, modifications to improve access might alter an area's demeanor and the long-term impact may not always be positive. For example, roads or trails of any kind into semi-primitive or primitive areas will induce changes in recreation activity and experience expectations (see Figures 8, 9, and 10 on pages 28-31). These changes may ultimately change an area's ROS classification beyond acceptable criteria.

For these reasons, modifications should not always be made solely for the purpose of accessibility. When such modifications will deleteriously impact the setting's "demeanor," environmental visage, or historic character,[7] efforts should be made to allow people with disabilities alternative access to the activity, or alternate representative activities should be provided, such as films, architectural models of upstairs rooms, or tactile maps and models.

A decision-making procedure should be followed in such instances to ensure that accessibility expectations are met without impacting the characteristics that make the site a desirable setting for recreation. Chapter III, *Applying the Guidelines to Your Site*, provides direction to help designers and managers determine the appropriate level of accessibility modifications in outdoor recreation sites.

Technical Information

Technical information, unlike scope, is based on anthropometrics, human performance data, and ergonomics. For example, the average adult wheelchair user requires a clear ground space of at least 60 inches diameter to negotiate a pivot turn. This space requirement remains constant irrespective of environment—wheelchair users require the same clear ground space to negotiate a pivot turn whether they are in the foyer of a building or on a fishing platform.

II

the outdoor recreation environment

---

7.   Accessibility requirements for historic sites and structures are addressed in Section 4.1.7 of both UFAS and ADAAG. They are also discussed on pages 95-100 of this document.

developing standards for outdoor environments

UFAS and ADAAG are intended to provide scope and technical information for the built environment only. However, certain elements and spaces provided in the built environment, such as parking lots and toilet rooms, are also commonly provided in the outdoor recreation environment. In addition, some elements and spaces common to outdoor recreation, though not addressed directly in UFAS and ADAAG, are also provided in the built environment. Picnic tables, for example, are as likely to be found in the courtyard of an office building as in a campground. Other components of outdoor recreation, however, such as fishing platforms and hiking trails, are exclusive to recreational activities and unique to the outdoor recreation environment.

Many elements and spaces that are provided in both the built environment and the outdoor recreation environment, along with those elements and spaces that are unique to outdoor recreation, have not yet been directly addressed by the Architectural and Transportation Barriers Compliance Board (ATBCB). As a result, there are no official accessibility requirements for many of the elements and spaces found in the outdoor recreation environment.

The ATBCB is awaiting further developments in accessibility research and technology to support the development of appropriate accessibility criteria for outdoor recreation settings. The ATBCB began addressing the development of standards for outdoor recreation environments in 1993. The Board will be actively reviewing this document and other published information, in conjunction with a thorough review of contemporary design considerations and participation from the general public, as a starting point for developing appropriate accessibility criteria.

Because some elements and spaces common to the built environment are also provided at outdoor recreation sites, and because compliance with UFAS or ADAAG is required by law, these standards must be directly applied, where appropriate, across the spectrum of recreation opportunity settings. In this manner, though these elements and spaces might look different between sites in different ROS settings, accessibility—as defined by law—will transcend the spectrum of recreation settings. Thus, elaborate flush toilet facilities at highly developed urban/rural campgrounds and rustic outhouses provided in semi-primitive settings will both be accessible (i.e., they will conform to UFAS or ADAAG).

UFAS and ADAAG also provide the basis for establishing accessibility criteria for elements and spaces that are not currently addressed by accessibility standards but which nonetheless can be found in both the outdoor recreation environment and the built environment (e.g., picnic tables and barbecues). However, these criteria must be extrapolated. For example, picnic tables are not directly addressed in UFAS and ADAAG, but section ADAAG 4.32 considers general information relevant to seating, tables, and work surfaces that may be applied to picnic tables.

The accessibility criteria presented in UFAS and ADAAG may also be extrapolated for those elements and spaces that are unique to the outdoor recreation environment. The extent of extrapolation must be determined based on the item in question within the context of the recreation site and its ROS classification. For example, hiking trails are not directly addressed, but accessible routes are. The extent to which the requirements for accessible routes are applied to a particular hiking trail will depend on the expected level of accessibility, as evoked by the site's ROS classification. Hiking trails in urban/rural settings, where an easy level of accessibility is expected, will follow UFAS and ADAAG requirements more closely (both in terms of direct application and extrapolation) than trails in settings that are farther down the spectrum, where expectations of moderate, difficult, and most difficult accessibility prevail.

The applicability of existing standards to the outdoor recreation environment diminishes as the gulf between the built environment and the outdoor recreation environment becomes wider. There may also be cases where elements and spaces in the outdoor recreation environment cannot be addressed even through extrapolation of existing standards. In these cases, new accessibility criteria must be developed.

The need for extrapolation or development of new criteria increases as one moves along the spectrum of recreation opportunity settings. Settings at the urban/rural end of the spectrum have more development and modification of the natural environment; they more closely resemble the built environment and can more likely be addressed directly by UFAS and ADAAG. Settings that are farther down the spectrum are increasingly different from the built environment; there is a corresponding increase in the need to extrapolate accessibility criteria and the need to develop new criteria altogether.

II

the outdoor recreation environment

applying the guidelines to your site

introduction

This chapter will help you better understand and apply the design guidelines presented in Chapter IV within the context of customer expectations and levels of accessibility as discussed in Chapters I and II. It presents a process for incorporating universal design in the design process and discusses the ways in which potential conflicts between protecting the environment and designing for accessibility can be resolved. It then discusses how the guidelines presented in Chapter IV can be applied to achieve the appropriate level of accessibility in the most common recreation activities. While examples are provided, they should not be interpreted as "standard" designs for use in any site. Proper application of the guidelines to your site will require critical analysis, individualized site planning and design, and customer involvement. These activities are also discussed.

The chapter is presented in four sections:

■   **The Design Process** provides an overview of the site planning process and illustrates how the universal design philosophy can be incorporated in all stages of project planning, development, and maintenance.

■   **Integrating Universal Design In the Outdoor Environment** discusses the dilemmas that are often associated with incorporating universal design into natural settings. It defines scoping provisions and a decision-making process to address situations where the desired level of accessibility cannot be met because of environmental features, presenting an objective and systematic approach for determining when, given a certain set of conditions, it is appropriate and desirable to design to a higher or lower level of accessibility.

■   **Applying the Guidelines** provides examples of how the technical specifications and guidelines presented in Chapter IV can be applied to the settings most commonly encountered in outdoor recreation. It discusses many of the fundamental issues that must be considered when designing accessible outdoor environments. Areas that are addressed in detail include: paths, picnic areas and campgrounds, fishing areas, play areas, and signs. General recommendations are also provided for boating and swimming areas and equestrian facilities. The section does not cover all aspects of outdoor recreation environments. Rather, it provides examples to help designers develop a better understanding of how the guidelines presented in this book can be interpreted and applied to the widest possible range of outdoor settings.

■   **Other Issues and Considerations** discusses several areas of special concern in regard to the design and management of the outdoor environment. These include special considerations related to historic structures, retrofitting existing facilities, and providing accessibility in semi-primitive and primitive settings. A discussion of safety and risk management is also included. It presents current thinking and applicable guidelines for reducing risk to reasonable levels and minimizing the potential for injury or death.

III

applying the guidelines to your site

the design process

Good site planning blends human needs and desires with environmental considerations, while respecting the visual character and integrity of the natural landscape. Activities and functions are organized based on the site's unique characteristics, with constructed features added as necessary to meet program objectives. These constructed features can be located and designed in the site so that they appear to be natural, human-influenced, or human-made. In urban or more developed areas, architectural themes and constructed features may tend to dominate the landscape. In settings where nature is the primary focus and attraction, constructed facilities, if provided at all, should be subordinate to the surroundings and should use natural or natural-appearing features and materials.

Regardless of the setting, selection of the appropriate design style and level of development is best determined through an understanding of customer expectations and a familiarity with the site and related environmental and social factors. This approach responds to user needs while developing a design that evolves from the site organically, ensuring a good "fit" on the land. The development must complement rather than compete with the environment.

The universal design approach helps ensure that site design strives to meet the needs of all visitors while respecting the integrity of the natural environment. It should be incorporated in all stages of the design process to ensure that accessibility is a central concern in the design of both facilities and programs, not an add-on during design development or construction. The result will be a quality product that provides each visitor with a sense of dignity, independence, and the opportunity to socialize with others.

Universal design's goal is to provide an integrated recreation experience for all users; it specifically avoids creating segregated or "special" areas. It strives to provide the highest level of accessibility that is practicable consistent with customer expectations and the constraints and opportunities presented by the natural environment. To achieve these goals, designers must follow a universal design approach throughout the design process.

The following discussion outlines eleven steps in the process of designing outdoor recreation sites, focusing on universal design considerations that should be addressed in each step. These steps are not all-inclusive; they highlight issues particular to universal design. Many of these issues are expanded upon later in this chapter.

1.   **Project Initiation.** Universal design should be incorporated in the earliest stages of project planning. In new construction, site selection criteria should include consideration of the recreation setting and customer expectations of accessibility. When possible, select sites that will facilitate provision of the expected level of accessibility to the primary recreation activities under consideration. The process of designing accessible facilities, programs, and services must involve those groups that will ultimately be users. Such involvement can be critical to ensuring a successful outcome and can help to avoid costly mistakes. The project manager should organize an integrated, interdisciplinary design team, including: landscape architect(s) and engineer(s), an accessibility specialist, other resource specialists, and consumers of accessible outdoor recreation. These consumers should represent a diversity of skills, interests, and disabilities, and should have appropriate technical knowledge.

2.   **Scoping and Research.** Existing sources of information and direction related to the project site(s) should be inventoried and reviewed. These might include Forest Plans, Transition Plans, regional and statewide plans, the State Comprehensive Outdoor Recreation Plan (SCORP), and budgets. Customer needs and the project's purpose, feasibility, and priority should also be identified and documented, and an approach to project planning established. This phase can also assist state, regional, and local recreation managers in identifying or assessing potential deficiencies in the availability of accessible recreation sites and programs. This information can be critical in considering budget priorities and related tradeoffs.

3.   **Site Analysis.** The design team should conduct an objective study of the project site and adjacent areas to gain a thorough understanding of the setting. Information from this study can help ensure that human needs are balanced with environmental concerns. The analysis may reveal issues that could impose constraints on or provide opportunities for accessibility, and guide the selection and location of necessary modifications.

At this point, the site's recreation setting should be classified as urban/rural, roaded natural, semi-primitive, or primitive. These are the four recreation settings defined in the Recreation Opportunity Spectrum (ROS). Descriptions of each setting are provided in Chapter II, "The Outdoor Recreation Environment." These descriptions should be used to determine the classification most applicable to the project site.

The ROS classification indicates the overall preliminary level of accessibility that customers will expect at the site (i.e., an "urban/rural" classification implies an easy level of accessibility; "roaded natural" implies a moderate level of accessibility; "semi-primitive" implies difficult access; and "primitive" implies the most difficult level of accessibility). The operative word at this point is preliminary. The ROS classification alone does not determine the appropriate level of accessibility. The site's topography and natural features must also be considered. Universal design modifications must be incorporated in ways that will not diminish the quality of the environment.

The expected levels of accessibility associated with the ROS classifications are intended as guidelines, not absolutes. For example, if the terrain in a roaded natural setting is gently rolling or flat, designers should not feel compelled to provide a moderate level of accessibility when an easy level would be more appropriate. Likewise, an easy level of accessibility may not be possible in all areas of an urban/rural setting. Steep slopes or other environmental factors might make an easy level of accessibility unachievable in some areas. Again, the primary goal is to provide the highest level of accessibility practicable, based on customer expectations for the type of outdoor recreation the setting is designed to provide. (See "Integrating Universal Design in the Outdoor Environment" on pages 53-56 for a more detailed discussion of this issue.)

4. **Program Development.** Once the broad planning issues and specific characteristics of the site are identified, the program elements and objectives—the desired recreation experience—must be defined in consultation with user groups and management. Questions to address include: What recreation activities should be made available? Are there natural features that must be preserved, protected, or modified? Is the expected level of accessibility appropriate for the site, at least by initial appearances?

This is the stage when a universal design approach can help ensure that unnecessary limitations or barriers are not imposed on either the proposed activities or participants. To this end, a comprehensive list of proposed facilities and relevant design guidelines should be compiled and analyzed from a user needs perspective.

5.   **Conceptual Design.** This phase determines the functional relationships between activities and facilities proposed for the site. Program elements are adapted to site conditions and the paths connecting facilities and activity areas are laid out and designed to meet the expected level of accessibility. Several alternative design concepts are generated and successive iterations are undertaken, each building on the positive features of the last. Preliminary cost estimates are also developed to assist in the evaluation of alternatives. In the end, a preferred alternative is developed that best responds to the program requirements and site conditions. The selected design concept is evaluated and further refined through review by peers, management, consumer groups, and plan-in-hand visits to the site.

6.   **Path Analysis.** Before the concept plan is finalized, the proposed "accessible routes" connecting basic program elements must be analyzed. This analysis considers general circulation and movement through the site as well as accessibility requirements related to slopes, surfaces, cross slopes, widths, and distances. This will help ensure that accessibility considerations, which are often overlooked, are corrected early in design. This analysis must also identify situations where provision of the expected levels of accessibility may significantly alter the character of the natural environment. A more thorough discussion of path-related issues is provided on pages 58-67.

7.   **Final Site Plan and Design Detailing.** After the concept plan has been tested and refined for accessibility, the final site plan and final cost estimate are prepared for review and critique by managers. Materials, surfaces, and other design details are specified as part of this plan. These should also be in keeping with the site's ROS classification. For example, designs in urban/rural sites might use paved surfaces extensively, while less developed sites might use surfacing materials such as modified or unmodified native soil or compacted crushed gravel to provide a natural-appearing yet firm, stable, and slip-resistant surface. Designers are

encouraged to fully explore options and possibilities when selecting design elements. Excellence in universal design results from all of the site components working together as a unit.

The site plan and detailing can be considered "fully accessible" and approved if it meets any of the following conditions: 1) All aspects of the site are designed to the guidelines for the recreation setting; 2) The design provides alternative equivalent recreation experiences when the guidelines are impossible to meet; or 3) A decision is made to manage the site for multiple levels of accessibility. In the latter case, each level must be applied with consistency and clearly signed. It would not be appropriate, for example, to reach a highly developed visitor center by an undeveloped footpath.

8. **Contract Preparation.** After the final site plan has been approved, the contract package is prepared, including working drawings and specifications. It is imperative that the construction documents clearly indicate the level of work and detail required by the contractor to ensure that the concepts of universal design are not lost or negated during construction. Included in the specifications should be the requirement that the contractor submit an "as-built" drawing of the project prior to closing out the contract.

9. **Construction and Contract Administration.** Before the contract is awarded, the contract administration team is usually identified. This group is responsible for administering the contract and ensuring that construction proceeds according to specifications. Ideally, the contract administration team will be the same as the design team. Serious complications can arise if those responsible for administering the contract have not been involved previously in the project. If this is not possible (as is often the case), it is important to select contract administrators who have both experience and sensitivity for recreation construction.

Once the contract administration team is chosen and the contract awarded, a pre-work meeting should be held between the contractor and contract administrators to review the purpose, objectives, and desired outcome of the project. This is a good time to review specifications, details, and other elements related to universal

III

applying the guidelines to your site

design to ensure that the contractor understands them completely. Once construction has begun, contract administrators must pay close attention to detail and conduct frequent inspections to ensure that the scope of the contract is being met during construction, particularly with respect to universal design considerations.

10.   **Post–Occupancy Evaluation.** One of the most important but often overlooked steps in the design process is the follow-up review and critique of the project after the site or facility is opened to the public. This review considers the satisfaction of recreationists—the ultimate measure of the design's success. It should involve administrators, managers, the design team, users, and operators of the site, and should focus on questions such as "What works?"; "What doesn't work?"; and "If we could do it all over again, what would we do differently?" It should also consider whether or not universal design was successfully carried through in the project planning and implementation. Lessons from this review can help prevent problems from being repeated on future projects and can highlight aspects of the design that need to be corrected or refined through maintenance in order to better meet the needs of all visitors.

11.   **Ongoing Operations and Maintenance.** In terms of accessibility, ongoing operations and maintenance can be critical steps in the design process. Operators and maintenance staff must understand the original intent of the site design, program requirements, and factors affecting site and program accessibility. It is especially critical that staff have an in-depth understanding of the connection between maintenance and accessibility guidelines so that maintenance tasks, such as resurfacing a portion of a trail or pathway, do not create new barriers to accessibility. An "Operations and Maintenance Guide" can be a valuable reference for conveying this information. It should include source references for design components, preventive maintenance procedures, considerations for accessibility, and a copy of the "as-built" drawings. Routine maintenance of the site, particularly surfacing materials (e.g., sweeping sand from beach walkways, repairing cracked or crumbling asphalt, keeping trails and paths clear of branches, etc.) is critical to ensure that normal use and wear do not deteriorate the level of accessibility below that for which the site has been designed.

integrating universal design in the outdoor environment

Current accessibility standards, including the Uniform Federal Accessibility Standards (UFAS) and the Americans with Disabilities Act Accessibility Guidelines (ADAAG), address the "built" environment—areas where a high level of development and modification is necessary and expected. According to these standards, all new facilities and any existing facilities that are altered must be made fully accessible.

Such standards and expectations are unrealistic for outdoor spaces. Natural elements, such as water, geologic features, steep terrain, or cultural resources, can make sites naturally inaccessible. Modifying the site for accessibility using guidelines for the built environment can undermine the very recreation experience that is being sought. These sites require a design approach that can address and resolve the seemingly inherent conflicts between providing accessibility and respecting the integrity of both the natural environment and the recreation experience.

Conflicts between accessibility and preservation of the recreation environment are most common in urban/rural and roaded natural settings, where easy to moderate levels of accessibility are expected but may not be achievable without excessive modification of the site. Typically, the most problematic design elements will be the paths that connect the site's various elements and spaces.

In these cases, designers must decide whether to:

- Modify the site in order to achieve the expected level of accessibility;

- Preserve that part of the site and change the level of accessibility to a different classification (for that part of the site only); or

- Find a middle ground where modifications are kept to a minimum and accessibility is provided, albeit at a level which is less than what would be expected.

III

applying the guidelines to your site

Applying the ROS

There is a direct correlation between customer expectations and levels of accessibility, which implies that the level of accessibility may vary between sites. This approach is consistent with one of the primary tenets of accessibility regulations which states that modifications for accessibility are not required if they would "change the fundamental nature of the activity." The fundamental purpose of many outdoor recreation experiences is to enjoy the outdoor environment in its most natural and untouched condition.

The Recreation Opportunity Spectrum (ROS), discussed at length in Chapter II, provides a framework for balancing universal design considerations with the concerns and opportunities encountered in outdoor recreation settings. This framework affords a number of advantages for site planning and design:

- It establishes criteria for determining the degree of accessibility modification that will be required in a given area;

- It balances customer expectations for accessibility with concerns for recognizing and protecting the "fundamental nature of the outdoor recreation environment;" and

- It provides a spectrum of opportunities for all people and a diversity of challenge and risk (an important component of the outdoor recreation experience).

To determine the level of modification that is appropriate at a particular site to ensure accessibility, designers must consider the three criteria reflected in the ROS framework:

1. **Customer Expectations.** When people go to a highly developed campground or visitor center, they expect an environment that has a level of accessibility similar to facilities in urbanized areas, where they can participate independently in all activities. In a rustic campsite nestled in the woods, they expect a greater emphasis on the natural landscape and fewer developments and amenities. Greater challenge and risk and fewer amenities are expected in primitive areas.

2.   **Degree of Structural Modification to the Site.** This is closely related to the previous criterion, but focuses more closely on the actual physical attributes of the site. Essentially, the level of accessibility at the site should be consistent with the level of development at the site. As the degree of structural modification increases or decreases, so does the level of accessibility.

3.   **Natural Features.** One of the primary reasons that people participate in outdoor recreation activities is to enjoy the natural beauty and environmental features that outdoor areas provide. Site modifications that destroy or compromise the integrity of these features will undermine the very reasons behind people wanting to access them.

Designers must consider these criteria to determine whether modifications are necessary and appropriate. If the expected level of accessibility will result in unacceptable impacts on the site's natural features, it must be determined whether alternative access can be provided or if it will be necessary to design the facility for a decreased level of accessibility.

The Case of Campground X

As an example, Campground X is in a roaded natural setting, which has a "moderate" expected level of accessibility. Since the site is relatively flat, an easy level of accessibility can be provided throughout most of the site because excessive earthwork is not required. Although the expected level of accessibility is "moderate," most of the paths on the site provide an "easy" level of accessibility, exceeding customer expectations of accessibility without modifying the site's natural features.

In the same campground, one area has extremely steep slopes and clumps of large, healthy, specimen trees. Providing a moderate level of accessibility will require extensive earthwork and removal of several trees. This level of modification may be excessive and require a fundamental alteration to the setting. The situation must be evaluated in light of the design criteria—customer expectations, degree of structural modification, and natural features—and the relative importance of each criteria must be weighed. If the earthwork and tree removal will undermine the desired recreation experience, it may be appropriate

III

applying the guidelines to your site

to lower the level of accessibility in that area. The decision is then documented and included in the project's public files. Decision documents should include the names of the individuals on the planning and design team, the design solution, the decision official, and the concurrence of the reviewing officials.

If an exception to the expected level of accessibility is approved, it is critical to ensure that equivalent accessible experiences are provided in the recreation area and fully integrated in the site. In Campground X, some campsites are secluded, some are by the water, and others are nestled in the trees. Ideally, all of these campsites would be connected to each other and to the site's other activities and facilities by paths that provide a moderate level of accessibility. However, because of the terrain, this may not always be possible. In such situations, the guidelines recommend that a majority of the campsites that provide each type of camping opportunity be made accessible by a path that provides a moderate level of accessibility.

The final site design for Campground X might include paths that are designed to three different levels of accessibility—easy, moderate, and difficult. However, the majority of the site continues to provide—as a minimum—the expected moderate level of accessibility and preserves the natural features that recreationists come there to enjoy.

applying the guidelines

The preceding sections of this chapter discussed the framework and decision-making processes by which universal design can be incorporated in the design of outdoor recreation environments. The following discussions focus on specific aspects of recreation settings that are critical to ensuring accessibility, including:

■ Paths *(page 58)*

■ Picnic Areas and Campgrounds *(page 68)*

■ Fishing Facilities *(page 78)*

■ Boating and Swimming Areas *(page 84)*

■ Equestrian Facilities *(page 84)*

■ Signage and Interpretation *(page 85)*

■ Play Areas *(page 91)*

Most of these discussions apply to the construction of new facilities. A special discussion on "Retrofitting Existing Sites" is provided on pages 101-102.

Paths

Most people enter recreation sites in a car, van, or bus and then transfer to other modes of travel (e.g., feet, wheelchair, bike, walker, cane, stroller) to access the various facilities and recreation activities via the site's path system. Paths are often the single most critical factor in providing accessibility in the outdoor environment and can be divided into two distinct categories: (1) paths that provide access to the primary activities and elements at a site, called Outdoor Recreation Access Routes, and (2) paths that provide access to the site's other, or nonprimary, recreation activities and elements, called Recreation Trails.

Chapter IV, Section 4 ■ **Outdoor Recreation Access Routes (Access To Primary Elements and Spaces).** Outdoor recreation access routes are the paths that connect the spaces and elements that are basic to the recreation experience being offered at the site. For example, the paths at a picnic ground that link the parking area, restrooms, picnic units, and water hydrants. While many of these elements—parking area, restroom, and water hydrant—are not the primary reason for a person to visit the site, they are basic elements that serve all visitors.

Designers and managers must determine which of the activities and elements at a recreation site are "basic to the recreation experience being offered." This determination must be based on visitor expectations regarding levels of accessibility. For example, a fishing area that is located at the far end of a picnic ground may not need to be accessible via an outdoor recreation access route. However, if the fishing area is one of the site's primary features and is in a developed area of the site, it should be considered a primary activity and be serviced by an outdoor recreation access route.

Chapter IV, Section 5 ■ **Recreation Trails (Access to Nonprimary Recreation Elements and Spaces).** Recreation trails provide access to recreation activities and elements that are not the primary activities at the site. They provide varying levels of accessibility, based on the site's ROS classification and visitors' expectations. The accessibility guidelines for recreation trails balance accessibility and recreation considerations and expectations so that efforts towards improving access do not undermine the very nature of the recreation activity being pursued.

In addition to providing access to recreation activities that are not among the site's primary activities, many recreation trails are considered a recreation activity in and of themselves (i.e., hiking trails). Recreation activities served by a recreation trail might include scenic overlooks, interpretive sites, and fishing platforms. Recreation trails can be short, more developed trails—such as a trail connecting a trailhead, visitor center, or parking area with a recreation activity—or longer, less developed trails that provide for hiking in the natural outdoors. Recreation trails are generally longer than outdoor recreation access routes, typically 1/4-mile or longer.

■ **Multiple Levels of Accessibility.** To protect the integrity of a site, paths should be designed to blend with the site's topography to the greatest extent possible. As a result, not all paths can be designed to the guidelines presented in sections 4 and 5 of Chapter IV. However, all paths must be designed and constructed to provide a stable and maintainable facility.

Universal design in outdoor settings is accomplished through the integration of a variety of outdoor recreation access routes and recreation trails at different levels of accessibility. Some may be primitive trails while others are graded and paved to provide easy accessibility. Individuals are then free to choose a trail that provides the recreation experience and degree of challenge and difficulty that they desire.

A single recreation area may have several trail standards. For example, a picnic ground designed into a hillside in a roaded natural setting might have an outdoor recreation access route that connects it to parking, water, and restrooms. That same path might continue as a recreation trail designed for a moderate level of accessibility to a nearby scenic overlook and then become a hiking trail with a difficult level of accessibility through a semi-primitive area.

Because the site is a roaded natural setting, people visiting the site will expect a moderate level of accessibility. However, the design guidelines for the different paths will vary based on the type of access being provided. To determine the appropriate design guidelines to apply on each segment of the path system, you must first identify the site's primary recreation activities. In this case, picnicking is

III

applying the guidelines to your site

the primary activity. The scenic overlook and hiking into the semi-primitive or primitive area are nonprimary recreation activities. These activities are important, but they are not critical to the recreation experience of picnicking.

The paths connecting the picnicking areas with the site's other primary activities and elements (parking, water, restrooms, etc.) are outdoor recreation access routes and must provide at least a moderate level of accessibility. The guidelines for outdoor recreation access routes are provided in section 4 of Chapter IV. The path leading to the scenic overlook is a recreation trail and should be designed to provide a moderate level of accessibility in accordance with the design guidelines in section 5 of Chapter IV. These guidelines provide greater flexibility for blending the trail into the natural environment. In places where the paths overlap in use (serving both as an outdoor recreation access route and as a recreation trail), apply the strictest set of guidelines (i.e., the guidelines for outdoor recreation access routes).

For the recreation trail that continues into the semi-primitive area, there are two design options. These same options apply to all lesser developed trail systems, including trails for hiking, equestrian use, ATVs, and bicycles. The first option is to design the trail in accordance with the applicable design guidelines for recreation trails in section 5 of Chapter IV. In a semi-primitive setting, these guidelines would provide a "difficult" level of accessibility. The second option would apply if site topography or customer expectations are such that modifications for accessibility would alter the fundamental recreation experience. In this case, the trail may be designed to a lesser guideline in accordance with agency trail management guidelines.

■   **Path Surfacing.** Surfacing materials for constructed pathways should be selected to achieve the highest level of accessibility practicable, commensurate with the amount of structural modification to the site, the recreation experience being sought, and the characteristics of the site's natural setting.

In general, surfacing materials for pathways in urban/rural settings should be pavement or other hard-surfaced material, while in roaded natural and semi-primitive settings materials that are more natural-appearing will be preferred. Trails in primitive settings will most likely be native soil. The selected material for developed pathways must provide a firm, stable, and slip-resistant surface throughout the primary season of use and must provide a continuous surface free of abrupt level changes. Attention to these factors is extremely important both during construction and during routine maintenance.

Following is a list of some surfacing materials that can be used for outdoor recreation access routes:
- Concrete
- Asphalt
- Brick, tile, or concrete pavers on concrete
- Brick, tile, concrete pavers, or other paving material set in sand
- Chip seal
- Wood decking
- Compacted gravel
- Soil cement or other soil hardeners
- Crushed stone with cement binder
- Grass
- Native soil

Not all of these materials are appropriate or suitable for every level of accessibility. While guidelines for accessible surfacing are provided in section 4 of Chapter IV, the selection, design, and installation of the proper material for any site must be based on specific site conditions, application requirements, material availability, and applicable regional or local guidelines. Additional guidelines can be found in the Forest Service's *Trails Management Handbook* (USDA Forest Service 1991) and various industry publications. Designers should also keep up-to-date on new products for universal design applications as they become available. Manufacturers and distributors of surfacing materials should be consulted to identify new technologies that might better meet the needs of a specific site or application.

Pathways in urban/rural settings should be firm, stable and slip-resistant

Natural-materials are preferred in roaded natural and semi-primitive settings.

III

applying the guidelines to your site

■   **Other Path Design Considerations.** Paths in developed settings require the consideration of additional design factors, such as edge protections, ample vertical clearance, elimination of protruding objects, and tactile distinctions. These design features help to ensure safe travel for recreationists with visual disabilities and are addressed in the guidelines for outdoor recreation access routes (section 4) and, to an extent, in the guidelines for recreation trails (section 5).

While curbs are not always necessary, the edges of paths in developed settings should be easily discernible through changes in the surface texture (e.g., from asphalt to dirt or grass) or through use of a textured edge on the path surface. Such changes can also serve to mark points of interest or areas where visitors should use special caution, such as at the intersection of two paths. If the path surface is a natural material, then curbs or berms can be used to distinguish the trail edge. Alternatively, a natural surface that is discernible from the surrounding surface can be used. For example, well-compacted gravel is appropriate in locations where it contrasts with the native soil and duff. This treatment can work well for outdoor recreation access routes in roaded natural settings where a moderate level of accessibility and use of natural materials is desired. In semi-primitive and primitive areas, these edging treatments may not be desirable or appropriate.

Signage is also an important aspect of path design and is critical to path accessibility. Issues related to the design and location of signage are discussed on pages 85-90.

Concept Illustrations: Paths and Overlooks

The illustrations on the following four pages show how different levels of accessibility can be integrated in a recreation site.

1)   The illustration on pages 64-65 shows a site in which a path system of outdoor recreation access routes provides an easy to moderate level of accessibility from accessible parking to the site's primary activities (visitor's center, play area, scenic overlook), while recreation and equestrian trails provide a difficult to more difficult level of accessibility to the site's other recreation activities.

2)   The illustration on pages 66-67 shows how overlooks have been incorporated into the same path system at different levels of accessibility.

An easy level of accessibility is expected in developed areas of the site.

Lesser developed areas provide a moderate level of accessibility and emphasize the use of natural materials.

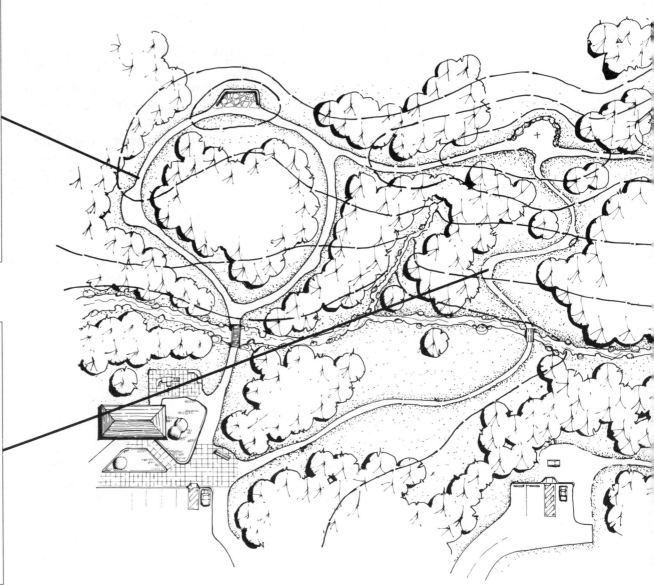

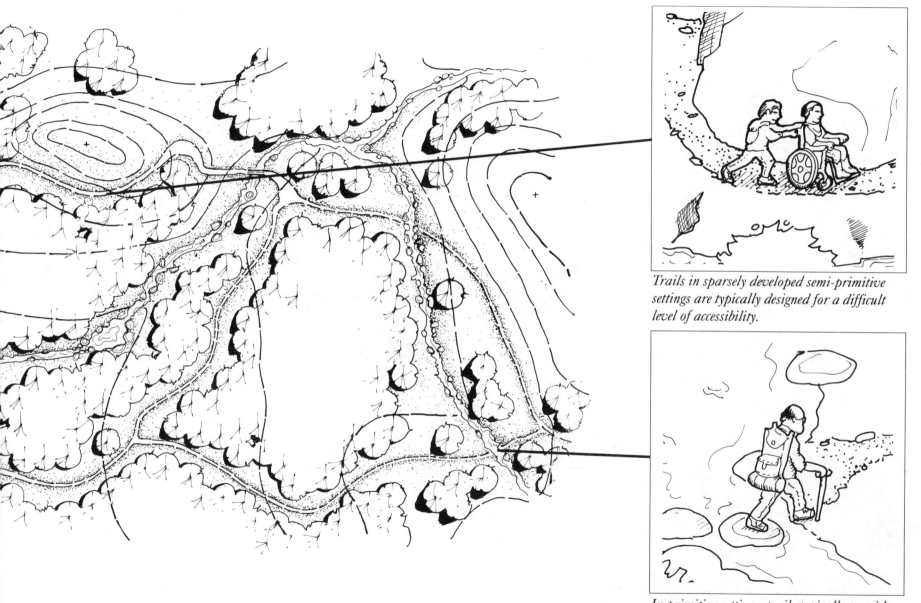

Trails in sparsely developed semi-primitive settings are typically designed for a difficult level of accessibility.

In primitive settings, trails typically provide the most difficult level of accessibility.

III

applying the guidelines to your site

Outlooks in highly developed settings maximize accessibility and safety.

As the site becomes less developed, the design of overlooks places greater emphasis on the environment while continuing to ensure safety.

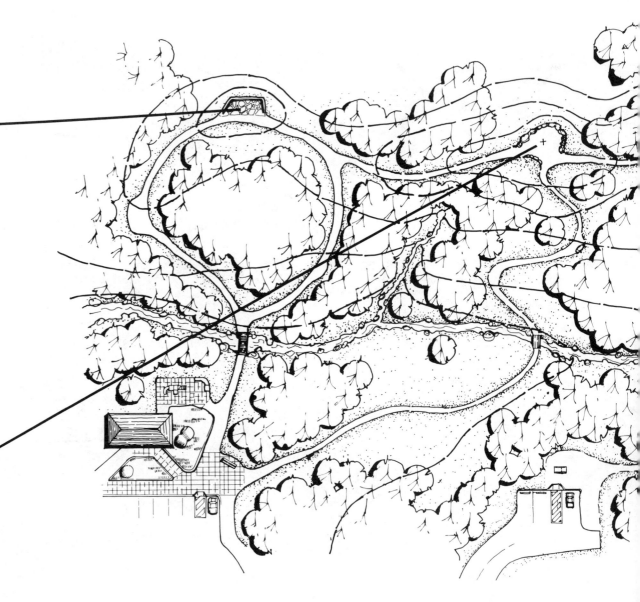

III

applying the guidelines to your site

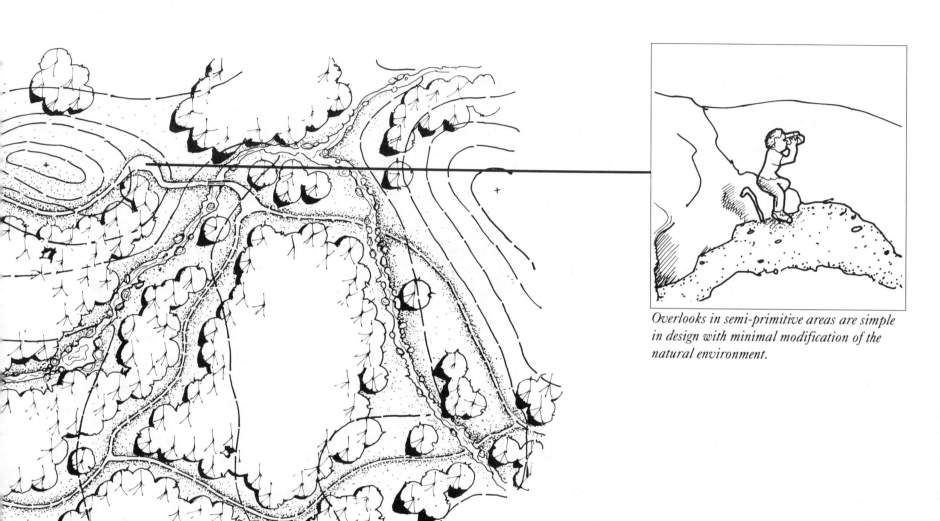

Overlooks in semi-primitive areas are simple in design with minimal modification of the natural environment.

III

applying the guidelines to your site

Picnic Areas and Campgrounds

Picnicking and camping are two of the most popular recreation activities in America. They provide settings in which individuals, families, and groups can relax, eat, and play together in the out-of-doors. To ensure that all people are able to participate in these important group activities, it is critical that these areas be designed using universal design concepts.

When picnic areas, day use sites, and campgrounds are provided in urban/rural and roaded natural settings, they should follow the basic performance standards set forth in ADAAG (e.g., clear space, reach ranges, etc.). These standards can be applied to tables, water sources, fire rings and grills, trash receptacles, and restrooms. Guidelines for each of these elements, based on ADAAG, are provided in section 3 of Chapter IV. In addition, the paths that provide access to these areas should be designed to provide an easy (urban/rural) or moderate (roaded natural) level of accessibility in terms of gradient, width, cross-slope, and surface material (see sections 4 and 5 of Chapter IV).

Whenever camping or picnic units are provided, they should be situated in different locations throughout the site to provide a variety of choices and to take advantage of the area's natural features. For example, some picnic areas should be provided in shady areas and others should be located where they will have direct sunlight; some picnic units should be clustered together to accommodate large groups or located near other site amenities, such as athletic facilities or indoor cooking facilities. Other picnic units should be in secluded areas, where people can enjoy bird watching, studying nature, or simply being alone. However, it may not be possible to provide the expected level of accessibility in all areas of the site due to environmental constraints. In that case, it is critical to ensure that paths meeting the expected level of accessibility connect a majority of the units in each of the different recreation experiences to the site's primary activities and elements. Segregated "special" areas are neither appropriate nor desirable.

The furnishings in picnic areas and camp units vary depending on the site's ROS classification and level of development. Some of the most common elements are addressed in the following discussion. References to the relevant design guidelines are provided in the margins.

Chapter IV, Section 2 ■ **Accessible Parking Spaces.** Most people travel to recreation sites by car. Therefore, parking is the first place where accessibility issues are confronted. ADAAG has set forth detailed standards for the design of accessible parking spaces and their relation to the site. These guidelines must be adhered to in developed parking areas so that all visitors may freely enter the site. In summary, accessible parking spaces must be adequate in number to accommodate expected use levels and must be located and designed to facilitate transfers from vehicles to the accessible path and accessible site entrances. The path from parking to the site must be clear of obstructions and must not require that visitors cross behind other visitors' parked cars. Spaces must also be clearly identified with appropriate signs. In areas where parking is user-established, the guidelines do not need to be followed.

Chapter IV, Section 4.3 ■ **Parking to Provide Alternative Access.** Parking may also be used as an alternative means of providing access to facilities that may otherwise be inaccessible. This form of alternative access has been used in a number of different settings where site topography makes the provision of accessible pathways difficult or impossible without significant alteration of the site. For example, the terrain at a given campground or picnic area may be too steep to provide easy access between the campsite or picnic unit and the restroom, even though the facilities themselves are accessible. A solution would be to provide parking adjacent to the restroom and a path that provides an easy or moderate level of accessibility between the parking and the restroom.

Chapter IV, Section 2.3.5 ■ **Parking at Camp Sites.** Requirements for back-in parking spurs at camp sites are different from the requirements for standard vehicle parking spaces. Because these spaces are used regularly by recreational vehicles (RVs), many of which have awnings or wheelchair lifts, accessible parking spurs require both a greater length and greater width than typical parking spaces. In urban/rural campgrounds, a single back-in spur should be a minimum of 16 feet wide and 50 feet long. In roaded natural settings, where appropriate to the setting, a majority of the units in each loop or in each area of the campground that offers different camping experiences should be at least 16 feet wide and 50 feet long.

III

applying the guidelines to your site

Chapter IV, Section 3.1   ■   **Restrooms.** Whenever restrooms are provided in developed settings, they must comply with all applicable accessibility standards. The building's architecture, materials, and system (i.e., compost, vault, or flush) should be compatible with the site's recreation setting and overall management direction.

Chapter IV, Section 3.7   ■   **Picnic Tables.** All new picnic tables must meet accessibility requirements. Depending on visitor and designer preference, seating for people in wheelchairs can be provided at one or both ends of the table or along the side of the table by removing a section (36 inches minimum) of the bench. This "cut-out" design allows people to get up close to the table for food preparation and serving. Benches and table tops should be made of materials which are comfortable to touch in both hot and cold weather and that are appropriate to the setting.

Chapter IV, Section 3.8   ■   **Fire Rings and Grills.** All new fire rings and grills must meet accessibility requirements. To ensure safety, they must be located off the path and should never be installed in the heavily traveled areas between parking or outdoor recreation access routes and the camping or picnic unit. In addition, fire rings and grills should be located downwind from camping and seating areas (based on the predominant wind direction at the site) and grills on post-mounted grills should rotate to allow for changes in wind direction. Also, handles on fire rings and grills must be easy to grasp and should not conduct heat.

In urban/rural settings, the surfacing that is used under and around the fire ring or grill must be tactually distinct from adjacent surfaces. For example, the accessible route leading up to the fire ring in a camp unit may be asphalt, whereas the fire ring itself may be installed on a heat-resistant concrete pad of exposed aggregate. This will provide a tactile indication that a different element is being approached along the path. In roaded natural settings, such treatments may not be as appropriate, particularly in areas that are less developed. In these areas, designers may want to use a base of well-compacted, crushed gravel around fire rings and grills. In any case, some type of surface treatment other than native soil is recommended. Soil should be avoided as a surfacing around fire ring areas because campers will use the soil to douse fires and hot embers, not realizing that the holes they are creating will be safety and tripping hazards for the next visitors to the site.

Chapter IV, Section 3.9   ■   **Tent Pads.** The accessibility guidelines for tent pads should be applied whenever such facilities are provided. Requirements for size and slope will ensure that tent pads can accommodate a tent and camping supplies, with ample room remaining for a person in a wheelchair to maneuver. While tent pads should be located adjacent to hard surface areas, they do not need to be hard-surfaced themselves. Although the selected material must provide a firm, stable, and slip-resistant surface, it should also be comfortable and should make it easy to pound in tent stakes. Raised pads help facilitate transfers from wheelchairs to the pad surface, but are not required. When appropriate to the setting and topography, some raised pads may be provided, giving attention to aesthetics, natural terrain, drainage, maintenance, and erosion control.

■   **Hookups.** Water and utility hookups are important amenities in camp sites. When provided, they must be designed in accordance with accessibility guidelines, including requirements for clear ground space, reach ranges, and operation. Hookups should be located to the back of the driver's side of back-up parking spurs.

■   **Lantern Hooks.** Lantern hooks must be placed so that they do not create safety hazards. They must not protrude into paths, must be mounted at appropriate heights based on reach ranges, and must not encroach upon required clear ground spaces. In addition, they should be located in areas where they will not pose a fire hazard.

Chapter IV, Section 3.4 and 3.5   ■   **Drinking Fountains, Hydrants, and Hand Pumps.** Water sources are important amenities in both picnic areas and camp sites. These elements must be located adjacent to an accessible route and must be designed to facilitate independent use. Design requirements include a hard-surfaced pad of appropriate size and slope, ample clear ground space, drain grates that will not pose hazards to wheels or cane tips, and appropriate heights for controls and spouts. The location and number of hand pumps are reserved since there are no hand pump designs currently available to provide the 5-pound maximum operating force necessary to ensure accessibility.

III

applying the guidelines to your site

Chapter IV, Section 3.3 ■   **Trash Receptacles.** If a receptacle is located along a heavily used path, it should be positioned so that there is enough room adjacent to the receptacle such that traffic flow will not be interrupted by people dumping their trash. A set-back of 12 inches minimum from the edge of a pedestrian path may be sufficient. However, if the receptacle is located adjacent to a vehicle road, a minimum 36 inches of clear ground space must be provided between the receptacle and the road edge to ensure safety. The surfacing material under and around the trash container should also be firm, stable, and slip-resistant.

Chapter IV, Section 3.11 ■   **Assembly Areas.** All assembly areas must comply with accessibility requirements, although the particular design and selection of materials will vary depending on the recreation setting. Accessibility requirements are largely concerned with the location and design of accessible seating and the paths connecting these seating areas with accessible entrances and other facility amenities. The key goal in relation to seating is to provide a variety of views and choice of seats to meet the widest possible range of needs and desires.

Another issue of concern is the path. Steps and narrow aisles can be troublesome for everyone, but they pose formidable barriers for people in wheelchairs or with strollers. The circulation system to and through an assembly area must meet accessibility guidelines. If steps are necessary, the path must also include a ramp, treated as an integral design element, not as a detail added on as an afterthought.

■ **Distances Between Facilities.** The following chart offers suggestions to assist designers in locating the primary elements in a campground or picnic area (Nordhaus et al. 1984; Wolf et al. n.d.). These distances relate to the energy consumption that is required for a person to move from one location to another. These are not absolutes! Distances are a greater consideration in urban/rural settings. In roaded natural settings, distances need to be tailored to reflect the increased emphasis on the natural landscape.

	urban/rural	roaded natural
Maximum distance from camp unit to toilet	250 ft.	500 ft.
Maximum distance from camp or picnic unit to potable water	100 ft.	200 ft.
Maximum distance from camp to trash receptacle	200 ft.	300 ft.
Minimum distance from camp unit to main roads	50 ft.	100 ft.
Maximum distance from vehicle space to camp unit living area	25 ft.	50 ft.
Maximum distance from vehicle to picnic unit	250 ft.	500 ft.

Concept Illustrations: Restrooms and Camping

The illustrations on the following four pages show how different levels of accessibility are integrated in a camping or picnic area.

1)   The illustration on pages 74-75 shows how the design of restroom facilities might become simplified as the level of development decreases in different areas of the same site. While all restrooms are accessible, the design of each is in keeping with its context in the outdoor recreation environment.

2)   Likewise, the illustration on pages 76-77 shows the camping unit designs at the same site. As the level of development decreases, camping units become increasingly rustic and the level of accessibility increasingly difficult.

Restroom facilities in developed settings use forms and materials common to the built environment.

Restrooms in lesser developed, roaded natural settings are simple in design and emphasize use of natural materials.

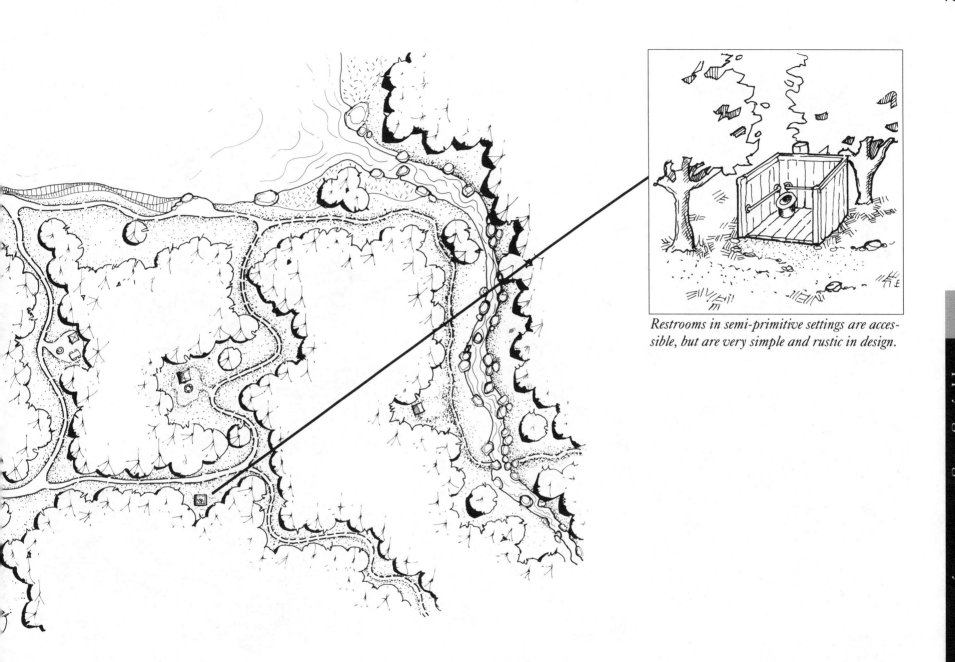

Restrooms in semi-primitive settings are accessible, but are very simple and rustic in design.

applying the guidelines to your site

Camping units in developed settings have an easy level of accessibility for people of all ages and abilities.

This camping unit is in a roaded natural setting and provides a moderate level of accessibility.

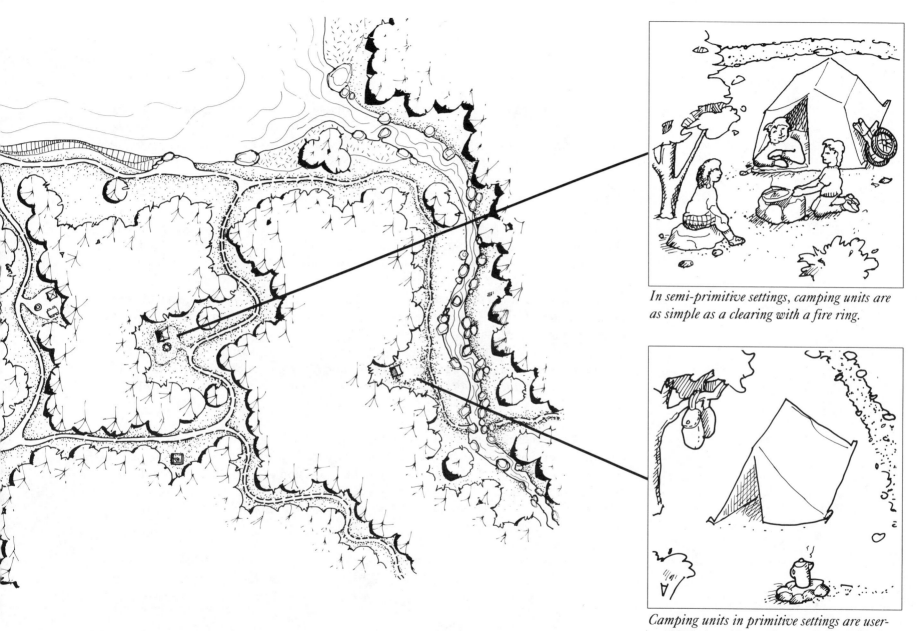

In semi-primitive settings, camping units are as simple as a clearing with a fire ring.

Camping units in primitive settings are user-established and have the most difficult level of accessibility.

III

applying the guidelines to your site

Chapter IV, Section 3.14   **Fishing Facilities**

Fishing is a favorite American pastime that continues to grow in popularity. For many anglers, catching a fish is actually a secondary benefit to the opportunity to relax and unwind with friends, family members, or by themselves. Fishing facilities can provide a variety of integrated recreation experiences if they are carefully planned and managed using universal design concepts. If ample variety is provided, each angler will be able to match his or her abilities to the challenges offered at different fishing stations.

Fishing is a recreation activity that can be found in each type of recreation setting. However, modifications to improve accessibility to fishing facilities are primarily found in urban/rural and roaded natural sites, and rarely in semi-primitive areas.

Planning and design decisions about appropriate improvements to specific fishing sites must consider the ROS setting, recreation demands and expectations, environmental issues, and management concerns. If developed fishing areas are provided, they should be interspersed within the existing pattern of fishing spots along a stream or lake shore, so that an integrated fishing experience and desirable fishing locations are available to all anglers. The specific location of developed areas should respond to the quality of fishing, the desired recreation experience, topography, and proximity to other facilities.

The issues that need to be addressed when designing accessible fishing facilities include: safety; proximity to other facilities; accessible routes; design of the fishing site and amenities; seating and resting areas; and the provision of shade and shelter. Design guidelines for fishing facilities are provided in section 3.14 of Chapter IV. The following discussion highlights how design and planning considerations vary according to the ROS class and customer expectations.

Chapter IV, Section 3.14.1   ■   **Urban/Rural Sites** generally have a high level of structural modification and receive fairly heavy use. Accessibility and safety considerations will be central to the design of facilities so that anglers may expect to find a safe and easy level of accessibility.

- *Accessible Route.* If fishing is the primary activity at the recreation area, then the path connecting developed fishing facilities with the site's support facilities (e.g., parking, restrooms, etc.) will be designed according to the guidelines for outdoor recreation access routes. If fishing is not a primary site activity, then the accessible route leading to developed fishing stations may be designed according to the guidelines for recreation trails.

- *Proximity to Other Facilities.* Designers must consider the proximity of the fishing site to other on-site recreation facilities. When possible, the distance between the fishing site and accessible parking and between the fishing site and an accessible toilet should be limited to no more than 1/8-mile (Nordhaus et al. 1984).

- *Fishing Site Design.* The surfacing at the fishing site must be firm, stable, and slip-resistant. It is also helpful if there is a tactile distinction between the accessible route leading to the site and the site itself. The size of the site will vary based on the amount of space available and the desired capacity. The desired capacity should be determined based on the scale of the lake or river on which it is located and a typical day's demand for fishing. Urban/rural sites may need to be designed to accommodate two, three, or more anglers. There must be a minimum of 5 linear feet along the water's edge for a single angler, 12 feet for two anglers. The minimum depth of the fishing area must be 8 feet so that pedestrians can pass safely behind anglers. In addition, there must adequate room for a person in a wheelchair to access and maneuver around the fishing pad, pier, or dock.

- *Safety Rails and Curbs.* Regardless of the height of the fishing site above the water or the type or depth of the water itself, it is essential that safety rails and some form of edge protection be provided, designed for both accessibility and safety. While the guidelines for safety rails require a 42-inch height, the safety rails at fishing sites may be lowered to a 32-inch height. In addition, safety rails at fishing sites should incorporate arm rests that can be used by both standing and seated anglers. These armrests should be inclined at 30 degrees toward the angler.

-   *Other Amenities.* Tackle box shelves and fishing rod holders can be valuable amenities at fishing sites and can be incorporated into the design of safety rails.

-   *Seating.* Seating, if provided, should include backs and armrests and should be located adjacent to (but not within) the clear path. Seating should also be provided on the outdoor recreation access route or recreation trail leading to the fishing site in accordance with the guidelines for rest areas at passing spaces (see guidelines 4.4.5 and 5.3.5).

-   *Shade and Shelter.* Fishing sites should be located to take advantage of natural shade or shelter. In addition (or if none exists), it may be appropriate to provide constructed shade structures. Shade vegetation or structures must not obstruct the 12-foot minimum overhead clearance required for casting.

Chapter IV, Section 3.14.2 ■ **Roaded Natural Sites** have minimal constructed improvements and are designed to maintain a natural appearance. Considerations for accessibility are balanced with, or sometimes superseded by, the desired recreation experience and the natural beauty of the area. Consistent with a minimal level of structural development, anglers can expect a moderate level of accessibility.

-   *Accessible Route.* If fishing is not a primary site activity or is located more than 1/4-mile from accessible parking, then the accessible route leading to developed fishing stations may be designed according to the guidelines for recreation trails. If fishing is the primary activity at the recreation area, then the path connecting developed fishing facilities with the site's support facilities (e.g., parking, restrooms, etc.) should be designed according to the guidelines for outdoor recreation access routes.

-   *Proximity to Other Facilities.* Fishing sites should be located within reasonable proximity of other on-site recreation facilities, if allowed by the site's natural setting. As a general guideline, the distance between the fishing site and accessible parking and between the fishing site and an accessible toilet should not exceed 1/4-mile (Nordhaus et al. 1984).

- *Fishing Site Design.* The size of fishing pads should be based on the same crite-ria as listed under urban/rural sites, although the scale of development will gen-erally be less in roaded natural settings due to the increased emphasis on the recreation experience and natural landscape. Many sites may be designed to accommodate only one angler and a companion. However, larger sites may be appropriate depending on use, popularity of the area, and recreation demands.

- *Safety Rails and Curbs.* Consistent with the decreased level of structural modifi-cation and increased emphasis on the natural environment, safety rails may be replaced by natural materials such as boulders, providing a greater sense of risk, challenge, and being "out on the water." However, if the site is highly devel-oped (for example, a fishing platform is provided), then safety should be emphasized and safety rails should be provided in accordance with section 4.9.

- *Other Amenities.* If provided, tackle box shelves and other amenities should be rustic in design. For example, a large, flat boulder extending 9 to 15 inches above the ground works well and is in keeping with the overall site aesthetics.

- *Seating.* Seating with backs and armrests should be provided near the fishing site, but need not be incorporated in the design of the site itself.

- *Shade and Shelter.* Sites should be located to optimize natural shade and shelter. In rare instances, a shelter structure may be provided, although it should be designed to be in keeping with the site's natural environment. Another option is to specify native deciduous trees as a means of creating shade and shelter. As in urban/rural sites, both structures and vegetation should be located so as not to interfere with casting ranges or obstruct the clear path.

Concept Illustration: Fishing

The illustration on the following two pages shows how different levels of accessi-bility are integrated in a recreation site that provides opportunities for fishing. As the recreation setting becomes less developed, the design of fishing facilities becomes increas-ingly simple and the level of accessibility more difficult.

III

applying the guidelines to your site

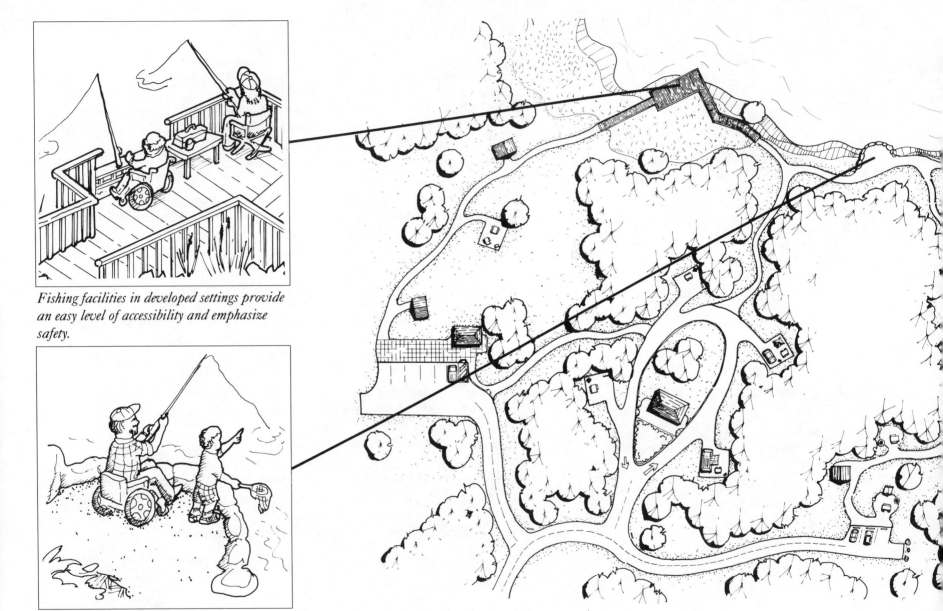

Fishing facilities in developed settings provide an easy level of accessibility and emphasize safety.

In lesser developed settings, the design of fishing facilities helps ensure safety and accessibility, but emphasizes natural materials.

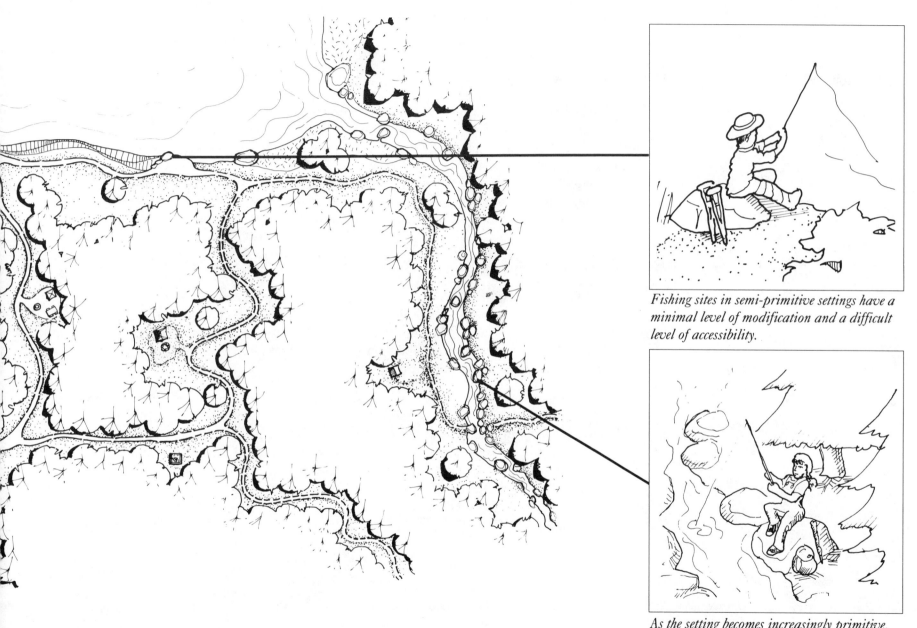

Fishing sites in semi-primitive settings have a minimal level of modification and a difficult level of accessibility.

As the setting becomes increasingly primitive, fishing sites become entirely user-established.

Chapter IV, Sections 3.12 and 3.13   **Boating and Swimming Areas**

Accessibility and safety must be the central focus in the design of boating and swimming areas if all recreationists are to fully participate. Access to these facilities is usually provided by ramps and stairs, with handrails provided. Although stairs are not usually included as part of an accessible route, they can provide valuable alternative access in swimming pools if a ramp is not feasible. In addition, it is extremely important that the surfacing material around swimming pools be very slip-resistant, yet nonabrasive, and absorb a minimal amount of heat when exposed to sunlight.

Chapter IV, Section 3.15   **Equestrian Facilities**

For equestrian activities to be accessible, access must be provided to the place where horses are available and a method for transferring onto and off of the horses must be available. In addition, related facilities such as water hydrants, gates, and openings must be accessible. The extent of accessibility modifications will vary based on customer expectations and the recreation setting.

The primary design issue in equestrian facilities is providing a method for riders to transfer onto and off of the horses with as much ease and independence as possible. For some people, mounting and dismounting is made easier by getting to the level of the horse's stirrups. A level mounting platform can be very helpful. The specifications for such a platform are provided in section 3.15.1 of Chapter IV.

Chapter IV, Sections 4.10 and 5.6

Signage and Interpretation

The following discussion focuses on design issues related to conveying messages to the public through the appropriate design of signs and similar information devices. It does not cover issues related to programmatic access. An excellent reference for program access guidelines is the National Center on Accessibility's *Handbook on Universal Interpretation* (NCA 1994).

Land managers must provide accurate, concise information to potential visitors so that they can make informed decisions about participating in a specific activity or site, including information on the site's recreation opportunities, setting, and level of accessibility.

- ■ **Location.** Interpretive displays, signs, and related materials should be installed at site entrances, along trails, and in visitor centers in keeping with the guidelines in section 4.10 of Chapter IV. The paths that lead to signs and displays must meet the level of accessibility that is consistent with the recreation setting, as posted.

- ■ **Text.** Characters and numbers on signs must be sized according to the viewing distance from which they are to be read. Signs that are mounted or projected overhead should have characters that are at least 3 inches high. Sans serif or simple serif typefaces are preferred. All characters should have a width-to-height ratio between 3:5 and 1:1 and a stroke-width-to-height ratio between 1:5 and 1:10.

- ■ **Color and Contrast.** Interpretive displays and signs should use sharply contrasting colors for text and background (i.e., light-colored images on a dark background, or vice-versa). Colors that "vibrate" off each other, such as red and green together, should be avoided.

- ■ **Restroom Signs.** The requirements for signs identifying restrooms vary by ROS classification:

  — In urban/rural settings, signs for restroom facilities should include gender and wheelchair pictograms, raised text, and Grade 2 Braille.

— In roaded natural settings, restroom signs should include gender and wheel-chair pictograms and raised text. Braille is optional.

— In semi-primitive and primitive settings, restroom signs generally are not necessary.

■ **Signs and Interpretation in Developed Settings.** The following methods of interpretation should be used as appropriate in highly developed recreation settings based on customer expectations:

— *Audio "Signs" and Captioned Material.* Signs that provide audio text or captioned material should be provided wherever possible in urban/rural settings. However, they are out of place in semi-primitive and primitive settings.

— *Displays.* Important artifacts, labels, and graphics should be placed at comfortable viewing levels relative to their size, with important text positioned so that it is viewable by all visitors. Display cases should be designed so that short or seated people can easily view the contents and labels. Video monitors associated with exhibits should be positioned so that they can be viewed comfortably by all visitors. A mounting height of 24 to 30 inches with a 30 to 45 degree inclination toward viewers will make displays and video monitors accessible to most visitors.

— *Lighting.* Lighting should be selected and positioned to reduce glare and reflections from all viewing angles. This is especially important to people with limited vision. Where feasible and appropriate, visitor-controlled, rheostat-type lighting should be provided to augment general room lighting.

— *Information Desks.* Information desks and sales counters should be designed to facilitate use by visitors and employees in wheelchairs. Information about the accessibility of the exhibit and any adjoining recreation site should be available at the information desk.

■ **Communication Accessibility.** Printed information regarding the site's communication accessibility should be available for people with hearing disabilities at primary site entrances and information desks. As applicable, the International Symbol for Deafness (ear with slash), the Text Teletype (TTY) symbol, the amplified telephone symbol, and the closed caption symbol should be visible at appropriate locations. When exhibits include audio information, that information should be duplicated in a visual medium, either on the exhibit or in a printed handout. All new narrated audio-visual programs should be captioned. In addition, exhibit areas should be designed to minimize background noise and listening systems should be provided at staffed interpretive sites.

■ **Multi-Sensory and Participatory Signs.** Whenever possible, sign systems should be designed to communicate to all of the senses and should be understandable without having to read text. Bold graphics and colors can be used on maps and other displays to communicate simple messages and directions. Tactile and participatory elements can be included on signs and in exhibits to enhance other forms of communication and allow visitors who do not speak English, people with visual limitations, and people with learning disabilities to more fully enjoy and understand the exhibit. In developing the text for signs and exhibits, it is best to avoid unnecessarily complex and confusing topics as well as unfamiliar expressions and technical terms. Where appropriate, it is helpful to provide pronunciation aids for unfamiliar words.

■ **Audio-Visual Programs.** Audio-visual programs include motion pictures, sound-slide programs, video programs, and oral history programs. All audio-visual programs should include some method of captioning, which should be incorporated into the program's development at an early stage in the planning process. To the maximum extent possible, an open-captioned version of the program should be provided. In outdoor settings, such as a campfire program, prearranged sign language interpretation or scripts may suffice. In addition, audio amplification and listening systems should be provided where feasible or applicable. The best approach will vary according to the conditions of the installation area and the media being used.

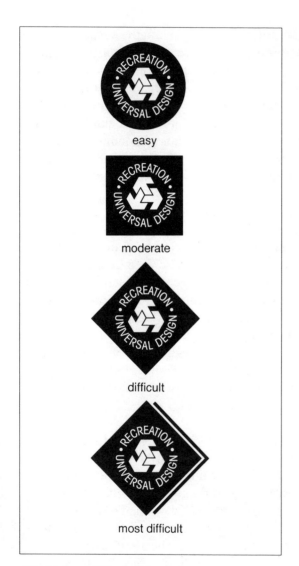

The Universal Design Symbols.

easy

moderate

difficult

most difficult

Areas where audio-visual programs are shown should be designed to accommodate general space allowances and reach ranges (see section 1, Chapter IV). The space layout and seating arrangement should provide a variety of viewing spaces and seating with clear sight lines to provide a range of viewing locations for people of all abilities. If control mechanisms or interactive components are used, they should be mounted in accessible locations.

Overall, the design of audio-visual programs should use the same principals as the design of signs and interpretive media. Graphics should be used to communicate key messages and narration should be concise, free of jargon and unnecessary technical information.

■   **Signs on Paths: the Universal Design Symbols.**   Signs on paths must inform visitors of site conditions related to accessibility. The level of accessibility for each path should be identified using the Universal Design Symbols shown at left.

The Universal Design Symbols should be used instead of the International Symbol of Accessibility in outdoor settings where the international symbol is not required. The International Symbol for Accessibility is required to be posted in four areas—accessible parking spaces, accessible loading zones, accessible restrooms, and accessible entrances when they are not the primary entrance.

Use of the Universal Design Symbols is preferred to the International Symbol of Accessibility because of the meanings attached to each. The International Symbol of Accessibility is seen by many as meaning "reserved for people with disabilities." The Universal Design Symbols, on the other hand, do not reserve sites or facilities for use by certain individuals. Rather, they provide visitors with specific criteria from which informed decisions with regard to participation can be made.

When the International Symbol of Accessibility is used, the color and overall size of the sign and symbol should be designed to blend into the outdoor setting, as long as this does not conflict with ADAAG requirements. For example, Forest Service signs utilize the standard Forest Service colors of brown and cream or white unless otherwise required by ADAAG.

To support public education and safety, the universal design symbols must be used consistently. All signs in urban/rural and roaded natural settings must be designed in accordance with the guidelines presented in section 4.10 of Chapter IV, and all paths must be identified according to the level of accessibility to which they were designed (based on the guidelines presented herein). In addition, to help people better understand the levels of accessibility system and the meaning of the universal design symbols and signs, more in-depth information and other site-specific details should be provided in displays, brochures, and maps at information nodes or kiosks, trailheads, and entrance stations.

■   **Trail Difficulty Rating System.** Individuals can determine when trails are within their range of ability and interest if they have accurate and complete information on trail conditions and characteristics. This information is particularly important for enhancing accessibility in semi-primitive and primitive settings.

Beneficial Designs Inc., a research and design firm working under a grant from the National Institute of Health's National Center for Medical Rehabilitation Research, in partnership with the U.S. Forest Service and National Parks Service, has developed a system to inventory, assess, and map information related to levels of difficulty for park and recreation trails. It can convey necessary information to people who use wheelchairs, have heart conditions or respiratory limitations, are accompanied by children, and others who want to know the level of difficulty.

—   *Inventory and Assessment.* Data related to trail conditions must be inventoried based on objective, quantifiable measures and presented in clear, concise terms. Information should be collected on the average and the minimum or maximum value of four attributes: grade, cross-slope, width, and surface. The trail's total distance and change in elevation should also be documented, as should be any obstacles and their magnitude (e.g., steps, roots, ruts, embedded rocks, vertical obstructions, and water crossings).

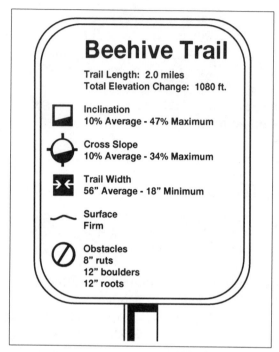

Example of a sign based on the trail difficulty rating system.

— *Mapping and Signing.* Data on trail attributes and features should be posted at information areas and trailheads and provided in trail guides, maps, and brochures. The sign at left illustrates how this information could be displayed. In addition, a route map and grade profile should be provided when possible. Specific obstacles such as large rocks, vertical obstructions, water crossings, steps, drop-offs, ruts, and roots should also be identified on maps wherever possible.

To further assist a user in determining the appropriateness of a particular trail, maps should identify the locations of the minimum trail width and maximum values for grade and cross-slope. If the most demanding trail attributes occur at the end of the trail or in a particular direction on a loop trail, users with limited mobility or endurance can use this information to determine the direction and distance they wish to travel.

— *Rationale.* Different groups will use trails for different purposes at different times throughout the year. Qualitative measures such as easy, moderate, difficult, and most difficult will vary according to the type of use (pedestrian, snowmobile, equestrian, etc.), the functional abilities of the user (age, ability to walk, stamina, etc.), the season of use, and weather conditions. That is why a quantifiable trail rating system, such as the one advocated by Beneficial Designs, is preferred. Posting the minimum and maximum values for the four attributes—grade, cross-slope, width, and surface—will allow individuals to decide for themselves if they have the ability and interest to continue.

Play Areas *(Moore, Goltsman, and Iacofano 1992)*

Play is the raw material of education—helping children to express, apply, and assimilate knowledge and experience. A rich, integrated play environment can encourage all children to take the first experimental steps toward growth and development.

It is essential that play and learning environments provide activities and stimulation for children of all ages and abilities. They should include natural and artificial features, encourage active and passive play, and offer places to play alone or in groups. All play elements, individually and collectively, should provide a sense of dignity, independence, and social integration while supporting children's mental, emotional, social, and physical development.

Play areas must also be designed to meet program needs and safety requirements. Parents and program staff, regardless of ability level, should be able to interact directly with children in their play activities. Safety must be a central concern in design, maintenance, and ongoing management of all play environments.

General considerations include the following:

■ **Level of Accessibility**. Since play sites are associated with a higher level of development and structural modification, they are most common in urban/rural settings, where an easy level of accessibility is expected and the ADAAG standards should be applied. However, since ADAAG was developed according to the needs of adults, not children, it may be appropriate to exceed ADAAG when designing play environments. The following recommendations are based on the report "Recommendations for Accessibility Standards for Children's Environments" developed by the Center for Accessible Housing at North Carolina State University (CAH, 1992).

■ **Paths.** Children who use wheelchairs and other mobility aids require wider paths than adults because they have greater difficulty controlling their chairs, walkers, and crutches. Paths in children's environments should be at least 60 inches wide to allow a child in a wheelchair and a walking companion to travel together.

III

applying the guidelines to your site

Smooth, level, hard-surfaced paths are essential for accessibility. However, in children's environments, they can also be wonderful racetracks for bicyclists, skateboarders, and other wheeled toys. To minimize potential conflicts of use, design the entire path keeping in mind its value as a play element. Provide a diversity of path lengths, alignments, and slopes. Any combination of these characteristics will invite a different play behavior and experience of place. If possible, design one path system as an accessible circulation route and one or more auxiliary routes as play opportunities.

Whenever an accessible path comes within 8 feet of a piece of play equipment that is more than 20 inches off the ground, the path surface must also be shock-absorbing. See the discussion of surfacing at the end of this section.

■ **Ramp Slopes.** The maximum slope for ramps in environments used by children should be 1:20. Where this is not practicable because of the natural terrain or other environmental constraints, a maximum of 1:16 is permitted.

■ **Rest Areas.** Play areas should include comfortable seating areas with plentiful shade and water where children can take a break from their play activities and supervising adults can sit comfortably in close proximity to different play elements. To the maximum extent possible, different seating arrangements and locations should be provided. Some should be designed especially for children (both alone and in groups) while others are designed for parents. Seating for adults is particularly important in infant and toddler play areas.

■ **Play Equipment.** Manufactured equipment can be a valuable addition to a play site if properly selected, sited, programmed, and managed. The best play structures support more than just physical activity; they also support opportunities for social interaction, dramatic play, and education. A good piece of play equipment in the right location can be adapted to meet the needs of a variety of program activities.

Manufactured equipment can pose serious safety hazards if it is not properly installed and maintained. All equipment settings should meet the playground safety guidelines of the U.S. Consumer Product Safety Commission (CPSC) and

A low platform helps children transfer onto play equipment.

the American Society for Testing and Materials (ASTM). Manufactured equipment must also be inspected and maintained on a regular basis.

There are three critical issues regarding accessibility for manufactured equipment:

— *Approach* to play equipment requires an accessible path leading to a specially designed transfer point. In areas where the path lies within the fall zone of play equipment, the path surfacing must be both accessible and shock-absorbing, meeting the CPSC and ASTM requirements for impact attenuation.

— *Transfer* onto the play equipment can be facilitated by provision of a low platform where children can transfer from a wheelchair or other mobility aid onto the play equipment. This platform should be 11 to 14 inches above the ground when designed for use by children under age 5, and 12 to 17 inches above the ground for children ages 5 to 12. The platform surface should be at least 2 feet wide and at least 14 inches deep, and there should be an adjacent clear ground space at least 5 feet in diameter. Handholds should also be provided to help a child maneuver onto the equipment, and a "parking space" that is 30 inches by 48 inches should be provided outside the equipment fall zone where wheelchairs can be left. There must also be a path from the transfer platform onto the rest of the equipment.

— *Use* of play equipment will be different depending on the age and ability of the child. The best equipment settings are those that provide a full range of activities and a graduated series of physical challenge. These settings allow children to enter the setting at a level of challenge that is comfortable to them, and then progress to more difficult challenges at their own pace. In such settings, every child may not be able to reach every part of a piece of play equipment because of ability or age.

■ **Surfacing.** A diversity of surfacing materials, both hard and soft, are needed to support different types of play activity. The surfacing in each part of the play environment must respond to safety concerns and the needs of the intended activities and user groups. Selection of appropriate materials can ensure a wide variety of play opportunities for the widest number of users.

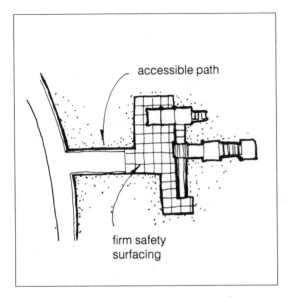

accessible path

firm safety
surfacing

*A firm, resilient, and slip-resistant surface
around play equipment helps ensure accessibility
and safety.*

Shock-absorbing surfacing materials are mandatory throughout the fall zones of all manufactured equipment and must meet or exceed the requirements set forth by the CPSC and ASTM standard specification F1292. These materials must be firm, resilient, and slip-resistant along accessible routes leading to transfer points onto equipment.

Surfacing is also critical to accessibility. Accessible surfaces must be firm, resilient, and slip-resistant. An inappropriate surface can make any environment or setting inaccessible. However, natural ground covers must not be overlooked, as they can be extremely valuable in creating a diverse play environment. They can allow contact with nature, create habitats for small animals, and are an excellent source of play props.

A number of materials can provide appropriate shock-absorbing surfacing in the fall zones of play equipment, including organic materials, such as bark nuggets and wood chips, and inorganic materials, such as sand and chopped tire. Some of these materials, such as wood chips and chopped tire, can also provide a moderate level of accessibility for people in wheelchairs, but their uneven surfaces can cause difficulties for children using other walking aids. The only materials that can provide both shock-absorbancy and complete accessibility are synthetic compact materials, such as rubber mats, synthetic turf on foam mats, poured-in-place urethanes, and rubber compositions. Because of their cost, these materials are often used on the portion of accessible routes that lie within the fall zones of play equipment, ensuring access to the play equipment, while other less accessible but equally safe materials are used elsewhere beneath the play equipment.

Regardless of the surfacing material chosen, it is imperative that the material be properly installed (at proper depths for the height of equipment in the area) and properly maintained. Inadequate surfacing beneath play equipment can lead to death. Designers and managers should consult the *Play For All Guidelines, 2nd Edition* (Moore, Goltsman, and Iacofano 1992) for a more extensive discussion of surfacing materials and issues, as well as the Consumer Product Safety Commission's *Handbook for Public Playground Safety* and ASTM standard specification F1292.

other issues and considerations

Historic Properties *(USDI National Park Service 1992, 1990; U.S. Dept. of Justice 1992a,b)*

Buildings and sites of historical significance offer a special challenge to accessibility. Since historic properties are not exempt from accessibility requirements, balancing accessibility with historic preservation requires great care.

Substantial modifications for accessibility can usually be made to most historic properties with little or no impact. When this is not possible, ADAAG's special provisions will help ensure that efforts to make facilities accessible do not destroy the features and materials that convey the historic significance of the property.

Both ADAAG and UFAS include alternative minimum requirements for accessibility that may be used when a State Historical Preservation Officer (SHPO) determines that complying with the full accessibility requirements would threaten or destroy the historical nature of the property. To be eligible to use the less restrictive guidelines, a facility must either be listed in or be eligible for listing in the National Register of Historic Places, or must be designated as a historical place by state or local law. However, the decision to allow use of alternative minimum guidelines is made at the discretion of the proponent in consultation with the SHPO.

In unique cases, even compliance with the less restrictive minimum alternative requirements for physical access may threaten or destroy the historical significance of a property. In these cases, the proponent, in consultation with the SHPO, may elect to allow the use of alternative methods of providing access. While these may not provide full or even partial physical access, they do represent a good faith effort to allow people with disabilities to enjoy historical properties.

As with all properties, the ADA requires varying levels of retrofitting of historic properties. The extent of renovations required depends primarily on what the facility is used for and who owns the property. Buildings and properties that are not in use do not require accessibility renovations. Furthermore, religious entities, private clubs, and private residences are exempt from the requirements of the ADA. Bed and breakfasts that have five or fewer rooms are also exempt if the proprietor occupies the residence.

■ **Requirements for Public Accommodations.** Public accommodations are facilities which are privately owned but used by the public (e.g., inns, theaters, restaurants, stores, private museums, parks, and other commercial establishments). These facilities are covered by the requirements in Title III of ADA, which are different from the accessibility requirements under ADA's Title II, which addresses facilities operated by government agencies. In general, required renovations for public accommodations are limited to what is "readily achievable." This obligation is ongoing, with modifications being required as they become readily achievable.

In addition, new construction and renovations to historical properties triggers certain other accessibility requirements. If new construction (e.g., an addition to a historic structure) is undertaken, the new construction must fully comply with current accessibility standards. In some instances, additions to historic structures may provide opportunities to increase the accessibility level of the original structure. The new construction must also meet the Secretary of the Interior's *Standards for Rehabilitation of Historic Properties* (USDI 1990). These standards require that new construction:

— Preserve historic materials that characterize the property;

— Be differentiated from the existing facility;

— Be compatible with the massing, size, scale, and architectural features of the historic property; and

— Be undertaken in a manner which would allow its removal at a future date without impairing the integrity or essential form of the historic property.

Alterations and renovations to historic properties must follow the accessibility requirements outlined in ADAAG and UFAS. Essentially, these guidelines require that access improvements be made to the path from the parking area to the facility entrance whenever alterations are undertaken to primary use areas of the facility. Restrooms, drinking fountains, and telephones must be made accessible when additions are made to a facility. The extent of the improvements required depends on the cost of the alterations to the primary use area. Building owners are not required to spend more than 20 percent of the total project cost on these improvements. Maintenance work, such as reroofing and painting, does not trigger these requirements.

If the building owners feel that complying with these requirements would threaten or harm the historical nature of the property, they may petition to use the alternative minimum standards or alternative methods of access.

■ **Requirements for State and Local Government Facilities.** Buildings and facilities that are owned by state or local governments are required to comply with Title II of ADA. Title II requires that programs, activities, and services be readily accessible to people with disabilities. ADA requires that state and local governments make their programs accessible no later than January 26, 1995. Physical modifications to the structure are only required when access cannot be provided through other means. In the case of historic properties, where historic preservation is the primary goal, the controlling agency must attempt to provide physical access to the facility. However, the extent of required renovations is also limited. Agencies are not required to make modifications that would pose an undue financial burden, fundamentally alter the program in question, or threaten to destroy the historical significance of the facility.

When making improvements, government agencies may choose between following ADAAG or UFAS standards. Whichever standard is used, it must be followed throughout the facility. In addition, ADAAG's elevator exception does not apply to state and other government agencies.

■ **Minimum Alternative Requirements.** When compliance with the regular standards of ADAAG or UFAS would threaten the historical nature of a property (as determined in consultation with the SHPO), the following alternative minimum guidelines may be used:

— One accessible route must be provided from the site entrance to an accessible entry to the facility. Ramps that have a maximum slope of 1:6 may be used to provide entry, providing that the ramp run does not exceed two feet.

III

applying the guidelines to your site

— One accessible entry must be provided. If the main public entry cannot be made accessible, a separate unlocked entry is permissible. In this case, directional signs to the alternate entry must be provided.

— If public toilets are provided, an accessible toilet facility must also be provided. This may be a separate unisex facility.

— All public spaces on the entry level must be accessible and other levels should be made accessible whenever practical.

— Displays and other written information must be located where they can be seen by a person seated in a wheelchair. Horizontal signs should be no higher than 44 inches above the floor.

These guidelines are far less restrictive than normal ADA guidelines. While they may also help to reduce the expense of making the property accessible, their primary benefit is to allow access to historic properties without undertaking major alterations that could threaten or destroy the historical significance of the property.

■ **Alternative Methods of Access.** When the proponent, in consultation with the SHPO, determines that even compliance with the less restrictive alternative minimum guidelines would threaten or destroy the historic nature of a property, the use of alternative methods of access may be provided. While these methods may not provide physical access to a facility, they will increase the overall level of accessibility of the facility. However, it is always preferable to provide full, unassisted access to a facility. Some examples of alternative methods of access are:

— Using audio-visual materials, presentations, or displays to show areas of the facility that are inaccessible to people with disabilities.

— Assigning an aide or guide to help people with disabilities enter or maneuver through spaces that are not fully accessible.

■ **Procedures.** There are formal procedures that must be followed in order to make use of either the alternative minimum guidelines or the alternative methods of access. These procedures vary slightly depending on whether or not the facility is subject to Section 106 of the National Historic Preservation Act of 1966. Section 106 applies when the entity responsible for the historic property is a Federal agency, when the property owner receives Federal assistance, or when the property owner is federally licensed. Regardless, it is important to include interested persons in the consultation process. This may include state or local accessibility officials, people with disabilities, agencies or organizations representing people with disabilities, or other interested persons.

Section 106 requires that Federal agencies that have jurisdiction over Federal, federally assisted, or federally licensed facilities consider the impact of all renovations on historic properties. In addition, the Advisory Council on Historic Preservation must be given a reasonable opportunity to comment on the proposed alterations. If after following the Section 106 process, the SHPO agrees that the application of standard accessible guidelines would threaten the historical nature of the property, the use of the alternative minimum guidelines or alternative methods of access may be authorized.

When alterations are undertaken on a facility that is not subject to Section 106, the property owner may initiate consultation with the SHPO. Before consultation is initiated, the property owner must gather all relevant information for use by the SHPO in making a determination. This information may include, but is not limited to: interior and exterior photographs of the property; floor plans and elevations; explanations of alternatives considered; and documentation of consultation with interested parties. If the SHPO agrees that application of standard accessible guidelines would threaten the historical nature of the property, the use of the alternative minimum guidelines or alternative methods of access may be authorized. Typically, a three-step process is followed in making the decision to authorize use of alternative minimum guidelines. These steps are:

III

applying the guidelines to your site

1. Identify the historical significance of the property.

2. Evaluate compliance with accessibility requirements.

3. Evaluate accessibility options.

First, the eligibility of the property owner to apply for use of the alternative minimum guidelines is verified and a prioritized list of the significant features, materials, and spaces is prepared. This list is important because ADA requires that evaluation of proposed alterations be done on a feature-by-feature basis.

Second, the existing level of accessibility in the facility is evaluated. This is often done concurrently with step one. In the case of state and local governments, this must be a formal survey; public accommodations may make an informal survey of their facilities (although a survey must be conducted). The list of access barriers that results from this survey can help building owners determine which areas are most in need of access improvements. Recognizing that it is impractical to require full and immediate access to all existing facilities, the Department of Justice has identified four priorities that should be applied to the list of access barriers to develop a plan of action for renovation and retrofit:

1. Entry to the facility.

2. Access to goods and services provided by the facility.

3. Access to public telephones, drinking fountains, and restrooms.

4. Elimination of other barriers.

Finally, the plan of action developed in the second step and the list of significant historical elements from step one should be analyzed together to determine the appropriate actions for ensuring access without endangering the facility's historic character. All proposed actions must be evaluated under the Secretary of the Interior's *Standards for Rehabilitation of Historic Properties* (USDI 1990).

applying the guidelines to your site

III

Retrofitting Existing Facilities and Sites

Agencies may find that many existing recreation facilities, even those constructed fairly recently, are not accessible by today's standards. Bringing those facilities into compliance and achieving universal designs is the focus of this next section.

First, in compliance with Section 504 and ADA, existing facilities, programs, and activities must be surveyed for accessibility. The survey team should include universal design specialists who are also consumers of accessible outdoor recreation. Information gathered during the survey will be used to develop an Accessibility Action Plan or Transition Plan. The plan must, at a minimum:

■ Identify physical obstacles in the agency's facilities that limit the accessibility of its programs or activities to individuals with disabilities; and

■ Describe in detail the methods that will be used to make the facilities accessible.

Elements and spaces to be surveyed include parking, paths, restrooms, signs, utilities, grading/drainage, and associated site furnishings. The site's recreation setting and ROS classification, which will indicate the overall preliminary expected level of accessibility, also need to be documented.

The Transition Plan outlines priorities for removing the access barriers identified in the survey, presents cost estimates for accomplishing this work, and indicates the official responsible for implementation of the plan.

The retrofitting needed to make the site accessible may be accomplished through routine maintenance and/or routine operation. In some situations, capital investment may be required. The extent of a site's noncompliance and the reality of barriers to access may mean that the only way to achieve full integration of universal design is to establish multi-year goals within the Transition Plan.

For a site to offer an equal opportunity to participate, a majority (at least 51 percent) of the elements and spaces that are fundamental to the recreation experience must

III

applying the guidelines to your site

integrate universal designs in accordance with the guidelines in this book. All developed sites must address this retrofit requirement. For example, the camp units in a campground must be connected to accessible parking, potable water, and accessible restrooms by an accessible path. In addition, managers must ensure that these accessible elements and spaces provide "equivalent experiences" to those offered in other areas of the recreation site.

The goal in retrofitting, as in other aspects of site planning and design, is to incorporate universal design throughout the entire recreation area under review. The challenge, however, is to accomplish this within existing facilities, often with limited resources. A critical element throughout this entire process is the full participation of consumers of outdoor recreation to determine deficiencies in site accessibility, develop the Accessibility Action Plan, and establish priorities. The guidelines presented in Chapter IV of this design guide should be used to ensure that the majority of the site offers accessible facilities and services, and fosters a sense of dignity, independence, and social integration.

Semi-Primitive and Primitive Settings

Thus far, this chapter has focused on universal design in urban/rural and roaded natural areas, where the environment has been modified to some extent. As mentioned earlier, the design guidelines presented in Chapter IV are most applicable in these settings.

Preservation of the natural environment is the dominant design criteria in semi-primitive and primitive settings, followed by the recreation experience itself. People of all ages and abilities visit these settings for the challenge, risk, and adventure associated with them. In these settings, ADA guidelines, and even the design guidelines presented in this book, are less applicable. The following discussion focuses on how people with disabilities may be affected by management policies in semi-primitive and primitive settings and offers recommendations for improving accessibility while respecting and preserving the natural environment.

■ **Balancing Access and Preservation.** In recent years, a perceived conflict between two major social movements has developed—the movement to preserve national wilderness areas and the movement to provide equal access and opportunity for persons with disabilities. Both of these movements have been embodied in various Federal laws, most notably the Wilderness Act of 1964 and the Americans with Disabilities Act of 1990.

Land managers must balance conflicting opinions from different constituencies regarding the accessibility of semi-primitive and primitive settings. However, the split between those who would like to preserve wilderness areas in their natural state and those who would like to make such areas more accessible is not as large as one might expect. There are many people with disabilities who would like to enjoy semi-primitive and primitive settings as they are, without alterations that would fundamentally change the natural environment. The type of accessibility improvements they would like to see are more programmatic than they are physical.

The ADA specifically addresses the issue of wilderness access in section 507(c). However, this section applies only to the National Wilderness Preservation System

(NWPS), a jointly managed Federal lands system that is generally composed of primitive recreation settings. Section 507(c) states:

> "(1) In General — Congress reaffirms that nothing in the Wilderness Act is to be construed as prohibiting the use of a wheelchair in a wilderness area by an individual whose disability requires use of a wheelchair, and consistent with the Wilderness Act no agency is required to provide any form of special treatment or accommodation, or to construct any facilities or modify any conditions of lands within a Wilderness area to facilitate such use, outside current existing laws pertaining to disability access to Federal agency facilities, programs, and activities.

> (2) Definition — For the purpose of paragraph (1), the term wheelchair means a device designed solely for use by a mobility-impaired person for locomotion, that is suitable for use in an indoor pedestrian area."

As a result of this statement and definition, mechanically and electrically powered wheelchairs must be considered an extension of the individual and their use may not be restricted. However, beyond the issue of wheelchair access to constructed features (outhouses, etc.), no Federal agency is required to provide special treatment or accommodation to persons with disabilities who wish to visit the NWPS. By inference, ADA affirms that resource preservation should take precedence over access—at least in the NWPS.

This does not, however, relieve Federal managers from the requirements of Section 504 and Title II and III of the ADA. Primitive and semi-primitive experiences, as programs, must be made available to persons with disabilities, commensurate with their experience and ability to participate.

Agencies are responsible for providing the setting in which recreation activities occur, but people of all ages and abilities are responsible for obtaining any specialized equipment necessary for participation. For example, access to a primitive setting may require a canoe or a horse, just as specialized equipment may be required for individuals with disabilities to participate in a particular outdoor recreation activity. Obtaining and learning how to use this equipment is the individual's responsibility—not that of the land management agency.

■ **Universal Design Considerations.** In semi-primitive and primitive recreation settings, access issues focus primarily on people with mobility impairments.

Estimates regarding current levels of participation are difficult to confirm, but there are at least 15 outfitters that specialize in serving persons with disabilities in semi-primitive and primitive areas. Managers of the NWPS estimate that more than 16,000 persons with disabilities use the system lands annually. In reality, the number may actually approach 50,000 (Lais, McAvoy, and Fredrickson 1992). With relatively few improvements in access design and accurate information pertaining to trail difficulty, more people with disabilities would be able to enjoy these areas.

Semi-primitive and primitive settings may be designed for a difficult level of accessibility when this does not negatively impact the environment. Factors that must be considered include: trail width, grade, and cross slope; surface conditions and characteristics; water crossings and bridges; impacts on resources (i.e., erosion control, existing vegetation, environmental features); and ease of maintenance.

Designs for trails in the NWPS should be consistent with the Wilderness Opportunity Class delineations, which are generally categorized as pristine, primitive, semi-primitive, and transitional. A narrow trail in an area of sparse vegetation may be unobtrusively widened to 28 inches (the standard maximum width for wheelchair design established by the National Wheelchair Standards Committee, ANSI/RESNA) when it is appropriate to the opportunity class within which it occurs. On the other hand, a 28-inch wide trail in a thicket of vegetation, in a pristine setting, or in an area constrained by natural geologic formations might be out of place and inappropriate.

■ **Primitive Developments.** At trailheads and other sites that access semi-primitive and primitive settings, all developed features (e.g., restrooms, picnic tables, cooking units, water hydrants, trail information, etc.) should be fully accessible and paths should meet the expected level of accessibility consistent with the recreation

III

applying the guidelines to your site

setting. However, these guidelines generally do not apply within semi-primitive and primitive settings.

Structural modifications within semi-primitive and primitive settings are rare. Thus, design guidelines for accessibility are generally not applicable. The few developed features that may be provided serve only to mitigate human impacts to the natural environment. In these instances, basic accessibility considerations should be incorporated when practicable.

A case in point is the heavily used Boundary Waters Canoe Area, a congressionally-designated Wilderness, where wooden box toilets were installed several years ago in response to sanitation concerns. Design details such as a wide seating platform and a toilet lid that provided back support made these structures somewhat accessible to many visitors, albeit in a very primitive way. Recently, these toilets were replaced with conical-shaped, fiberglass toilets that are easier to transport, install, and maintain. However, since back rests and other features that would help people with balance and mobility impairments were not provided, these new toilets are much less accessible than the old wooden box toilets. This problem might have been avoided if designers involved people with disabilities who recreate in these settings in the development or selection of accommodations so that at least a minimal or "primitive" level of accessibility could be provided whenever practicable.

More research is needed to establish universal design guidelines for semi-primitive and primitive settings, particularly since the primary concern of resource protection may be at odds with accommodating a primitive level of accessible design. For example, standard methods of handling surface run-off and minimizing erosion, such as water bars, check dams, drainage dips, and trail cross-slopes, may eliminate access entirely for many people with disabilities.

■ **Signage at Trailheads.** Signs at trailheads can help individuals determine when trails in semi-primitive and primitive settings are within their range of ability. See the discussion of the "trail difficulty rating system" on pages 89-90.

applying the guidelines to your site

III

Safety and Risk Management

The following discussion focuses on issues of safety and risk management in each of the four ROS settings. It also offers suggestions, guidelines, and examples to help land managers ensure safety while promoting accessibility.

At this point, there are no absolute answers or established processes. However, as with other phases of universal design, many pitfalls can be avoided and workable solutions developed when designers, people with disabilities, safety personnel, and managers work together to address issues of safety and risk management.

Standards, codes, and regulations are established, in part, to ensure that safety considerations are addressed. These standards and codes rely on quantitative measures (e.g., height, width, depth, etc.). However, qualitative measures must also be considered. Basic civil rights legislation requires equal opportunity for all to participate in activities, programs, and services without regard to disability or other social, cultural, or personal factors. Universal design in outdoor settings incorporates both quantitative and qualitative measures, developing and applying "common sense" design solutions. A similar blending of quantitative and qualitative approaches is necessary to develop and apply "common sense" responses to safety and risk management issues in outdoor settings.

■ **Safety Standards and the Outdoor Recreation Environment.** Safety and risk are critical, complex issues that must be addressed when incorporating universal designs in the outdoor recreation environment. In this discussion, the term "safety" is used in relation to conditions that may cause accidents resulting in bodily harm. It is important that safety issues be addressed in the design process. However, it is also important that elements of risk not be eliminated, since they are often important components of the outdoor recreation experience and the reason why many recreationists choose to pursue a particular activity.

In the built environment, safety standards are defined by the Uniform Building Code (UBC), related state and local codes, Occupational Safety and Health Administration (OSHA), American National Standards Institute (ANSI), UFAS,

ADAAG, and others. These standards provide clear direction to designers and managers for providing a safe, relatively risk-free environment.

Such is not the case in the natural environment. No single authority has declared which, if any, of these codes takes precedence. As a result, recreation and park agencies must balance competing legal requirements when planning for operations. To further complicate the issue, existing codes may not be directly applicable to all situations in the outdoor recreation setting, and may actually be at odds with making the recreation experience accessible to all visitors. For example, safety rails at scenic overlooks or on viewing platforms attached to buildings or fishing sites can block the views for children and people in wheelchairs if they are installed to comply with ANSI and UBC standards. In addition, it is unclear to what extent OSHA codes are applicable when designing recreation sites where employees may be exposed to potential safety hazards.

■ **Guardrails, Handrails, and Grab Bars.** To accurately consider the components of safety and risk management, it is critical to clarify the functions, purposes, and requirements for guardrails, handrails, and grab bars.

— *Guardails*, also called safety rails, are used strictly for providing safety. They are not used to facilitate a particular function or activity. These rails are required as part of UBC when connected to a building, primarily to provide protection from an elevation change. A minimum height of 42 inches is required in developed settings and the built environment.

— *Handrails* are installed along ramps and stairs to assist with balance and support. As such, specifications established for handrails are performance standards—designed to perform a certain function. Handrails must be mounted 34 to 38 inches above ramp surfaces and stair nosings. This mounting height puts the handrails within easy reach of the majority of people needing assistance. Guardrails do not address the performance requirements of handrails. In cases where both safety restraints and handrails are needed, both must be provided.

— *Grab bars* are provided to assist people in transferring from one location to another (e.g., between a wheelchair and a bathtub). Since grab bars are used to facilitate a specific function, they must meet specific performance standards. Grab bars must be mounted between 33 and 36 inches above the floor and must meet all structural specifications.

Performance standards are absolutes. When providing features which require the use of handrails or grab bars, the specified performance standards must be followed. Noncompliance could result in a hazardous situation.

There is more leeway to tailor safety standards to site-specific needs. Guardrails provide an important restraint in areas designed for congested, heavy use or where safety is a primary design consideration. The specified height is based on providing safety, not on facilitating a particular function. Guardrails can be raised to provide an unobstructed view and still provide a safety barrier. It might also be appropriate to lower safety standards, if consistent with customer expectations, to ensure equal participation and compliance with civil rights legislation in less developed outdoor recreation settings or in areas not associated with buildings.

■   **The Recreation Setting, Safety, and Risk Management.** Some recreationists seek settings which offer high risk and challenge. Those who camp or hike the backcountry of some of the nation's most popular areas, such as the national forests of Alaska or Yellowstone National Park, recognize the inherent exposure to risks (from grizzly bears to rocky cliffs) associated with pursuing their recreation interests. In these settings, it is neither possible nor even desirable to design a risk-free environment. To do so would deny the recreation experience people are seeking and fundamentally alter the natural setting. On the other hand, some visitors prefer secure, comfortable surroundings. Because the desired level of risk varies among individuals, it should not be imposed upon a participant.

To determine the acceptable level of risk at a particular site, designers and managers must balance several factors: the recreation setting's ROS classification (based on the degree of structural modification and customer expectations for accessibility); preservation of natural features; primary purpose of the site; antici-

A lowered guardrail at a developed fishing site minimizes hazards while ensuring views for people in wheelchairs.

pated amount of use; and customer expectations for risk and safety. For some visitors and some settings, simply viewing the scenery from a safe, secure distance is appropriate. For others, a sense of exposure and being "on the edge" is the experience being sought. Designers must be able to recognize the difference so that they can strike the right balance between accessibility and risk. Creative design solutions, developed through collaborative efforts of designers and people with disabilities, can often resolve the perceived conflict between access and safety, as the following examples illustrate:

— *Urban/Rural: Easy Access, Low Risk, High Safety.* The dominant design goal in urban/rural settings is to provide full access to all of the site's primary activities, programs, and facilities. Features and qualities of the natural environment are a secondary concern. People choosing to recreate in these settings are looking for a high level of safety with a low level of risk. Therefore, careful attention should be paid to safety considerations and a formal safety management program should intensively monitor site conditions (e.g., hazard tree assessment, daily checking for hazardous surface conditions, etc.).

Routes that connect the site's primary elements and spaces (e.g., parking area, visitor center, campsites, restroom, etc.) should be fully accessible and safe. For example, in areas of concentrated pedestrian traffic, a 42-inch minimum high safety rail as specified by UBC or ANSI standards should be provided where abrupt drop-offs or other hazardous conditions exist. Because guardrails are required by safety standards, not performance standards, they can be slightly modified in response to accessibility concerns. For example, guardrails can be lowered slightly along walkways or at fishing sites to ensure both safety and an unobstructed view of the surrounding scenery or fishing from a seated position (illustrated at left). Likewise, both safety and accessibility issues can be addressed at scenic overlooks by providing a multilevel scenic viewing area that incorporates guardrails to ensure safety and a raised platform to allow individuals to see over the guardrail.

Natural features such as boulders can provide protection at drop-offs in roaded natural settings.

— *Roaded Natural: Moderate Access, Moderate Risk, High Safety.* Roaded natural settings are less developed and have fewer built-in safety features than urban/rural sites. Equal emphasis is placed on accessibility and the natural environment. Guardrails or other edge protection are most likely not provided on maximum grade segments of paths except in the presence of a hazardous edge condition (i.e., a sharp drop-off). At fishing pads or viewing platforms, railing heights could be lowered to ensure full participation by all visitors. Alternatively, natural barriers such as boulders could be used to ensure safety and maintain the rustic character of the site (illustrated at left). Roaded natural settings may also use signs rather than physical barriers to alert users to potential hazards.

— *Semi-Primitive: Difficult Access, High Risk, Moderate Safety.* These settings provide a difficult level of accessibility with few if any structural modifications. Isolation from other people, challenge, high risk, and increased emphasis on the natural environment are the qualities people are seeking. Users assume a greater responsibility for personal safety. Recreation providers should use personal contact, signs, maps, and other information channels to inform users of existing natural conditions and potential hazards. Conditions may vary due to infrequent removal of barriers (fallen limbs, rocks, snow, etc.) that may create a high safety hazard for some users. Physical barriers to hazardous conditions are seldom provided.

— *Primitive: Most Difficult Access, Very High Risk, Low Safety.* In these settings, users assume full responsibility for site information pertaining to personal safety, including information about unusual hazards and unexpected conditions. Monitoring and corrective action are usually done only for protection of the wilderness resource, not for user safety or convenience.

■ **Liability Control.** Much has been said about the current siege of lawsuits against public recreation providers. The insurance industry has often raised rates to private providers and in some cases no insurance is made available. In deciding cases of legal liability, courts seek to establish the presence of four elements:

III

applying the guidelines to your site

1. A duty to protect must be owed the visitor.
2. A standard must be identified and shown to be in violation.
3. An act must take place.
4. Some real damage must occur.

Typically, all four elements need to be proven for an award to be made under common law principles of liability and negligence.

Almost universally, federal courts have recognized that recreation and park agencies have a duty to protect the visiting public, even trespassers, from inherent and imposed dangers. The degree of protection required and the resulting modifications to outdoor recreation areas vary. Courts have held that the more developed an area, the greater must be its compliance with established public safety standards. In some cases, liability has been attached to operations even in wilderness areas, where managers have failed to warn visitors adequately.

■   **Documentation of Decisions.** All decisions and decision-making processes related to safety and risk management issues must be properly documented. Because existing safety codes may compete with each other and with accessibility requirements, designers, safety officials, people with disabilities, and site managers must work together to determine applicable codes and standards on a case-by-case basis, considering also the desired levels of accessibility and risk.

Documentation must include all information pertaining to the analysis of potential hazards; input from people with disabilities; design and safety decisions; and concurrence of managers with final decisions. The most powerful legal defense, recognized by the courts, is to demonstrate the good faith efforts of administrators (1) to produce management plans which identify where conflicts among established safety codes occur, and (2) to address those conflicts in a responsible manner.

Concern for customer safety must be the highest concern. In the absence of clear direction, a "common sense" process should be followed that integrates risk facilitation, safety management, and liability control to effectively and proactively balance concerns for public safety, customer expectations, and the unique characteristics of the natural landscape. The final result will be quality customer service.

III

applying the guidelines to your site

Summary

The design of recreation sites must incorporate the universal design philosophy and match expectations with experiences to offer a full range of recreation opportunities. The decision to participate in an activity at a certain facility is made by the individual, not the designer, and is based on the individual's particular needs, skills, and interests. Technology changes at an astounding rate and individual abilities vary so greatly that designers and land managers should no longer make assumptions of who will be able to get to and enjoy a particular recreation site.

Current guidelines and standards specify only minimum requirements to achieve accessibility. True social integration, dignity, and independence will not be fully realized until designers and land managers, who have the most impact on the way outdoor spaces are shaped, make the commitment to go beyond the letter of the law and implement the spirit of the law.

Universal design can benefit well over half the American population. Use of universal designs in outdoor recreation settings makes good business sense. Buildings and outdoor facilities that are designed using a universal design approach, following the intent of the law rather than the minimum legal requirements, have a longer useful life and built-in adaptability. As standards change, they are less likely to require redesign, ultimately saving both time and money.

design
guidelines

IV

introduction

This chapter presents design guidelines for the various elements and spaces of outdoor recreation environments. The guidelines were developed based on the Americans with Disabilities Act Accessibility Guidelines (ADAAG), with modifications and additions in response to the special context and requirements of outdoor recreation settings. Many guidelines, such as those for outdoor recreation access routes and recreation trails, provide different measurements for use in different ROS settings. Other guidelines, such as those for restrooms and picnic tables, require the same set of measurements regardless of the ROS setting in which they are applied.

These are guidelines, not standards. They have been developed through a process that has involved numerous public and private organizations and individuals of all ages and abilities. As with any guidelines document, the information presented here must be applied within a planning and design context that takes into consideration issues of safety and risk as well as accessibility. In all planning processes the input and involvement of those who will use the environment—including people with disabilities—is critical. In addition, designers and managers must ensure that all applicable standards, codes, and other requirements—at the local, regional, state, and federal levels—are properly applied and implemented. Under no circumstances should these guidelines be used to supersede existing standards applicable in a particular setting or be applied in a manner inconsistent with local conditions and visitor safety.

The guidelines are presented in five sections, as listed below. Definitions of terms used in the guidelines are provided in the glossary.

IV

design guidelines

IV

design guidelines

IV

design guidelines

1
space allowances and reach ranges

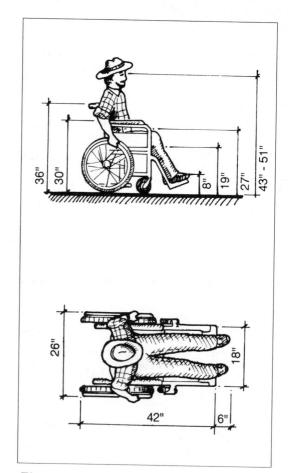

Figure 1-1

Designers should be familiar with the basic spatial dimensions necessary to accommodate people using wheelchairs and other mobility aids. The guidelines in *Universal Access to Outdoor Recreation* were developed based on anthropometric data for adults using wheelchairs and other types of mobility aids, as presented below. These measurements should be followed when designing any space or element not covered by specific guidelines. Because these measurements are based on adult anthropometrics, they may not be appropriate for environments that are intended for use by children.

1.1   Space Allowances

1.1.1   General Dimensions

Figure 1-1 illustrates the typical dimensions for a large adult male in a wheelchair. Figure 1-2 illustrates the typical range and pace of an adult using a cane.

1.1.2   Clear Width (ADAAG 4.2.1)

The minimum clear width for passage of a single wheelchair is 36 inches (915 mm). The width may reduce to 32 inches (815 mm) at a point (Figure 1-3). The 36-inch clear width is also necessary for people who use mobility aids other than a wheelchair (e.g., crutches, walkers, canes) to ensure adequate room for a comfortable gait and safety. Crutch tips, often extending down at a wide angle, are a hazard in narrow passageways where they might not be seen by other pedestrians.

1.1.3   Clear Width at Door and Gate Openings (ADAAG 4.2.1)

The clear width of openings at doors, gates, and similar elements must be at least 32 inches (815 mm) (Figure 1-3). While many people who use wheelchairs need only a 30-inch (760 mm) clear width at such openings (when entered head-on), the addition of an inch of leeway on both sides ensures adequate room for maneuvering. This is especially important for people who are unfamiliar with the facility, for areas in which there is heavy traffic, for situations in which frequent movements are needed, and for situations where a wheelchair must be turned at the opening.

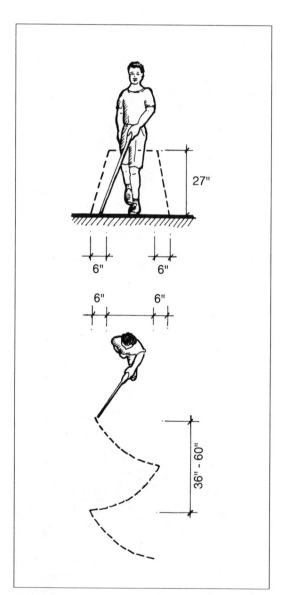

Figure 1-2

If the door opening or reduced area extends for a distance greater than 24 inches (610 mm), it is considered a passageway and must meet the minimum clear width requirement of 36 inches (915 mm).

1.1.4   Passing Width (ADAAG 4.2.2)

The minimum width required for two wheelchairs to pass is 60 inches (1525 mm) (Figure 1-4). This provides just enough space for two people using wheelchairs to pass one another. To provide a more comfortable passage for two streams of traffic, 64 inches (1625 mm) of clear width should be provided. This allows 32 inches (815 mm) for each person, which is the width needed by an able-bodied person in winter clothing, walking straight ahead with arms swinging. This includes 2 inches (50 mm) on either side for sway and another 1 inch (25 mm) tolerance on either side for clearing nearby objects or other pedestrians. Most people who use wheelchairs or other mobility aids can also manage within this 32 inch (815 mm) width for short distances. A minimum of 48 inches (1220 mm) is needed for an ambulatory person to pass a nonambulatory or semi-ambulatory person (Figure 1-5). Even then, an ambulatory person will have to twist to pass a person using a wheelchair, walking aid, or service animal. There will be little leeway for swaying or missteps.

1.1.5   Turning Space (ADAAG 4.2.3)

A person using a wheelchair requires a clear space of 60 inches (1525 mm) diameter to make a 180-degree turn (i.e., to turn around) (Figure 1-6).

Alternatively, a T-shaped intersection of two passageways can provide space for a pivoting, 180-degree turn of a wheelchair. Both passageways must be 36 inches (915 mm) wide and clear for a distance of at least 60 inches (1525 mm) at the point of intersection (Figure 1-7).

While both of these alternatives will provide enough space for turning around, many people will not be able to turn without repeated tries and bumping into surrounding objects. If possible, it is best to provide a space that is 60 inches (1525 mm) wide by 78 inches (1965 mm) long. This will allow most people in wheelchairs to make a U-turn without difficulty (Figure 1-8).

IV

design guidelines

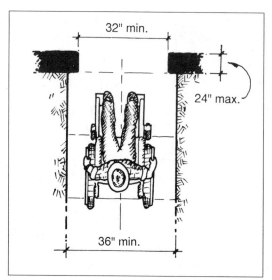

Figure 1-3

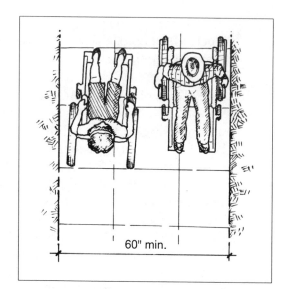

Figure 1-4

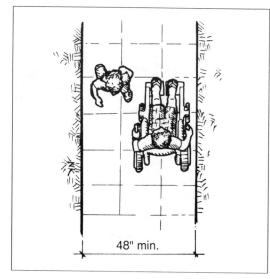

Figure 1-5

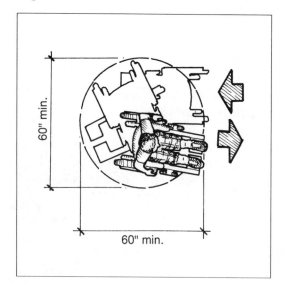

Figure 1-6

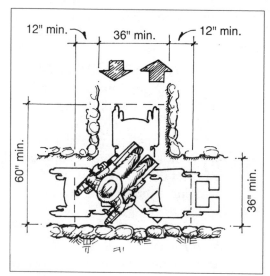

Figure 1-7

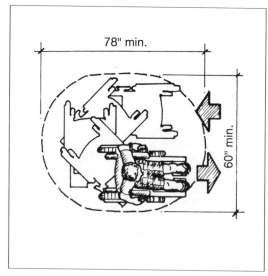

Figure 1-8

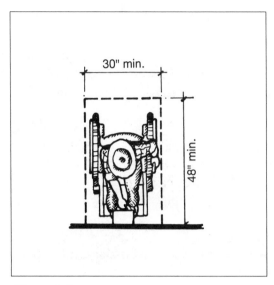

Figure 1-9

1.1.6   Clear Ground or Floor Space (ADAAG 4.2.4)

A single person in a stationary wheelchair requires a clear ground or floor space 30 inches (760 mm) wide by 48 inches (1220 mm) long. This space may be positioned to allow for a forward approach (Figure 1-9) or a parallel approach to an object (Figure 1-10). It may also be positioned so that part of the clear ground or floor space is part of the knee space required under some objects.

One full, unobstructed side of the clear ground or floor space must adjoin or overlap an accessible route or adjoin another wheelchair clear ground or floor space. If the space is located in an alcove or is otherwise confined on all or part of three sides, additional maneuvering clearances may be necessary. For foreward approach, if the clear ground or floor space extends more than 24 inches into the alcove, then 6 inches of additional maneuvering clearance must be provided (Figure 1-11). For parallel approach, if the clear ground or floor space extends more than 15 inches into the alcove, then 12 inches of additional maneuvering clearance must be provided (Figure 1-12).

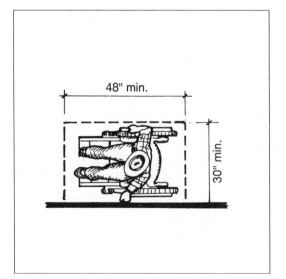

Figure 1-10

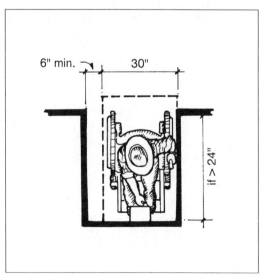

Figure 1-11

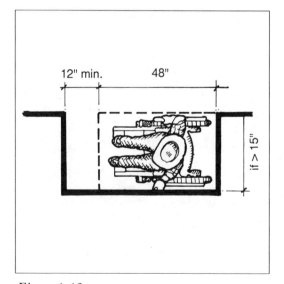

Figure 1-12

IV

design guidelines

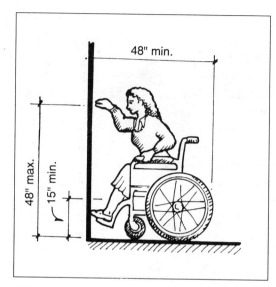

Figure 1-13

1.2   Reach Ranges

"Reach range" refers to the maximum and minimum height that a person in a seated position can reach. Objects that must be reached (telephones, elevator buttons, braille signs, etc.) must be positioned within the appropriate reach range to be accessible to people in wheelchairs.

There are two types of reach range—forward reach and side reach—which refer to the direction in which the object can be approached. If a person using a wheelchair can approach alongside the object and reach it from the side of the chair, the reach range will be greater than if the object can only be approached from the front.

1.2.1   *Forward Reach (ADAAG 4.2.5)*
If the clear ground or floor space is positioned such that the object can only be reached from the front of a wheelchair, the object must be positioned no higher than 48 inches above the ground or floor surface (1220 mm) and no lower than 15 inches (380 mm) (Figure 13). If a person must reach over an obstruction to access the object, the reach range is reduced and the object should be positioned accordingly, as shown in Figure 1-14.

1.2.2   *Side Reach (ADAAG 4.2.6)*
If the clear ground or floor space allows parallel approach to the object by a person in a wheelchair, the object may be positioned up to 54 inches (1370 mm) above the ground or floor surface and as low as 9 inches (230 mm) above the ground or floor (Figure 1-15). If a person must reach over an obstruction to access the object, the reach range is reduced and the object must be positioned accordingly, as shown in Figure 1-16.

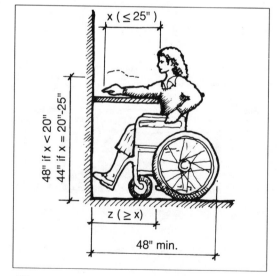

Figure 1-14

IV

design guidelines

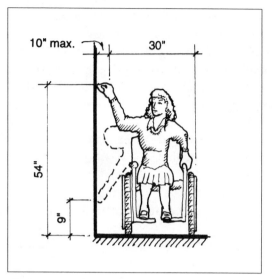

Figure 1-15   *Figure 1-16*

2

parking areas and loading zones
(ADAAG 4.6)

Most people travel to recreation sites in cars, vans, and buses. Therefore, it is important that parking areas and loading zones be designed and constructed in accordance with the following design guidelines to ensure accessibility. Based on ADAAG, these guidelines should be applied to all parking areas, regardless of the site's ROS classification. The only situations in which these guidelines need not be followed are (1) in areas where parking facilities are entirely user-established, as is often the case in semi-primitive recreation settings, and (2) in areas where motor vehicles are prohibited. However, if developed parking is provided adjacent to sites where motor vehicles are prohibited, accessible spaces should be provided.

2.1   Number of Accessible Parking Spaces   (ADAAG 4.1.2(5)(a))

Total Spaces	Accessible Spaces
1 to 25	1
26 to 50	2
51 to 75	3
76 to 100	4
101 to 150	5
151 to 200	6
201 to 300	7
301 to 400	8
401 to 500	9
501 to 1000	2% of total
1001 and over	20 + 1 for each space over 1000

The number of accessible parking spaces that must be provided is determined based on the total number of parking spaces available, as shown in the table above. One in every eight accessible spaces (but at least one) must be "van and RV accessible," as described in section 2.2, *Location of Accessible Parking Spaces*, which follows.

IV

design guidelines

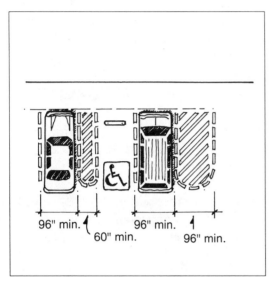

Figure 2-1

Figure 2-2

2.2   Location of Accessible Parking Spaces (ADAAG 4.6.2)

Accessible parking spaces must be located on the shortest accessible route to the recreation site or activity. If the parking area does not serve a particular recreation site, the accessible parking spaces should be located nearest the parking area's accessible pedestrian entrance. When recreation sites have more than one accessible entrance, the accessible parking spaces must be dispersed and located nearest each accessible entrance.

2.3   Parking Space Design (ADAAG 4.6.3)

2.3.1   Car Accessible Spaces

An accessible parking space must be at least 96 inches (2440 mm) wide and must have an adjacent access aisle that is at least 60 inches (1525 mm) wide. Two accessible parking spaces may share a common access aisle (Figure 2-1).

All parking spaces that are adjacent to accessible routes must be designed so that parked vehicles do not overhang and reduce the clear width of the accessible route (Figure 2-2).

2.3.2   Van and RV Accessible Spaces (ADAAG 4.1.2(5)(b), 4.6.4)

Vans and recreational vehicles (RVs) with side-mounted lifts or ramps are becoming increasingly popular among people with disabilities. These vehicles require wider access aisles to permit proper use of the lift or ramp.

To provide a minimum standard of accessibility, a "van and RV accessible" parking space must be 96 inches wide (2440 mm)—same as a car accessible space—and must have an adjacent access aisle that is 96 inches (2440 mm) wide. The combined parking space and access aisle width of 192 inches will be just wide enough to accommodate use of most side-mounted lifts. If a 96-inch (2440 mm) access aisle is placed between two spaces, both spaces will be accessible for vans and RVs. Alternatively, if the wide access aisle is provided at the end of a row, it may be possible to provide the wide access aisle without having to allocate additional space (Figure 2-1).

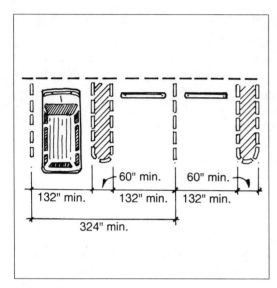

Figure 2-3

A sign must identify the space as van and RV accessible (see guideline 2.9.2, below), but the space should not be restricted to vans and RVs only.

2.3.3   Universal Design Spaces (ADAAG A4.6.3)

As an alternative to creating some accessible spaces that can accommodate vans or RVs, all accessible spaces can be designed as "universal design spaces." Under this design, all accessible spaces are 132 inches (3350 mm) wide with an adjacent access aisle that is 60 inches (1525 mm) wide (Figure 2-3). This design is recommended as a viable alternative across the spectrum of recreation settings because it increases choice for users. Cars, vans, and RVs can use any accessible space and users can choose to park to one side or the other within the 132-inch (3350 mm) space, allowing access from either the driver or passenger side (although, in some cases, this would require exiting or entering without a marked access aisle).

2.3.4   Access Aisle Design (ADAAG 4.6.3)

An access aisle, level with and adjacent to the parking space, is an essential consideration for any design. Access aisles must connect directly with an accessible route to the facility entrance. Therefore, the access aisle must be at the same level as the access route or, if separated by a curb, must be connected to the accessible route by a curb ramp. The curb ramp must not encroach on the required dimensions of the access aisle, must be located so that it is not blocked by parked vehicles, and must be designed in accordance with the specifications in section 4.5, *Curb Ramps*. The access aisle must be free of all obstructions, including curbs, ramps, planters, and wheelstops.

2.3.5   Campsite Parking Spaces

Parking for vans and RVs at campsites in urban/rural settings must be designed according to the universal parking space design. All spaces must be 132 inches (3350 mm) wide with an adjacent access aisle that is 60 inches (1525 mm) wide (Figure 2-3). In roaded natural settings, parking for vans and RVs should meet these requirements whenever practicable based on topography, natural features, and customer expectations. Accessible parking spaces at tent sites must

Figure 2-4

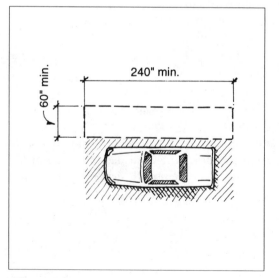

Figure 2-5

meet the requirements for car accessible spaces in guideline 2.3.1 above. In total, a majority of the parking at campsites must be accessible.

2.3.6   Parking at Scenic Overlooks (Kidd and Clark 1982)
     In urban/rural and roaded natural settings, roadside areas that are reserved for scenic overlooks or points of interest must provide at least one parking space from which the view or point of interest can be enjoyed without exiting the vehicle, if appropriate and feasible for the site. The sightlines from these spaces must be considered with respect to vegetation, guardrails, and fences (Figure 2-4).

2.4   Vertical Clearance (ADAAG 4.6.5)

A minimum vertical clearance of 98 inches (2490 mm) must be provided at accessible parking spaces and along the entire length of at least one of the vehicle routes connecting accessible parking spaces with site entrance(s) and exit(s).

2.5   Passenger Loading Zones (ADAAG 4.6.6)

If provided, passenger loading zones must have an access aisle adjacent and parallel to the vehicle pull-up space. The access aisle must be at least 60 inches (1525 mm) wide and 20 feet (6100 mm) long (Figure 2-5). To accommodate buses and vans that have been modified for accessibility, there must be a minimum vertical clearance of 114 inches (2895 mm) along the entire length of at least one of the vehicle routes connecting the passenger loading zone with site entrance(s) and exit(s).

2.6   Bus Parking and Loading Zones (Kidd and Clark 1982; Wisconsin 1991)

Bus parking should be located near the accessible entrance to a facility to minimize the need for people with disabilities to maneuver through parking areas or along roads. Where bus parking is provided, a loading zone should be designated to provide protected space

IV

design guidelines

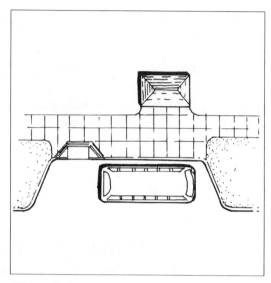

Figure 2-6

along the rear and door-side of the bus. In addition, if appropriate to the recreation site and setting, a small shelter with seating and wheelchair spaces may be provided adjacent to the bus parking area and loading zone as a comfortable place to wait and rest (Figure 2-6). Accessible toilets may also be provided within close proximity to bus parking.

2.7   Parking Area Surfacing

The surface of parking areas must be stable, firm, and slip-resistant. Soft, loose surfaces such as loose sand or gravel, wet clay, and irregular surfaces such as cobblestones, can significantly impede wheelchair movement and create slipping and tripping hazards for people using other mobility aids.

"Slip resistance" refers to the frictional force necessary to keep a shoe heel or crutch tip from slipping on the walking surface under conditions likely to be found on the surface. This frictional force is complex and varied in practice, but can be measured in terms of its "static coefficient" to provide a close approximation of the slip resistance of a surface. Contrary to popular belief, some slippage is necessary for walking, especially for persons with restricted gaits; a truly "non-slip" surface could not be negotiated. The Occupational Safety and Health Administration recommends that walking surfaces have a static coefficient of friction of 0.5. (ADAAG 4.5.1)

In recreation settings, surface materials should be aesthetically appropriate and commensurate with user expectations. Concrete, asphalt, and well-maintained, compacted crushed stone can meet these requirements. Other materials may also be used to achieve a stable, firm, slip-resistant surface. Departures from this guideline that use other materials, designs, or technologies are permitted where the alternative materials, designs, and technologies will provide substantially equivalent or greater access and usability.

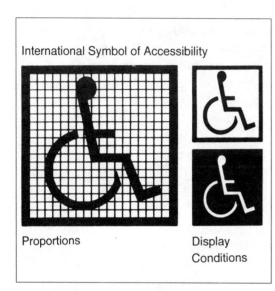

International Symbol of Accessibility

Proportions

Display
Conditions

Figure 2-7

2.8   Parking Area Slope (ADAAG 4.6.3)

The cross slopes of parking areas must not exceed 1:20 (5 percent). However, the cross slopes of vehicle standing spaces and access aisles for accessible spaces must not exceed 1:50 (2 percent) in urban/rural settings and 1:33 (3 percent) in roaded natural and semi-primitive settings.

2.9   Signs

2.9.1   *All Accessible Parking Spaces (ADAAG 4.6.4)*

Many states have specific signage requirements for accessible parking spaces. Designers and managers should consult these codes to determine applicable requirements. At a minimum, all accessible parking spaces in urban/rural and roaded natural settings must be designated as reserved by a sign displaying the International Symbol of Accessibility (Figure 2-7). If the parking area is paved, it is recommended that the International Symbol of Accessibility also be painted on the pavement (see 2.9.4).

2.9.2   *Van and RV Accessible Spaces (ADAAG 4.6.4)*

When an accessible parking space is designed to accommodate vans and RVs (in accordance with guideline 2.3.2), an additional sign with the words "Van and RV Accessible" must be mounted below the International Symbol of Accessibility.

2.9.3   *Location and Mounting Height (ADAAG 4.6.4)*

Signs designating accessible parking spaces must be located so that they are not obscured by parked vehicles. They should also be mounted high enough and in such a position so that they are visible from the driver's seat of a car or van. In urban/rural settings, a sign located at the front of the parking space and mounted with its bottom edge at least 80 inches above the ground is usually adequate. In urban/rural settings that experience heavy snowfall, signs designating accessible parking should be mounted at least five feet above the ground or up to ten feet

IV

design guidelines

Figure 2-8

required width

Figure 2-9

above the ground if local conditions warrant (Figure 2-8). In roaded natural settings, designers have greater latitude for designing and locating signs in keeping with the natural environment. However, when pavement markings are not possible, signs should be located so that they are visible from the driver's seat of a car or van.

2.9.4   Pavement Markings

If the parking lot is paved, the International Symbol of Accessibility should be painted on the parking stall surface. The paint used on the parking lot should always be slip-resistant.

2.9.5   Directional Signs

Signs directing people from accessible parking spaces to the accessible facility entrance should also be provided. Ready-made signs are available from sign companies, city traffic divisions, and state highway departments.

2.9.6   Colors and Materials (ADAAG 4.30.7)

All signs identifying accessible parking must be designed so that characters and symbols contrast with the sign background. However, apart from this requirement, designers may select materials and colors that are appropriate for the recreation setting. Designers should select materials and colors commensurate with the site's recreation setting (e.g., carved wood signs in a semi-primitive setting).

2.10   Tactile Warnings (ADAAG 4.29.5)

If a pedestrian route crosses or adjoins a vehicular way and the walking surface is not separated from the road surface by curbs, railings, or similar elements, designers may define the boundary between the areas with a continuous tactile warning on the vehicle side of the pedestrian route (Figure 2-9).

One recommended method for providing a tactile warning is to cut grooves or otherwise roughen the paved surface. However, care must be taken to ensure that such

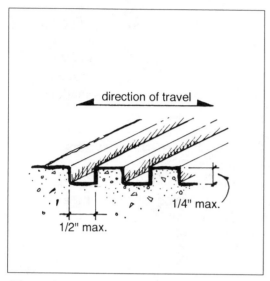

Figure 2-10

alterations to the surface texture do not create tripping hazards or impede travel by people in wheelchairs. If grooves are cut in the surface, they must be perpendicular to the dominant direction of travel and must not exceed 1/4 inch (6.5 mm) in depth or 1/2 inch (13 mm) in width (Figure 2-10).

Tactile warnings are recommended in urban/rural settings, roaded natural settings, and other locations where expectations of easy to moderate access prevail. In semi-primitive settings, motor vehicles may or may not be allowed, a difficult level of accessibility is expected, and parking areas are generally gravel. In these settings, facility managers must determine whether a warning system is necessary based on pedestrian and vehicle densities and common sense with respect to safety and risk management. If a warning system is desired, it can be achieved via appropriate changes in surface texture, provided that the materials used are stable, firm, slip-resistant, and do not present access barriers.

2.11   Lighting

Lighting should be installed in high-use areas in urban/rural settings and in roaded natural settings where electricity is available and night-lighting is appropriate. These areas may include parking areas, offices, visitor centers, restrooms, and the paths that connect them.

3
elements and spaces in the recreation environment

Many outdoor recreation environments contain a number of built features that provide various support services (restrooms, telephones, etc.) or that facilitate the pursuit of particular recreation activities (fishing platforms, swimming facilities, etc.). Because these elements and spaces are typically found in highly developed (urban/rural) or moderately developed (roaded natural) settings, they must be constructed for an easy or moderate level of accessibility.

The following are minimum guidelines for accessibility in the most common elements and spaces of the outdoor recreation environment. Scoping provisions are provided for each set of guidelines to assist designers in determining when a particular element or space must be constructed in accordance with these guidelines. Elements and spaces in urban/rural and roaded natural settings that are not addressed in these guidelines should be designed using the anthropometric data presented in section 1, *Space Allowances and Reach Ranges*.

3.1   Toilet Rooms

3.1.1   *Location and Minimum Number (ADAAG 4.22)*
All toilet rooms in developed sites must be accessible and must be located on an accessible route. When two or more single-user portable toilet units are clustered at a single location, at least 5 percent, but no less than one unit, must be accessible. Accessible units must be identified by the International Symbol of Accessibility.

3.1.2   *Doors (ADAAG 4.13)*
All doors and entries to toilet rooms must meet the minimum guidelines presented in section 4.7, *Gates, Doors, and Other Entryways*.

3.1.3   *Clear Floor Space (ADAAG 4.22.3)*
The accessible fixtures and controls required in accessible toilet rooms must be located on an accessible route and must have an adjacent clear floor space that is at least 30 inches (760 mm) by 48 inches (1220 mm). In addition, an

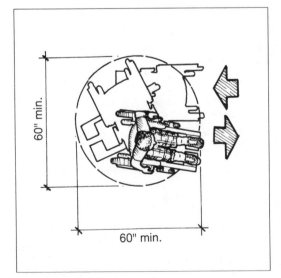

60" min.

60" min.

Figure 3-1

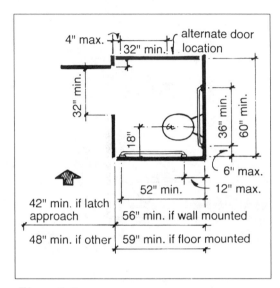

Figure 3-2

Figure 3-3

unobstructed turning space that is 60 inches (1525 mm) in diameter must be provided (Figure 3-1). The clear floor space at fixtures and controls, the accessible route, and the turning space may overlap. Departures from these guidelines through use of other designs and technologies are permitted where the alternative designs and technologies will provide substantially equivalent or greater access and usability (ADAAG 2.2).

3.1.4   Stalls (ADAAG 4.17)

Accessible toilet stalls must meet the following minimum requirements:

(1) Location. Accessible toilet stalls must be on an accessible route.

(2) Size and Arrangement of Toilet Stalls. The size and arrangement of a standard toilet stall must comply with Figure 3-2. The stall depth must be at least 59 inches (1500 mm) if the water closet is floor-mounted; it may reduce to 56 inches (1420 mm) if the water closet is wall-mounted. The layout shown in Figure 3-2 may be reversed to allow either a left- or right-hand approach. Figure 3-3 illustrates a standard stall at the end of a row. If 6 or more stalls are provided, then in addition to the standard stall, at least one stall must be 36 inches (915 mm) wide with an outward swinging, self-closing door (Figure 3-4) and parallel grab bars that comply with Figure 3-6 as well as with the requirements for accessible grab bars.

(3) Toe Clearances. In standard stalls, the front partition and at least one side partition shall provide a toe clearance of at least 9 inches (230 mm) above the floor. If the depth of the stall is greater than 60 inches (1525 mm), then the toe clearance is not required.

(4) Doors. Toilet stall doors, including door hardware, must comply with the general guidelines for doors and gates (section 4.7). If the toilet stall is approached from the latch side of the stall door, clearance between the door side of the stall and any obstruction may be reduced to a minimum of 42 inches (1065 mm).

(5) Size and Spacing of Grab Bars and Handrails. The diameter or width of the gripping surfaces of a grab bar must be 1-1/4 inches to 1-1/2 inches (32 mm to 38 mm), or the shape of the bar must provide an equivalent gripping surface. If grab bars are mounted adjacent to a wall, the space between the wall and the grab bar must be exactly 1-1/2 inches (38 mm) (Figure 3-7).

IV

design guidelines

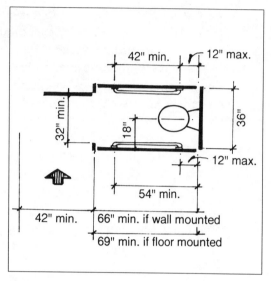

Figure 3-4

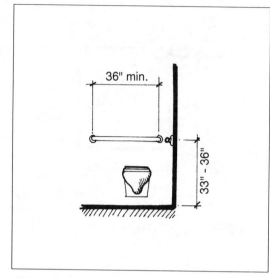

Figure 3-5

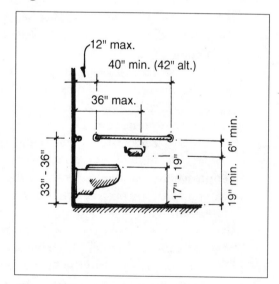

Figure 3-6

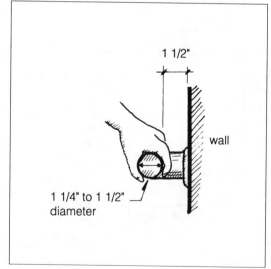

Figure 3-7

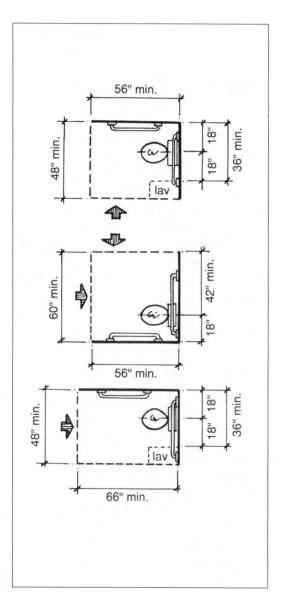

Figure 3-8

(6) *Structural Strength of Grab Bars.* The structural strength of grab bars, fasteners, and mounting devices must meet the following specifications:

(a) Bending stress in a grab bar induced by the maximum bending moment from the application of 250 lbf (1112N) must be less than the allowable stress for the material of the grab bar.

(b) Shear stress induced in a grab bar by the application of 250 lbf (1112 N) must be less than the allowable shear stress for the material of the grab bar. If the connection between the grab bar or seat and its mounting bracket or other support is considered to be fully stressed, then direct and torsional shear stresses shall be totaled for the combined shear stress, which must not exceed the allowable shear stress.

(c) Shear force induced in a fastener or mounting device from the application of 250 lbf (1112N) must be less than the allowable lateral load of either the fastener or mounting device or the supporting structure, whichever is the smaller allowable load.

(d) Tensile force induced in a fastener by direct tension force of 230 lbf (1112N) plus the maximum moment from the application of 250 lbf (1112N) must be less than the allowable withdrawal load between the fastener and the supporting structure.

(7) *Rotation of Grab Bars.* Grab bars must not rotate within their fittings.

(8) *Hazards.* All grab bars and all adjacent walls or similar surfaces must be free of sharp or abrasive elements. Edges must have a minimum radius of 1/8 inch (3.2 mm).

3.1.5 *Water Closets (ADAAG 4.16)*

All water closets in accessible stalls, and at least one water closet if no stalls are provided, must comply with the following where applicable:

(1) *Clear Floor Space.* Clear floor space for water closets that are not in stalls must comply with Figure 3-8. Clear floor space may be arranged to allow either a left-handed or right-handed approach. The slope of the clear floor space must not exceed 2 percent in all directions, with the exception of clear floor spaces in vault toilets and other outdoor toilet facilities, where the clear floor space may slope up to 3 percent.

IV

design guidelines

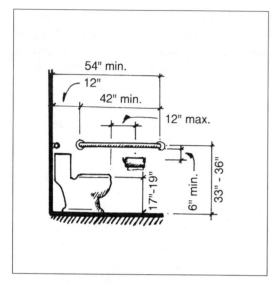

Figure 3-9

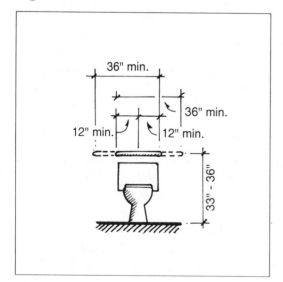

Figure 3-10

(2) Height. The top of the toilet seat on an accessible water closet must be 17 inches to 19 inches (430 mm to 485 mm) above the floor surface (Figure 3-9). Seats must not be sprung to return to a lifted position.

(3) Grab Bars. Grab bars for water closets not located in stalls must comply with the requirements in guideline 3.1.4 and Figures 3-9 and 3-10. The grab bar behind the water closet must be 36 inches (915 mm) minimum in length.

(4) Flush Controls. Flush controls, if provided, may be hand-operated or automatic. Hand-operated flush controls must be operable with one hand and must not require tight grasping, pinching, or twisting of the wrist. The force required to activate flush controls must not exceed 5 lbf (22.2 N). Flush controls must be mounted on the wide side of toilet areas and must be no more than 44 inches (1120 mm) above the floor.

(5) Dispensers. Toilet paper dispensers must permit a continuous sheet of paper to be obtained without pinching, grasping, or twisting of the wrist. Dispensers must be installed within reach of the water closet, as shown in Figure 3-9, and must be at least 6 inches below the grab bar so as not to interfere with its use.

3.1.6   Urinals (ADAAG 4.18)

If urinals are provided, at least one must comply with the following guidelines:

(1) Height. Urinals must be stall-type or wall-hung with an elongated rim at a maximum height of 17 inches (430 mm) above the finish floor.

(2) Clear Floor Space. A clear floor space of 30 inches by 48 inches (760 mm by 1220 mm) must be provided in front of urinals to allow forward approach. This clear floor space must adjoin or overlap an accessible route. If the clear floor space is located in an alcove or otherwise confined on all or part of three sides, additional maneuvering clearances must be provided as shown in Figures 1-11 and 1-12. The slope of the clear floor space must not exceed 2 percent in all directions, with the exception of clear floor spaces in vault toilets and other outdoor toilet facilities, where the clear floor space may slope up to 3 percent. Urinal shields may be provided if they do not extend beyond the front edge of the urinal rim and have a minimum clearance of 29 inches (735 mm) between them.

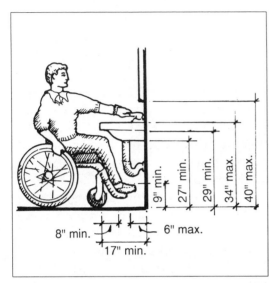

Figire 3-11

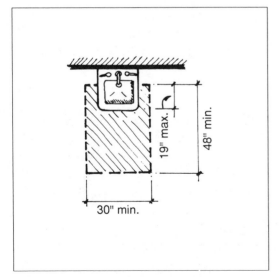

Figure 3-12

(3) Flush Controls. Flush controls, if provided, may be hand-operated or automatic. Hand-operated flush controls must be operable with one hand and must not require tight grasping, pinching, or twisting of the wrist. The force required to activate flush controls must not exceed 5 lbf (22.2 N). Flush controls must be no more than 44 inches (1120 mm) above the floor.

3.1.7   Lavatories and Mirrors (ADAAG 4.19)

If lavatories and mirrors are provided, at least one of each must comply with the following:

(1) Height and Clearances. Lavatories must be mounted with the rim or counter surface no higher than 34 inches (865 mm) above the finished floor and a clearance of at least 29 inches (735 mm) between the finished floor and the bottom of the apron. Knee and toe clearances must comply with Figure 3-11.

(2) Clear Floor Space. A clear floor space of 30 inches by 48 inches (760 mm by 1220 mm) must be provided in front of lavatories to allow forward approach. The clear floor space must adjoin or overlap an accessible route and must not extend more than 19 inches (485 mm) underneath the lavatory (Figure 3-12).

(3) Exposed Pipes and Surfaces. Hot water and drain pipes under lavatories must be insulated or otherwise configured to protect against contact. There must be no sharp or abrasive surfaces under lavatories.

(4) Faucets. Faucets must be operable with one hand and must not require tight grasping, pinching, or twisting of the wrist. The force required to activate controls must not exceed 5 lbf (22.2 N). Lever-operated, push-type, and electronically controlled mechanisms are examples of acceptable designs. If self-closing valves are used, the faucet must remain open for at least 10 seconds.

(5) Mirrors. Mirrors must be mounted with the bottom edge of the reflecting surface no higher than 40 inches (1015 mm) above the finished floor (Figure 3-11).

IV

design guidelines

3.1.8   Controls and Dispensers (ADAAG 4.27)

If controls, dispensers, receptacles, or other equipment are provided, at least one of each must be on an accessible route and must comply with the following:

(1) Clear Floor Space. A clear floor space of at least 30 inches by 48 inches (760 mm by 1220 mm) must be provided at controls, dispensers, receptacles, and other operable equipment. It may be positioned for forward or parallel approach. The slope of the clear floor space must not exceed 2 percent in all directions, with the exception of clear floor spaces in vault toilets and other outdoor toilet facilities, where the clear floor space may slope up to 3 percent.

(2) Height of Operating Controls and Mechanisms. The highest operable part of controls, dispensers, receptacles, and other operable equipment must be within at least one of the reach ranges specified in section 1.2, *Reach Ranges*. Electrical and communications systems receptacles on walls must be mounted no less than 15 inches (380 mm) above the floor. *EXCEPTION: These requirements do not apply where the use of special equipment dictates otherwise or where electrical and communications systems receptacles are not normally intended for use by building occupants.*

(3) Operation of Controls and Mechanisms. Controls and operating mechanisms must be operable with one hand and must not require tight grasping, pinching, or twisting of the wrist. The force required to activate controls must not exceed 5 lbf (22.2N).

IV

design guidelines

3.2   Telephones (ADAAG 4.31)

3.2.1   *Number of Accessible Telephones (ADAAG 4.1.3(17)(a))*

If public pay telephones, public closed circuit telephones, or other public telephones are provided, they must comply with the following guidelines to the extent required by the following table:

Number of each type of telephone provided on each floor or in each immediate area	*Number of telephones required to be accessible**
1 or more single unit	1 per floor or immediate area
1 bank (2 or more phones, often installed as a unit)	1 per floor or immediate area
2 or more banks	1 per bank

* Additional public telephones may be installed at any height.

(1) Accessible Phone in a Bank of Phones. An accessible phone unit that is part of a bank of phones may be installed as a single unit in close proximity to the bank. However, it must be visible from the main bank of phones or identified with signs.

(2) Forward Reach Phones. At least one public telephone per floor or immediate area must meet the requirements for a forward reach telephone. Other accessible phones may be either forward reach or side reach telephones. *EXCEPTION: For exterior installations, if dial tone-first service is available, a side reach telephone may be installed instead of the required forward reach telephone (i.e., one telephone in proximity to each bank must meet the requirements for accessibility).*

3.2.2   *Number of Accessible Text Telephones (ADAAG 4.1.3(17)(c))*

If public telephones are provided at the site, public text telephones must be provided in accordance with the following guidelines:

(1) If four or more public pay telephones (including both interior and exterior phones) are provided at a site, and at least one is in an interior location, at least one interior public text telephone must be provided.

IV

design guidelines

Figure 3-13

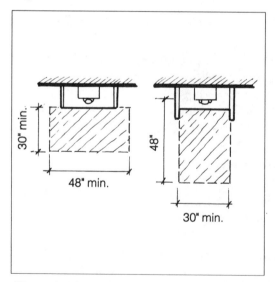

Figure 3-14

(2) If an interior public pay telephone is provided in a stadium, arena, convention center, hotel with convention center, or covered mall, at least one interior public text telephone must be provided in the facility.

(3) If a public pay telephone is located in or adjacent to a hospital emergency room, hospital recovery room, or hospital waiting room, one public text telephone must be provided at each such location.

(4) Where a bank of telephones in the interior of a building consists of three or more public pay telephones, at least one public pay telephone in each such bank must be equipped with a shelf and an electrical outlet.

3.2.3   Volume Controls (ADAAG 4.1.3(17)(b))

All accessible telephones must be equipped with a volume control. In addition, 25 percent, but never less than one, of all other public telephones provided must be equipped with a volume control and must be dispersed among all types of public telephones, including closed circuit telephones, throughout the building, site, or facility.

3.2.4   Hearing Aid Compatible and Volume Control Telephones (ADAAG 4.31.5)

Volume controls, capable of a minimum of 12 dbA and a maximum of 18 dbA above normal, must be provided on all telephones that are required to have volume controls, as set forth in guideline 3.2.3. If an automatic reset is provided, 18 dbA may be exceeded. Telephones required to have a volume control must be identified by a sign containing a depiction of a telephone handset with radiating sound waves (Figure 3-13).

3.2.5   Clear Ground or Floor Space (ADAAG 4.31.2)

A clear ground or floor space of at least 30 inches by 48 inches (760 mm by 1220 mm) that allows either a forward or parallel approach by a person using a wheelchair must be provided at accessible telephones (Figure 3-14). Bases, enclosures, and fixed seats must not impede the approach to the telephone by people who use wheelchairs.

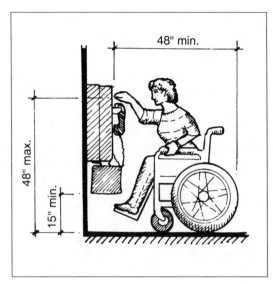

Figure 3-15

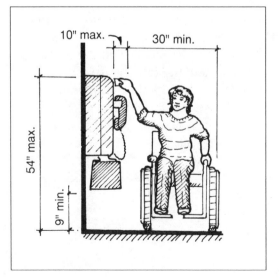

Figure 3-16

3.2.6   Mounting Height (ADAAG 4.31.3)

If the clear ground or floor space requires a forward approach to the telephone, the highest operable part of the telephone (maximum high forward reach) must be no more than 48 inches (1220 mm) and the lowest operable part of the telephone (minimum low forward reach) must be no less than 15 inches (380 mm) (Figure 3-15). If the high forward reach is over an obstruction, reach ranges and clearances must be as shown in Figure 1-14 on page 124.

If the clear ground or floor space allows parallel approach by a person in a wheelchair, the highest operable part of the telephone (maximum high side reach) must be no more than 54 inches (1370 mm) and the lowest operable part of the telephone (minimum low side reach) must be no less than 9 inches (230 mm) above the floor (Figure 3-16). If the side reach is over an obstruction, reach ranges and clearances must be as shown in Figure 1-16 on page 125.

3.2.7   Protruding Objects (ADAAG 4.4)

Telephones that project from walls with their leading edges between 27 inches and 80 inches (685 mm and 2030 mm) above the ground or finished floor must not protrude more than 4 inches (100 mm) into walks, halls, corridors, passageways, or aisles. Telephones mounted with their leading edges at or below 27 inches (685 mm) above the finished floor may protrude any amount (Figure 3-17). Free-standing telephones mounted on posts or pylons may overhang 12 inches (305 mm) maximum from 27 inches to 80 inches (685 mm to 2030 mm) above the ground or finished floor. Telephones must not reduce the clear width of an accessible route or maneuvering space.

3.2.8   Controls (ADAAG 4.31.6)

Telephones shall have push-button controls where service for such equipment is available.

3.2.9   Telephone Books (ADAAG 4.31.7)

Telephone books, if provided, must be located in a position within the reach ranges specified for forward approach and parallel approach (Figures 3-15 and 3-16).

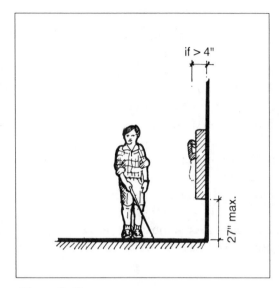

if > 4"

27" max.

Figure 3-17

International TTY Symbol (TDD)

Figure 3-18

3.2.10   *Cord Length (ADAAG 4.31.8)*

The cord from the phone to the handset must be at least 29 inches (735 mm) in length.

3.2.11   *Text Telephones (ADAAG 4.31.9)*

(1) When required (see 3.2.2) or provided, text telephones used with a pay telephone must be permanently affixed within or adjacent to the telephone enclosure. If an acoustic coupler is used, the telephone cord must be long enough to allow connection of the text telephone and the telephone receiver.

(2) Pay telephones designed to accommodate a portable text telephone must be equipped with a shelf and an electrical outlet within or adjacent to the telephone enclosure. The telephone handset must be capable of being placed flush on the surface of the shelf. The shelf must be capable of accommodating a text telephone and must have at least 6 inches (152 mm) vertical clearance in the area where the text telephone is to be placed.

(3) Alternatively, equivalent facilitation may be provided. For example, a portable text telephone may be made available in a hotel at the registration desk if it is available on a 24-hour basis for use with nearby public pay telephones. In this instance, at least one pay telephone shall comply with paragraph 2 of this section. In addition, if an acoustic coupler is used, the telephone handset cord must be long enough to allow connection of the text telephone and the telephone receiver.

(4) Text telephones required must be identified by the International TTY Symbol (TDD) (Figure 3-18). In addition, if a facility has a public text telephone, directional signs indicating the location of the nearest text telephone must be placed adjacent to all banks of telephones which do not contain a text telephone. Such directional signs must also include the International TTY Symbol (TDD). If a facility has no banks of telephones, the directional signs must be provided at the entrance (e.g., in a building directory).

Figure 3-19

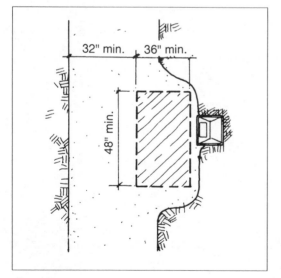

Figure 3-20

3.3   Trash Receptacles

3.3.1   Number

All new trash receptacles, whether being installed in new construction or replaced in retrofits, must comply with the following guidelines.

3.3.2   Location

Trash receptacles, if provided, must be located along an accessible route.

3.3.3   Height

If the trash receptacle can only be approached from the front by a person using a wheelchair, the usable opening of the trash receptacle must be between 15 inches (380 mm) and 36 inches (915 mm) from the ground surface. If the receptacle can be approached from the side, the usable opening may be located between 9 inches (230 mm) and 36 inches (915 mm) above the ground (see Figure 3-19).

3.3.4   Operating Mechanisms

Because trash receptacles in the outdoor recreation environment are often subject to scavenging animals, designers must balance the need for access with the need to inhibit scavengers. If lids are used, they should be hinged and easily operable with one hand. The force required to open the lid must not exceed 5 lbf (22.2 N).

3.3.5   Exposed Surfaces

Trash receptacles must not have sharp edges.

3.3.6   Clear Ground or Floor Space

A minimum clear ground or floor space of 36 inches by 48 inches (915 mm by 1220 mm) must be adjacent to the receptacle. This clear ground or floor space may be positioned for forward or parallel approach. The clear ground or floor space may overlap the adjacent accessible route but must be positioned so that a person in a wheelchair who is using the trash receptacle does not reduce the accessible route to less than 32 inches (Figure 3-20).

IV

design guidelines

3.3.7   Dumpsters

Dumpsters are important elements in recreation settings and should be selected and located for accessibility. However, since no designs are currently available that would meet accessibility requirements, no specific guidelines are provided.

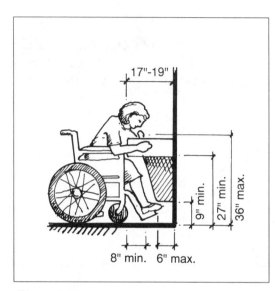

Figure 3-21

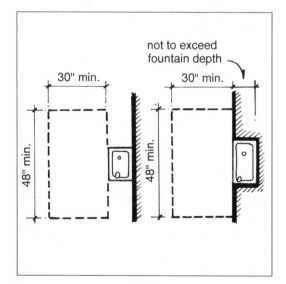

Figure 3-22

3.4   Drinking Fountains (ADAAG 4.15)

3.4.1   Location and Number (ADAAG 4.1.3(10))

Where drinking fountains are provided, at least one shall comply with the following guidelines.

3.4.2   Spout Height (ADAAG 4.15.2)

Spouts on water fountains must be no higher than 36 inches (915 mm), measured from the ground surface to the spout outlet (Figure 3-21).

3.4.3   Spout Location (ADAAG 4.15.3)

The spout must be at the front of the unit and must direct the water flow in a trajectory that is parallel or nearly parallel to the front of the unit. The spout must provide a flow of water at least 4 inches (100 mm) high so as to allow the insertion of a cup or glass under the flow of water. On an accessible drinking fountain with a round or oval bowl, the spout must be positioned so the flow of water is within 3 inches (75 mm) of the front edge of the fountain.

3.4.4   Controls and Operating Mechanisms (ADAAG 4.15.4)

Controls and operating mechanisms must be front-mounted or side-mounted near the front edge of the unit. Controls and operating mechanisms must be operable with one hand and must not require tight grasping, pinching, or twisting of the wrist. The force required to activate controls must not exceed 5 lbf (22.2 N).

3.4.5   Clear Ground or Floor Space (ADAAG 4.15.5)

Wall- and post-mounted cantilevered units must have a clear ground or floor space of at least 30 inches by 48 inches (760 mm by 1220 mm) to allow a person in a wheelchair to approach the unit facing forward. Freestanding or built-in units not having a clear space under them must have a clear ground or floor space of at least 30 inches by 48 inches (760 mm by 1220 mm) that allows a person in a wheelchair to make a parallel approach to the unit (Figure 3-22).

3.4.6   Knee Space (4.15.5)

Wall- and post-mounted cantilevered units must have a clear knee space between the bottom of the apron and the ground that is at least 27 inches (685 mm) high, 30 inches (760 mm) wide, and 17 to 19 inches (430 mm to 485 mm) deep (Figure 3-21).

3.5   Hand Pumps and Hydrants

3.5.1   *Location and Number*

All new *hydrants*, whether being installed in new construction or replaced in retrofits, must comply with the following guidelines.

There are no requirements for the location and number of *hand pumps* since there are no hand pump designs currently available to provide the 5 lbf maximum operating force necessary to ensure accessibility.

3.5.2   *Spout Height (Kidd and Clark 1982)*

The spouts of accessible hydrants and hand pumps must be no less than 28 inches above the ground and no more than 36 inches (915 mm) above the ground. Controls must not exceed a height of 40 inches (1017 mm) above the ground.

3.5.3   *Spout Location and Pad*

The spouts of accessible hydrants and hand pumps must be located at the front of the unit and must have an adjacent pad that is at least 60 inches square (1220 mm square). The pad surface must be stable, firm, and slip-resistant, and may not slope more than 3 percent. The pad slope should be designed to drain water away from the user (Figure 3-23).

3.5.4   *Controls and Operating Mechanisms (ADAAG 4.15.4)*

Unit controls and operating mechanisms on hydrants and hand pumps must be front-mounted or side-mounted near the front edge of the unit. Controls and operating mechanisms must be operable with one hand and must not require tight grasping, pinching, or twisting of the wrist. The force required to activate controls on *hydrants* must not exceed 5 lbf (22.2 N). The spout must provide a water flow not to exceed 60 psi.

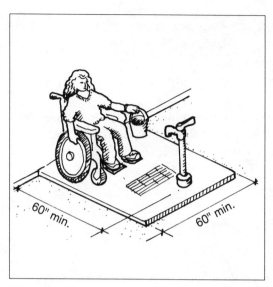

Figure 3-23

IV

design guidelines

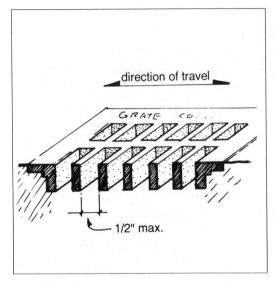

Figure 3-24

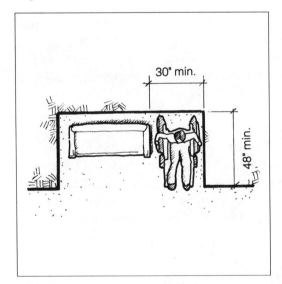

Figure 3-25

There is no force requirement for activation of controls on *hand pumps* since there are no hand pump designs currently available to provide the 5 lbf maximum operating force necessary to ensure accessibility.

3.5.5   Gratings (ADAAG 4.5.4)

If gratings are located on the spout pad, they must have spaces no greater than 1/2 inch (13 mm) wide in one direction. If gratings have elongated openings, they shall be placed so that the long dimension is perpendicular to the dominant direction of travel (Figure 3-24).

3.6   Benches

3.6.1   Backs and Armrests

When benches are provided in urban/rural and roaded natural settings, at least one must provide backs and armrests.

3.6.2   Clear Ground or Floor Space (ADAAG 4.15.5)

Benches must have an adjacent clear ground or floor space of at least 30 inches by 48 inches (760 mm by 1220 mm) to allow a person in a wheelchair to park near other seated people (Figure 3-25).

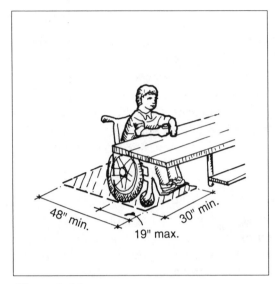

Figure 3-26

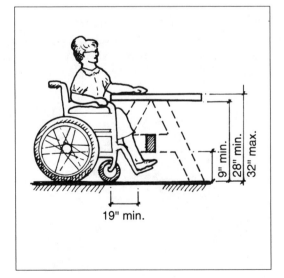

Figure 3-27

3.7 Picnic Tables (ADAAG 4.32)

Picnic tables provide a basic recreation opportunity for many people that allows them to enjoy the outdoors as well as friends and family. To the maximum extent possible, picnic table design should allow people of all ages and abilities to sit together at the same table. The following are minimum guidelines for accommodating people who use wheelchairs at picnic tables. Departures from these guidelines through use of other designs and technologies are permitted where the alternative designs and technologies will provide substantially equivalent or greater access and usability.

3.7.1 Number (ADAAG 4.1.1)

All new picnic tables, whether being installed in new construction or replaced in retrofits, must comply with the following guidelines.

3.7.2 Location

When picnic tables are provided in urban/rural or roaded natural settings, a majority of the tables must be located adjacent to an outdoor recreation access route.

3.7.3 Seating for People Using Wheelchairs (ADAAG 4.32.2)

To accommodate a person in a wheelchair, seating space at a picnic table must have clear ground space of 30 inches by 48 inches (760 mm by 1220 mm). This space may not overlap the required knee clearance space by more than 19 inches (485 mm) (Figure 3-26).

3.7.4 Table Height (ADAAG 4.32.4)

The top of an accessible picnic table must not be higher than 32 inches (865 mm) above the ground (Figures 3-27 and 3-28).

IV

design guidelines

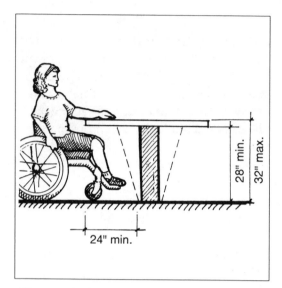

Figure 3-28

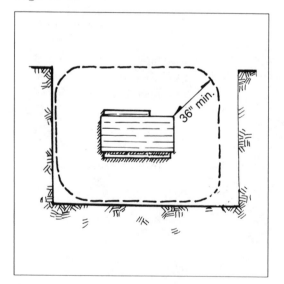

Figure 3-29

3.7.5   Knee Clearances (ADAAG 4.32.3)

To accommodate a person in a wheelchair, the seating space at a picnic table must have adequate knee space. The knee space requirements vary depending on whether the table design provides toe clearances as shown in Figure 3-27. For tables with toe clearance, the knee space must measure at least 28 inches (685 mm) high, 30 inches (760 mm) wide, and 19 inches (485 mm) deep (Figure 3-27). For tables without toe clearance, the knee space must be at least 28 inches (685 mm) high, 30 inches (760 mm) wide, and 24 inches (485 mm) deep (Figure 3-28).

3.7.6   Clear Area Around Picnic Tables

An accessible picnic table must have clear ground space of at least 36 inches (915 mm) around the perimeter of the table, although 48 inches is recommended. This space may overlap with the clear space required for other elements, but must never be encroached upon by another element (Figure 3-29).

3.7.7   Surface and Slope

The surface of the clear ground space around the picnic table must be stable, firm, slip-resistant, and evenly graded, with a maximum slope of 2 percent in all directions.

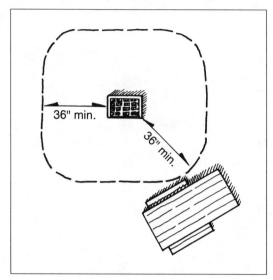

Figure 3-30

3.8   Fire Rings and Grills

The following guidelines should be applied in picnic areas and campsites where fire rings or pedestal grills are provided for public use. Departures from these guidelines through use of other designs and technologies are permitted where the alternative designs and technologies will provide substantially equivalent or greater access and usability. In all designs, two activities must be accommodated—fire building and cooking. In urban/rural settings, accessible fire rings must have a raised fire-building surface to allow independent use by people using wheelchairs; pedestal grills may also be provided. In roaded natural settings, the fire-building surfaces of fire rings need not be raised. However, if they are not raised, then an accessible pedestal grill must be provided to ensure an accessible cooking surface.

3.8.1   Number

All new fire rings and grills, whether being installed in new construction or replaced in retrofits, must comply with the following guidelines.

3.8.2   Location

Fire rings and pedestal grills, if provided, must be located adjacent to an accessible route.

3.8.3   Clear Ground Space

Fire rings and pedestal grills must have a clear, level ground space of at least 36 inches (1220 mm) on all sides, although 48 inches is recommended. This space may overlap with the clear ground space required for other elements, but must never be encroached upon by another element (Figure 3-30).

IV

design guidelines

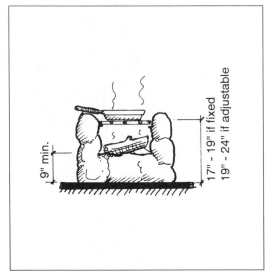

Figure 3-31

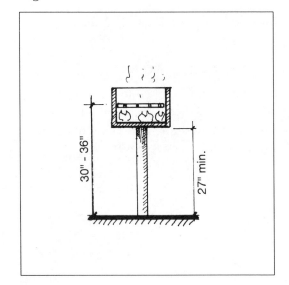

Figure 3-32

3.8.4 Heights

The height requirements for the fire-building surface and the cooking surface of fire rings and pedestal grills varies depending on whether the site is an urban/rural setting or a roaded natural setting.

(1) Guidelines in Urban/Rural Settings. In urban/rural settings, the following guidelines must be applied:

(a) The fire-building surface of all fire rings must be at least 9 inches (229 mm) above the ground (Figure 3-31).

(b) Fire rings with fixed grills must have cooking surfaces that are at least 17 inches (430 mm) above the ground and no higher than 19 inches (485 mm) above the ground (Figure 3-31).

(c) Fire rings with adjustable grills must have cooking surfaces that are at least 19 inches (485 mm) but no more than 24 inches (610 mm) above the ground (Figure 3-31).

(d) Pedestal grills must have cooking surfaces that are 30 to 36 inches above the ground and the grill must be able to rotate 360 degrees to allow users to adjust it based on wind direction. Pedestal grills must also provide at least 27 inches of knee clearance (Figure 3-32).

(2) Guidelines in Roaded Natural Settings. In roaded natural settings, the same guidelines apply, except that the fire-building surfaces need not be raised if doing so disrupts the site's character or natural features. If the fire-building surfaces of fire rings are not raised, then a pedestal grill must be provided as an accessible cooking surface (Figure 3-32).

3.8.5 Operating Mechanisms (ADAAG 4.27)

All operating mechanisms for adjusting the cooking surface must be operable with one hand and must not require tight grasping, pinching, or twisting of the wrist. The force required to adjust the grill must not exceed 10 lbf (22.2 N).

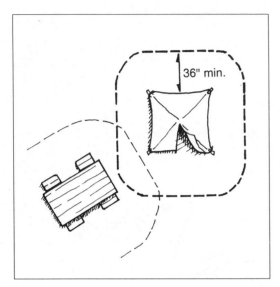

Figure 3-33

Figure 3-34

3.9   Tent Pads

3.9.1   Number

If tent pads are provided, a majority must comply with the following guidelines.

3.9.2   Location

Accessible tent pads, if provided, must be located adjacent to an accessible route.

3.9.3   Clear Ground Space

Accessible tent pads must be large enough to accommodate a tent and still provide at least 36 inches (915 mm) of clear ground space around the tent. This space may overlap with the clear ground space required for other elements, but must never be encroached upon by another element (Figure 3-33).

3.9.4   Surface and Slope

The surface of accessible tent pads must be stable and evenly graded, with a maximum slope of 3 percent in all directions.

3.9.5   Transfer Accommodations

In urban/rural and roaded natural settings, designers may provide tent pads that are 17 inches to 19 inches (432 mm to 483 mm) higher than the adjacent accessible route. This will facilitate transfer from a wheelchair to the tent pad. To ensure usability, a clear ground space that is at least 36 inches by 48 inches (915 mm by 1220 mm) should also be provided on the lower level, directly adjacent to the transfer point (Figure 3-34).

IV

design guidelines

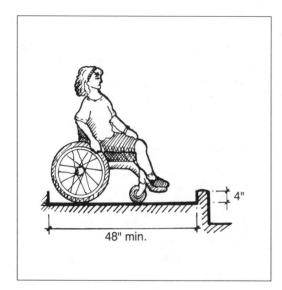

Figure 3-35

3.10   Terraces

Amphitheaters, assembly areas, and gardens are often provided in the outdoor recreation environment as terraced structures. Terraces are essentially stairs with higher than average risers and wider than average treads.

3.10.1   Terrace Width (Bunin et al. 1980)

Terraces intended for pedestrian use must be at least 48 inches (1220 mm) wide (Figure 3-35).

3.10.2   Edge Protection

The need for edge protection (e.g., curbs, walls, railings, or projecting surfaces) to prevent people from slipping off the terrace must be determined based on safety and risk management objectives. Edge protection, when provided, should consist of a 4-inch high minimum curb (Figure 3-35). Safety rails should also be provided, particularly in urban/rural settings. The materials used to construct edge protections should be commensurate with the setting's ROS classification. Metal, concrete, asphalt, brick, cut stone, boulders, dimensional lumber, logs, and native earth may all provide adequate and appropriate edge protection if properly constructed.

3.10.3   Surface and Slope

The terrace surface must be stable, firm, slip-resistant, and level, with maximum slope of 3 percent in all directions.

3.10.4   Access to Terraces

All terraces must have an accessible means of egress. A means of egress is a continuous and unobstructed path of travel from any point in a site or facility to a public way. An accessible means of egress is one that complies with ADAAG requirements and does not include stairs, steps, or escalators (ADAAG 3.5). Since terraces are a type of stairs, they cannot be part of an accessible means of egress. Changes in terrace levels greater than 1/2 inch (13 mm) must be accomplished by means of a curb ramp, ramp, elevator, or platform lift. Although developed elevators and platform lifts are generally not part of the outdoor recreation environment, they are found at various recreation sites in urban/rural settings. If elevators or platform lifts are required, designers should consult ADAAG 4.10 and 4.11.

3.11   Assembly Areas

Assembly areas are built facilities intended to accommodate large groups of people. They include permanent or semi-permanent seating and, typically, a stage or similar performance space. Assembly areas are found in urban/rural and roaded natural settings, and therefore should be designed to provide an easy to moderate level of accessibility, in accordance with the following guidelines.

3.11.1   Number of Wheelchair Seating Positions (ADAAG 4.1.3(19))

When permanent seating is provided, the number of required accessible wheelchair seating positions is determined based on the total seating capacity:

Capacity	Required wheelchair positions
4 to 25	1
26 to 50	2
51 to 300	4
301 to 500	6
501+	6, plus one additional space for each total seating capacity increase of 100.

3.11.2   Aisle Seats (ADAAG 4.1.3(19))

One percent of the total number of seats, but not less than one seat, must be aisle seats with no armrests on the aisle side, or removable or folding armrests on the aisle side. Each complying seat must be identified by a sign or marker. In addition, signs must be posted at the box office or ticket booth to notify patrons of the availability of such seats.

3.11.3   Location of Accessible Spaces (ADAAG 4.33.3)

All wheelchair spaces must adjoin an accessible route.

IV

design guidelines

Figure 3-36

Figure 3-37

3.11.4   Position of Accessible Space (ADAAG 4.33.3)

Wheelchair areas must be an integral part of any seating plan and must be located at a variety of positions to provide people who use wheelchairs a choice of admission prices and lines of sight comparable to those for members of the general public. When the seating capacity exceeds 300, wheelchair spaces shall be provided in more than one location. *EXCEPTION: Accessible viewing positions may be clustered for bleachers, balconies, and other areas having sight lines that require slopes of greater than 5 percent. Equivalent accessible viewing positions may be located on levels having accessible egress.*

3.11.5   Design of Wheelchair Spaces (ADAAG 4.33.2)

Each wheelchair location must provide a minimum clear ground or floor space as shown in Figures 3-36 and 3-37.

3.11.6   Removable Seats (ADAAG 4.33.3)

Readily removable seats may be installed in wheelchair spaces when the spaces are not required to accommodate wheelchair users.

3.11.7   Companion Seats (ADAAG 4.33.3)

A reserved regular seat must be provided next to each wheelchair space to accommodate a companion.

3.11.8   Continental Seating

Building safety codes specify the minimum distances required between rows of fixed seats based on the number of seats in a row, the exit aisle width and arrangement, and the location of exits. "Continental" seating is a seating pattern that places more seats per row with a commensurate increase in row spacing and exits. This facilitates emergency egress for all people and increases the ease of access to mid-row seats for people who walk with difficulty. When space allows, designers should use continental seating design to facilitate access for people of all abilities.

3.11.9 Access to Seating (ADAAG 4.33.3)

All seating areas must have an accessible means of egress. A means of egress is a continuous and unobstructed path of travel from any point in a site or facility to a public way. An accessible means of egress is one that complies with ADAAG requirements and does not include stairs, steps, or escalators (ADAAG 3.5). Since stairs cannot be part of an accessible means of egress, changes in level greater than 1/2 inch (13 mm) must be accomplished by means of a curb ramp, ramp, elevator, or platform lift. Although elevators and platform lifts are generally not part of the outdoor recreation environment, they are found at various recreation sites in urban/rural settings. If elevators or platform lifts are required, designers should consult ADAAG 4.10 and 4.11, respectively.

3.11.10 Edge Protection

The need for edge protection (e.g., curbs, walls, railings, or projecting surfaces) at drop-offs must be determined based on safety and risk management objectives. Edge protection, when provided, should consist of a 4-inch high minimum curb. Safety rails should also be provided, particularly in urban/rural settings. The materials used to construct edge protections should be commensurate with the recreation setting's ROS classification. Metal, concrete, asphalt, brick, cut stone, boulders, dimensional lumber, logs, and native earth may all provide adequate and appropriate edge protection if properly constructed.

3.11.11 Surfacing and Slope (ADAAG 4.33.4)

The surface of assembly areas must be stable, firm, slip-resistant, and level, with maximum slope of 3 percent in all directions.

3.11.12 Access to Performing Areas (ADAAG 4.33.5)

An accessible route must connect wheelchair seating locations with performing areas, including stages, arena floors, dressing rooms, locker rooms, and other spaces used by performers.

IV

design guidelines

3.11.13 Assistive Listening Systems (ADAAG 4.1.3(19)(b); 4.33.7)

    (1) Need for Assistive Listening Systems. ADA requires permanently installed assistive listening systems in assembly areas where (1) audible communications are integral to the use of the space (for example, a performance space or meeting room); (2) there is an audio-amplification system; (3) there is fixed seating; and (4) at least 50 people can be accommodated. In such spaces, the minimum number of receivers to be provided shall, at a minimum, be equal to 4 percent of the total number of seats, but in no case less than two seats. In outdoor recreation environments, all of these conditions are rarely met. Specific guidelines regarding the necessity for and placement of assistive listening devices in the assembly areas of outdoor recreation settings may be developed in the future, but are not currently available.

    (2) Types of Listening Systems (ADAAG, Bunin et al. 1980, Kidd and Clark 1982). Assistive listening systems (ALS) augment the standard public address and audio systems by providing signals which can be received directly by persons with special receivers or hearing aids. ALS help to eliminate or filter background noise. The type of ALS appropriate for a particular application depends on the characteristics of the setting, the nature of the program, and the intended audience. Magnetic induction loops, infrared, and radio frequency systems are types of listening systems which are appropriate for various applications.

    (3) Signage. Signs complying with applicable provisions shall be installed to notify patrons of the availability of a listening system.

3.12   Boat Launching Ramps and Boarding Docks

3.12.1   Boat Launching Ramps

The following guidelines for boat launching ramps should be applied in urban/rural settings. Guidelines for boat launching ramps in roaded natural settings are reserved.

Boat launching ramps serve two purposes. The primary purpose is to facilitate the launch and retrieval of boats. The secondary purpose is to serve as an access route to the boarding dock (if provided). The boarding dock is a fixed, floating, or adjustable structure on or adjacent to the launching ramp.

To fulfill its first purpose, a boat launching ramp must have a minimum slope of 12 to 15 percent. It is not practical to make a boat launching ramp accessible by reducing its slope; this would make launching and retrieving a boat extremely difficult. As a result, the slope of boat launching ramps will exceed the maximum allowable slope for maximum grade segments on outdoor recreation access routes. However, boaters with disabilities will find coping briefly with the steeper slope far less troublesome than attempting to launch and retrieve a boat from a ramp with a lesser grade. (Wilson 1991)

3.12.2   Boarding Docks and Gangways

Water elevations at boat launching facilities may fluctuate due to tides, seasons, or periodic releases from power dams. Fluctuations may vary from a few feet on a daily or seasonal basis to more than several hundred feet on reservoirs and lake impoundments. To accommodate fluctuations in water level, boarding docks are designed to float or to be manually slid along the launching ramp as the water elevation changes. As the water level drops, the boarding dock either moves (floats) by itself or is moved (skidded) away from the top (shore end) of the launching ramp, making the distance the boater must travel to reach the water increasingly long. (Wilson 1991)

IV

design guidelines

Skid piers are commonly used to manually change the position of the boarding dock when fluctuations are seasonal (resulting in only a 3- to 4-foot change in water level). Floating docks are used where daily fluctuations render skid piers impractical. Floating docks are typically attached to a fixed pier or abutment on the shore end by a gangway or pedestrian bridge. As the water level rises, the slope of the gangway joining the floating dock and the pier or shore structure is reduced to where it may be nearly horizontal. However, at lower water elevations, the slope of the gangway could possibly exceed the slopes allowable on maximum grade segments of outdoor recreation access routes and recreation trails (Figure 3-38).

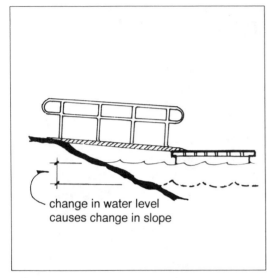

Figure 3-38

In general, accessible gangways should designed using the same guidelines as for accessible ramps in ADAAG 4.8. Because of the inherent danger posed by proximity to water, the slope of gangways should never exceed 1:12 (8.33 percent). For floating docks, maintaining a maximum slope of 1:12 requires careful planning and appropriate designs. It is possible to maintain an accessible slope on a gangway under all conditions if the gangway or series of gangways is long enough.

(1) In areas where water level fluctuations are slight, a single gangway may be sufficient if the run is long enough to provide a 1:12 maximum slope when the dock is at the mean low water level. If the gangway slope is accessible at mean low water level, it will be accessible at higher water levels as well.

(2) A series of gangways may be necessary to ensure an accessible gangway slope at low water levels. This can be accomplished by extending a gangway from the fixed pier or abutment to an interim floating structure to which a second gangway is affixed and extended to yet another interim structure or the floating dock. The number of gangways and interim structures can be increased as required. Switchbacks can also be employed (Figure 3-39).

Figure 3-39

change in water level causes change in slope

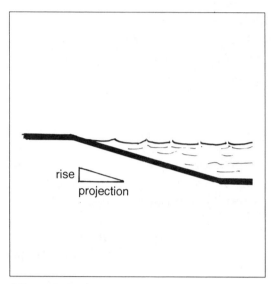

Figure 3-40

3.13   Swimming Areas

Swimming areas can be anything from highly developed pools in urban/rural settings to "swimming holes" in roaded natural or even semi-primitive settings. Access to swimming areas can be provided either by ramps or stairs. The following guidelines for ramps into water and stairs into water are applicable in urban/rural settings and in roaded natural settings where warranted by the level of development and customer expectations.

3.13.1   Ramps into Water

Ramps can facilitate access to outdoor pools, lakes, streams, or even the ocean. When provided, ramps into water must be designed to the following specifications:

(1)   Slope (Bunin et al 1980). The slope of ramps into water must not exceed 1:12 (8.33 percent).

(2)   Rise and Horizontal Projection. The maximum rise and horizontal projection for any run of a ramp into water must be as follows (Figure 3-40):

	rise	*projection*
urban/rural:	30 inches (760 mm)	30 feet (9 m)
roaded natural:	60 inches (1220 mm)	40 feet (12 m)

(3)   Clear Width. Ramps into water must have a clear width of at least 36 inches (916 mm).

(4)   Landings. Landings are required at the top and bottom of each ramp segment. Landings must meet the following specifications:

(a) The landing must be at least 60 inches (1525 mm) long, with no obstructions, and as wide as the ramp segment leading to it.

(b) If the ramp changes direction at the landing, the landing must be at least 60 inches by 60 inches (1525 mm by 1525 mm).

(5)   Handrails. The need for handrails must be determined by site designers and managers. If handrails are provided, they must meet the specifications listed in section 4.6.6, with the following exception:

(a) At the bottom (water end) of the ramp, the top handrail must end at water level, extending for twelve inches parallel to the water surface. In addition,

Figure 3-41

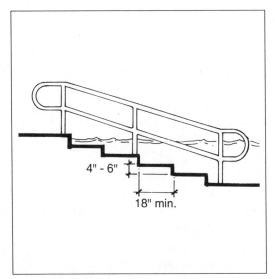

Figure 3-42

handrails must not end abruptly. They must return to a wall surface, a post, or the ground or they must be rounded. This will help prevent the possibility of a person inadvertently injuring themselves on an exposed end when entering or exiting the swimming area (Figure 3-41). (Bunin et al 1980)

3.13.2 Stairs into Water

Stairs can also facilitate access to swimming areas by allowing people with disabilities to lower themselves into the pool gradually. If a raised platform is also provided adjacent to the top of the stairs from which people can transfer from their wheelchairs to the stairway surface, many people will be able to enter the pool without assistance. When provided, stairs into water must be designed to the following specifications:

(1) Location. Stairs must be used to provide access to swimming areas, in lieu of ladders, when access cannot be accomplished or is not desired with a ramp.

(2) Width. Stairs into water must have a clear width of at least 36 inches (915 mm).

(3) Treads and Risers. Stairs into water must have steps with uniform riser heights and tread widths. Stair treads must be at least 18 inches (280 mm) wide, measured from riser to riser. Stair risers must be at least 4 inches (102 mm) high, but not higher than 6 inches (153 mm) (Figure 3-42). (Wisconsin 1991)

(4) Handrails. The need for handrails must be determined by site designers and managers. If handrails are provided, they must meet the same specifications as handrails on maximum ramp segments (section 4.6.6), with the following exception:

(a) At the bottom (water end) of the stairs, the top handrail must end at water level, extending for twelve inches parallel to the water surface. In addition, handrails must not end abruptly. They must return to a wall surface, a post, or the ground or they must be rounded. This will help prevent the possibility of a person inadvertently injuring themselves on an exposed end when entering or exiting the swimming area. (Bunin et al 1980)

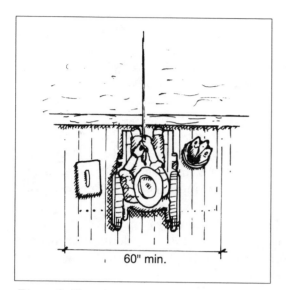

60" min.

Figure 3-43

3.14   Fishing Facilities

Fishing facilities should be planned and designed to provide a variety of integrated experiences and settings so that each angler has the opportunity to match his or her fishing skills to the challenges offered at different fishing stations. While fishing occurs in all types of settings, modifications to streambanks and shorelines to improve access are primarily found in urban/rural and roaded natural settings, and only occasionally in semi-primitive settings.

The decision to make a fishing site accessible must be made by site managers based on customer expectations and the characteristics of the recreation setting. Accessible fishing facilities should be interspersed within the existing pattern of fishing spots so that an integrated fishing experience and desirable fishing locations are available to all anglers. Specific location of accessible areas should respond to customer expectations, topography, and proximity to other facilities.

The following guidelines are for accessible fishing stations in urban/rural and roaded natural settings.

3.14.1   Urban/Rural Fishing Stations

Urban/rural fishing stations are in sites with a high level of structural modification where anglers expect a safe and easy level of accessibility.

(1) Location. The fishing station should be located on an accessible route commensurate with the ROS setting and should be located in close proximity (within 1/8 mile) to accessible parking and an accessible toilet facility.

(2) Fishing Station Design. The fishing station should be designed according to the following specifications:

(a) Determine the capacity of the fishing site based on the scale of the body of water on which it is located and a typical day's demand for fishing.

(b) Ensure that the surface of the fishing station is firm, stable, and slip-resistant, with a maximum slope of 1:33 (3 percent) in any direction. When possible, provide a tactile distinction between the surface of the fishing station and the surface of the adjacent accessible route.

(c) Provide a minimum of 5 linear feet (1525 linear mm) per angler (Figure 3-43), or 12 feet (3660 mm) for two anglers, along the water's edge.

IV

design guidelines

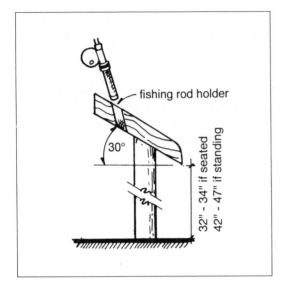

Figure 3-44

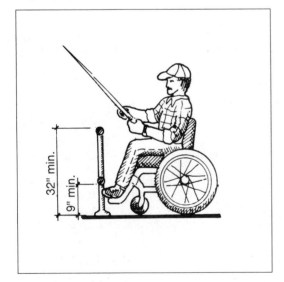

Figure 3-45

(d) Provide 8 feet (2440 mm) of clear space behind anglers to allow uncon-stricted pedestrian circulation.

(e) Provide adequate maneuvering space at the fishing site to accommo-date a person using a wheelchair. At a minimum, there must be a clear space of 60 inches (1525 mm) diameter.

(3) Safety Rails. Safety rails must be provided at the water's edge and at all drop-offs. Safety rail design should incorporate armrests, inclined at 30 degrees toward anglers, as well as other amenities, such as tackle box shelves and fishing rod holders. Armrests should be 32 inches (815 mm) to 34 inches (865 mm) high for seated anglers, 42 inches to 47 inches high for standing anglers (Figure 3-44). Safety rails should meet the guidelines in 4.9, with the exception that safety rail mounting height may be reduced to 32 inches (815 mm) (Figure 3-45).

(4) Curbs at Drop-offs. Edge protection from drop-offs should be provided in developed settings, commensurate with the setting's ROS classification. Protection should be accomplished with 4-inch (102-mm) high curbs at platform edges.

(5) Seating. Seating, if provided, should be on or adjacent to the fishing site to accommodate nonfishing companions. Seating design should comply with guideline 3.6. Seating location must not intrude upon required clear spaces for the fishing station or accessible routes.

(6) Shade and Shelter. Fishing stations should be located to take advantage of natural shade and shelter. In addition, or if none exists, it may be appropriate to provide constructed shade structures. Vegetation or structures for shade should not reduce the vertical clearance to less than 144 inches (3660 mm) above the fishing station (required for casting) or less than 80 inches (2030 mm) above an accessible route.

3.14.2 Roaded Natural Fishing Stations

Fishing stations in roaded natural settings are designed to maintain a natural appearance. Structural modifications in these sites are minimal and consid-erations for accessibility are balanced with—and sometimes superseded by—the desired recreation experience or the desire to preserve the natural setting. Anglers who visit these sites expect a moderate level of accessibility.

Figure 3-46

(1) Location. The fishing station should be located on an accessible route commensurate with the ROS setting and should be in close proximity (within 1/4 mile, if appropriate to the site) to accessible parking and an accessible toilet facility.

(2) Fishing Station Design. The fishing station should be designed according to the following specifications:

(a) Determine the capacity of the fishing site based on the scale of the body of water on which it is located and a typical day's demand for fishing. Fishing stations in roaded natural settings typically accommodate only one or two anglers, although larger stations may be appropriate based on site use and conditions.

(b) Ensure that the surface of the fishing station is firm, stable, and slip-resistant, with a maximum slope of 1:33 (3 percent) in any direction.

(c) Provide a minimum of 5 linear feet (1525 linear mm) per angler (Figure 3-43), or 12 feet (3660 mm) for two anglers, along the water's edge.

(d) Provide 8 feet (2440 mm) of clear space behind anglers to allow unconstricted pedestrian circulation.

(e) Provide adequate maneuvering space at the fishing site to accommodate a person using a wheelchair. At a minimum, there must be a clear space of 60 inches (1525 mm) diameter.

(3) Safety Rails/Protection from Drop-offs. Safety rails may be replaced with natural materials, such as boulders or logs, to provide protection from drop-offs without destroying the site's rustic character. Other amenities can also make use of natural materials. For example, a tackle box shelf may be provided by a large, flat boulder that extends 9 inches to 15 inches above the ground surface (Figure 3-46).

(4) Seating. Seating, if provided, should be on or adjacent to the fishing site to accommodate nonfishing companions. Seating design should comply with guideline 3.6. Seating location must not intrude upon required clear spaces for the fishing station or accessible routes.

(5) Shade and Shelter. Fishing stations should be located to take advantage of natural shade and shelter. While a shade structure might be constructed, it may be more appropriate for designers to specify shade vegetation, such as native deciduous trees, where none occurs naturally. Vegetation or structures for shade should not reduce the vertical clearance to less than 144 inches (3660 mm) above the fishing station (required for casting) or less than 80 inches (2030 mm) above an accessible route.

IV

design guidelines

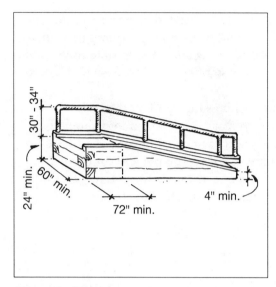

Figure 3-47

3.15 Equestrian Facilities

Accessible equestrian facilities should provide (1) access to the place where horses are available, (2) transfer capabilities onto and off of the horse, and (3) access to horse care areas and related facilities, such as water hydrants and corrals. The decision to make equestrian facilities accessible must be made by site managers based on customer expectations and the characteristics of the recreation setting.

3.15.1 Accessible Transfer Platform

A transfer platform will assist some people with disabilities in transferring onto and off of the horses by allowing them to get to the level of the horses' stirrups (Figure 3-47). An accessible transfer platform must meet the following specifications:

(1) Platform Size. The surface of an accessible transfer platform must be at least 60 inches (1525 mm) by 72 inches (1830 mm) and must be level.

(2) Platform Height. The platform must be raised at least 24 inches above the ground surface.

(3) Ramp-to-Platform Surface. The platform must be accessible by a ramp of maximum 1:12 (8.33 percent) slope.

(4) Handrail. A handrail that is 30 inches (760 mm) to 34 inches (865 mm) high should be provided on at least one side of the platform.

(5) Curbs at Edges. Edge protection from drop-offs should be provided in developed settings, commensurate with the setting's ROS classification. Protection should be accomplished with 4-inch (102-mm) high curbs at platform and ramp edges.

4

access to primary elements and spaces (outdoor recreation access routes)

The paths that provide access to the elements and spaces of a recreation site are among the most critical factors for ensuring accessibility. While the elements and spaces of a site may meet strict accessibility standards, a person with disabilities will be unable to access and enjoy those elements independently if the path leading to them is inaccessible.

Paths in outdoor recreation sites fall into two categories:

(1) Paths that provide access to the site's primary developed recreation elements and spaces, called *Outdoor Recreation Access Routes*, which are typically less than 1/4-mile in length; and

(2) Paths that provide access to the site's other, lesser-developed recreation elements and spaces, called *Recreation Trails*. These trails are typically 1/4-mile or more in length, connecting the lesser developed recreation activities with the site's access points and serving as part of the recreation experience itself.

Universal Access to Outdoor Recreation provides accessibility guidelines for both outdoor recreation access routes (presented in this section) and recreation trails (presented in the following section). These guidelines differ because of the different levels of accessibility that visitors will expect for each type of path.

The guidelines for outdoor recreation access routes are applicable in urban/rural settings, roaded natural settings, and semi-primitive settings where visitors will expect easy, moderate, or difficult access to the site's primary elements and spaces. Access to major structures, such as visitor centers and office complexes, should be provided by access routes that meet ADAAG requirements (ADAAG 4.3).

The accessibility guidelines for recreation trails should also be considered in urban/rural, roaded natural, and semi-primitive settings. These guidelines are less stringent than the guidelines for outdoor recreation access routes because recreation trails typically provide access to lesser-developed areas of a site, where natural features are to be emphasized along with customer expectations and level of development when determining accessibility modifications (see "Integrating Universal Design in the Outdoor Environment," pp. 53-56).

IV

design guidelines

Designers and managers must carefully identify the primary elements and spaces of each developed recreation site and ensure that there is a comprehensive system of outdoor recreation access routes that connects all primary elements and spaces with each other and with accessible parking spaces and facility entrances, as described in section 4.1.

4.1   Identifying Outdoor Recreation Access Routes

Outdoor recreation access routes are the paths that connect the developed spaces and elements that are basic to the recreation experience being offered at the site. For example, the outdoor recreation access routes at a picnic ground are the paths linking the parking area, restrooms, picnic units, and water hydrants. While many of these elements—parking area, restroom, and water hydrant—are not the primary reason for a person to visit the site, they are basic developed elements that serve all visitors.

Designers and managers must determine which of the developed activities and elements at a recreation site are "basic to the recreation experience being offered." This determination must be based on visitor expectations as well as the level of development at the site. For example, a fishing site that is located in an undeveloped area at the far end of a picnic ground may not need to be accessible via an outdoor recreation access route. It may be served by a recreation trail (see section 5, *Access to Other Recreation Activities and Elements*). However, if the fishing area is one of the site's primary features and is in a developed area of the site, it should be considered a primary activity and be serviced by an outdoor recreation access route.

Major structures at the site, such as a visitor center or office complex, should be served by access routes that meet the ADAAG standards for accessible routes (ADAAG 4.3).

4.2 Number and Location of Outdoor Recreation Access Routes (ADAAG 4.3.2)

At least one outdoor recreation access route, located entirely within the site boundary, must connect public transportation stops, accessible parking spaces, accessible passenger loading zones, and public streets or sidewalks with the accessible entrance(s) to the recreation site and its primary developed activities and elements. To the maximum extent feasible, the outdoor recreation access route must coincide with the route for the general public.

Within the site, at least one outdoor recreation access route must connect the accessible, developed primary activities and elements.

4.3 Alternative Routes

An alternative route may be provided in lieu of an outdoor recreation access route when:

1) Provision of an outdoor recreation access route is not feasible or practicable, or

2) Provision of an outdoor recreation access route would deleteriously impact the recreation site's demeanor, historic character, or environmental visage.

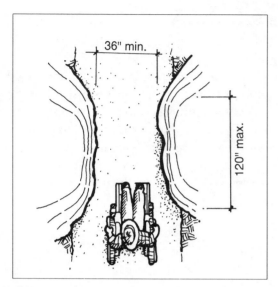

Figure 4-1

4.4   Design of Outdoor Recreation Access Routes

Summary of Design Standards for Outdoor Recreation Access Routes

	Easy *(urban/rural)*	**Moderate** *(roaded natural)*	**Difficult** *(semi-primitive)*
clear width (minimum):	48 inches	36 inches	36 inches
sustained running slope (maximum):	5 percent	5 percent	8.3 percent
maximum grade allowed:	8.3 percent	10 percent	10 percent
—for a maximum distance of:	30 feet	50 feet	50 feet
cross slope (maximum):	3 percent	3 percent	3 percent
passing space interval (maximum):	200 feet	300 feet	400 feet
rest area interval (maximum):	400 feet	900 feet	1200 feet
small level changes (maximum):	1/2 inch	1/2 inch	1 inch

Note: There are no guidelines for outdoor recreation access routes in primitive recreation settings.

4.4.1   Width (ADAAG 4.3.3)

The required minimum clear width for an outdoor recreation access route varies based on the expected level of access for each ROS setting:

Level of Accessibility	ROS	Required Clear Width
easy	urban/rural	minimum 48 in. (1220 mm)
moderate	roaded natural	minimum 36 in. (915 mm)
difficult	semi-primitive	minimum 36 in. (915 mm)
most difficult	primitive	not applicable

In all ROS settings, the clear width may reduce to 32 inches (815 mm) for a maximum distance of 2 feet. In urban/rural settings, if the route must pass through significant geological features (e.g., rock formations) or between aesthetically important vegetation (e.g., large trees), the route may reduce to 36 inches (915 mm) for a maximum distance of 10 feet (Figure 4-1).

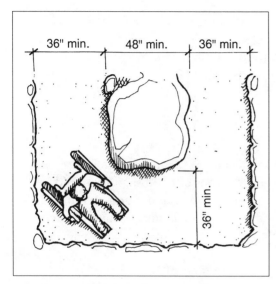

Figure 4-2

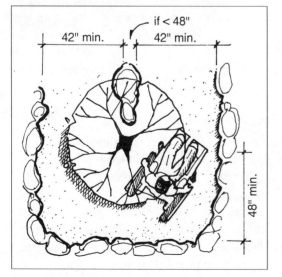

Figure 4-3

If a person in a wheelchair must make a turn around an obstruction, the minimum clear width of the outdoor recreation access route at that point shall be as shown in Figures 4-2 and 4-3.

4.4.2   Sustained Running Slope (ADAAG 4.3.7)

The slope of an outdoor recreation access route must not exceed 1:20 (5 percent) in urban/rural and roaded natural settings and 1:12 (8.33 percent) in semi-primitive settings. Segments of an outdoor recreation access route where the running slope is greater must be designed according to the guidelines for maximum grades in section 4.6, *Maximum Grade*.

4.4.3   Cross Slope (ADAAG 4.3.7)

Cross slope can make a pathway difficult to navigate for a person using a wheelchair or other mobility aid. Although some cross slope is desired to prevent water accumulation on the path surface, the cross slope should never exceed 3 percent (1:33) in all settings.

4.4.4   Passing Space (ADAAG 4.3.4)

If an outdoor recreation access route has less than 60 inches (1525 mm) of clear width, passing spaces must be provided at reasonable intervals, as shown below. Each passing space must be at least 60 inches by 60 inches (1525 mm by 1525 mm). A T-intersection of two corridors or walks is also an acceptable passing place. Designers are encouraged to use naturally occurring topographic features to provide passing spaces in recreation settings.

Level of Accessibility	ROS	Interval of Passing Spaces
easy	urban/rural	not to exceed 200 ft. (61 m)
moderate	roaded natural	not to exceed 300 ft. (91.5 m)
difficult	semi-primitive	not to exceed 400 ft. (122 m)
most difficult	primitive	not applicable

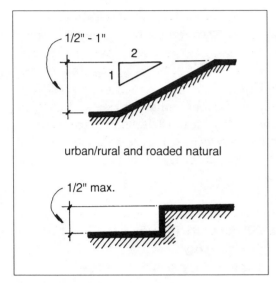

urban/rural and roaded natural

Figure 4-4

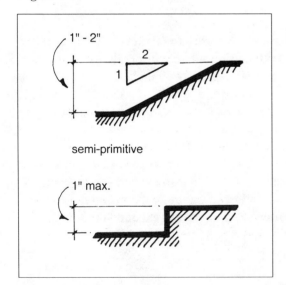

semi-primitive

Figure 4-5

An outdoor recreation access route with a clear width of 60 inches (1525 mm) allows the passage of two wheelchairs and eliminates the need for passing spaces. However, 60-inch (1525 mm) wide routes may not be appropriate in all recreation settings. The decision to construct a 60-inch (1525 mm) wide route should be commensurate with ROS considerations and expectations of accessibility.

4.4.5   Rest Areas at Passing Spaces

Passing spaces can provide valuable rest areas for all people. In urban/rural and roaded natural settings, benches and other types of fixed seating should be provided adjacent to passing spaces as a matter of convenience and accommodation. Along outdoor recreation access routes, rest areas should be incorporated into the design of passing spaces at reasonable intervals as follows:

Level of Accessibility	ROS	Interval of Rest Areas
easy	urban/rural	minimum every other passing space
moderate	roaded natural	minimum every third passing space
difficult	semi-primitive	minimum every third passing space
most difficult	primitive	not applicable

Benches and other types of fixed seating at rest areas should be accessible, designed in accordance with guideline 3.6.

4.4.6   Small Level Changes (ADAAG 4.5.2)

The surface of outdoor recreation access routes in urban/rural and roaded natural settings may have vertical changes in level of up to 1/2 inch (13 mm) without any edge treatment. In these settings, changes in level between 1/2 inch and 1 inch (13 mm and 25 mm) are allowed if they are beveled with a slope no greater than 1:2 (Figure 4-4). In semi-primitive settings, the surface of outdoor recreation access routes may have vertical changes in level of up to 1 inch (25 mm) without any edge treatment and changes in level between 1 inch and 2 inches (25 mm and 51 mm) must be beveled with a slope no greater than 1:2 (Figure 4-5).

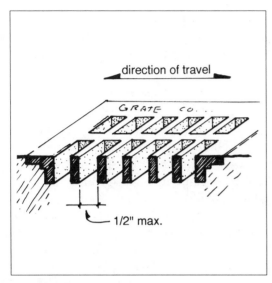

Figure 4-6

If the surface of an outdoor recreation access route changes in level more than 1 inch in urban/rural and roaded natural settings or more than 2 inches in semi-primitive settings, it must be accomplished by means of a curb ramp, graded surface, elevator, or platform lift. Although elevators and platform lifts are generally not part of the outdoor recreation environment, they are sometimes found in recreation sites in urban/rural settings. If elevators or platform lifts are used, designers should consult ADAAG 4.10 and 4.11. An outdoor recreation access route may not include stairs, steps, or escalators (ADAAG 3.5).

4.4.7 Gratings (ADAAG 4.5.4)

If gratings are located in the walking surface, they must have spaces no greater than 1/2 inch (13 mm) wide in one direction. If gratings have elongated openings, they shall be placed so that the long dimension is perpendicular to the dominant direction of travel (Figure 4-6).

4.4.8 Surfacing (ADAAG 4.5.1)

The surface of outdoor recreation access routes must be stable, firm, and slip-resistant. Soft, loose surfaces such as loose sand or gravel, wet clay, and irregular surfaces such as cobblestones, can significantly impede the movement of a wheelchair and create slipping and tripping hazards for people using other mobility aids.

"Slip resistance" refers to the frictional force necessary to keep a shoe heel or crutch tip from slipping on the walking surface under conditions likely to be found on the surface. This frictional force is complex and varied in practice, but can be measured in terms of its "static coefficient" to provide a close approximation of the slip resistance of a surface. Contrary to popular belief, some slippage is necessary to walking, especially for persons with restricted gaits; a truly "non-slip" surface could not be negotiated. The Occupational Safety and Health Administration recommends that walking surfaces have a static coefficient of friction of 0.5.

IV

design guidelines

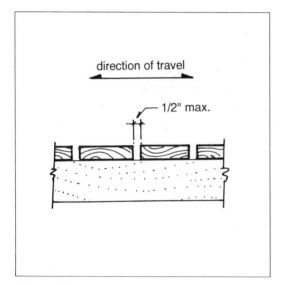

Figure 4-7

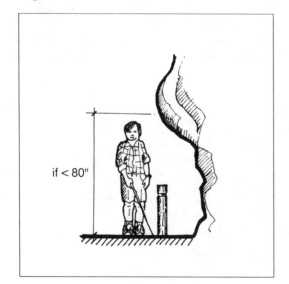

Figure 4-8

In recreation settings, surface materials should be aesthetically appropriate and commensurate with user expectations. Concrete, asphalt, pavers set on concrete, well-maintained compacted crushed stone, and wood decking can meet these requirements. Other materials may also be used to achieve a stable, firm, slip-resistant surface. Departures from this guideline that use other materials, designs, or technologies are permitted where the alternative materials, designs, and technologies will provide substantially equivalent or greater access and usability. For example, wood chips or fibrous material, held together with an appropriate binder and placed over a properly prepared and compacted substrate, may suffice under certain conditions. Guidelines may vary depending on local conditions and construction practices.

Wood decking may be used as a surfacing material, but planks must run perpendicular to the direction of travel and joints must be no more than 1/2 inch (13 mm) (Figure 4-7). Consideration should be given to the maximum expected shrinkage to ensure that the resulting gap between planks is 1/2 inch maximum. Planks must be securely fastened so they do not warp and treated with appropriate preservative to avoid decay and drying. Wood may not be slip-resistant when wet.

4.4.9   Vertical Clearance (ADAAG 4.4.2)

All outdoor recreation access routes must have clear head room of at least 80 inches (2030 mm). If vertical clearance of an area adjoining an outdoor recreation access route is reduced to less than 80 inches (2030 mm) as the result of overhanging objects or other obstructions, a barrier must be provided to warn people with limited vision (Figure 4-8).

4.4.10   Protruding Objects (ADAAG 4.4.1)

Individuals with visual disabilities often use long canes as mobility aids. The two principal cane techniques are the touch technique (the cane is arced from side to side, touching points outside both shoulders) and the diagonal technique (the cane is held stationary, diagonally across the body, such that the tip is just above or touching the ground at a point outside one shoulder and the grip extends to a point outside the other shoulder). The touch technique is used primarily in

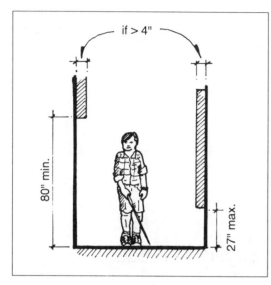

Figure 4-9

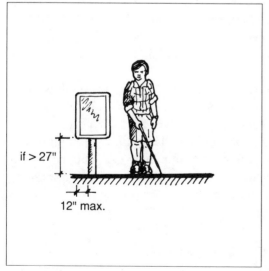

Figure 4-10

uncontrolled areas, the diagonal technique is used primarily in familiar, limited, and controlled environments. Cane users often use both techniques.

Objects that project from walls, such as telephones or signs, can create hazards for people with limited vision. These hazards are noticed only if they fall within the detection range of canes. The following standards must be followed to ensure that protruding objects are detectable:

(1) Objects Mounted Between 27 Inches and 80 Inches. An object that is mounted with the bottom of its leading edge between 27 inches and 80 inches (685 mm and 2030 mm) above the finished floor surface must not protrude more than 4 inches (102 mm) into walks, halls, corridors, passageways, or aisles (Figure 4-9).

(2) Objects Mounted Below 27 Inches. An object that is mounted with the bottom of its leading edge at or below 27 inches (685 mm) above the finished floor surface may protrude any amount, so long as it does not reduce the required clear width of an accessible route or maneuvering space.

(3) Post-Mounted Objects. A freestanding object mounted on a post or pylon may overhang 12 inches (305 mm) maximum from 27 inches to 80 inches (685 mm to 2030 mm) above the ground or finished floor (Figure 4-10).

(4) Clear Width. No object shall be mounted such that it reduces the required clear width of an accessible route or maneuvering space.

IV

design guidelines

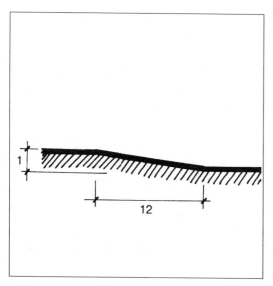

Figure 4-11

4.5   Curb Ramps (ADAAG 4.7)

4.5.1   Location (ADAAG 4.7.1)
Curb ramps must be provided wherever an outdoor recreation access route crosses a curb.

4.5.2   Clear Width (ADAAG 4.7.3)
Curb ramps must have a clear width of at least 36 inches (915 mm), exclusive of flared sides.

4.5.3   Slope (ADAAG 4.7.2)
All ramps must be designed with the least possible slope. The maximum slope allowed depends on the space available.
(1) New Construction and Existing Sites With Adequate Space. In new construction and in existing sites where space allows, the maximum slope shall be 1:12 (8.33 percent) (Figure 4-11).
(2) Existing Sites With Limited Space. Ramps that are constructed on existing sites or in existing buildings where space limitations prohibit the use of a 1:12 slope or less may have slopes and rises as follows:
(a) A slope between 1:10 (10 percent) and 1:12 (8.33 percent) is allowed for a maximum rise of 6 inches;
(b) A slope between 1:8 (12.5 percent) and 1:10 (10 percent) is allowed for a maximum rise of 3 inches.
(3) Maximum Slope. No slope may be steeper than 1:8 (12.5 percent).
(4) Transitions From Ramps to Adjacent Surfaces. Transitions from ramps to walks, gutters, or streets shall be flush and free of abrupt changes. The maximum slopes of adjoining gutters, road surfaces immediately adjacent to the curb ramp, and accessible routes shall not exceed 1:20 (5 percent).

4.5.4   Surfacing (ADAAG 4.7.4)
The surfacing of curb ramps must be stable, firm, and slip-resistant.

IV

design guidelines

Figure 4-12

Figure 4-13

4.5.5   Sides of Recessed Curb Ramps (ADAAG 4.7.5)
    If a curb ramp is located where pedestrians must walk across the ramp, or where it is not protected by handrails or guardrails, it must have flared sides. Flared sides may have a maximum slope of 1:10 (10 percent) (Figure 4-12). Curb ramps with returned curbs may be used where pedestrians would not normally walk across the ramp (Figure 4-13).

4.5.6   Built-up Curb Ramps (ADAAG 4.7.6)
    Built-up curb ramps must not project into traffic lanes.

4.5.7   Protection from Obstruction (ADAAG 4.7.8)
    Curb ramps must be located or protected to prevent them from being obstructed by parked vehicles (Figure 4-14).

4.5.8   Curb Ramps at Marked Crossings (ADAAG 4.7.9)
    Curb ramps at marked crossings must be wholly contained within the crosswalk markings, excluding any flared sides (Figure 4-15).

4.5.9   Diagonal Curb Ramps (ADAAG 4.7.10)
    Diagonal (or corner-type) curb ramps must have a clear and level bottom landing of at least 48 inches (1220 mm) square. If a diagonal curb ramp is at a marked crossing, the 48 inches (1220 mm) of clear space must be within the markings. If diagonal curb ramps have returned curbs or other well-defined edges, the curbs or edges must be parallel to the direction of pedestrian flow. If diagonal curb ramps have flared sides, they must have a segment of straight curb that is at least 24 inches (610 mm) long on each side of the curb ramp within the marked crossing (Figure 4-16).

4.5.10   Raised Islands in Crossings (ADAAG 4.7.11)
    If a pedestrian crossing bisects a raised traffic island, it must cut through level with the street or have curb ramps at both sides and a level area at least 48 inches (1220 mm) long between the curb ramps in the part of the island intersected by the crossings (Figure 4-17).

IV

design guidelines

Figure 4-14

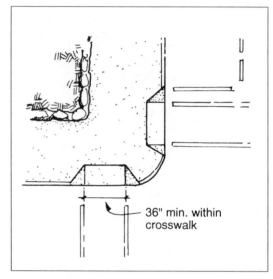

Figure 4-15

36" min. within
crosswalk

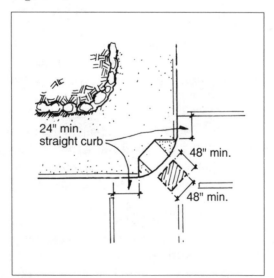

Figure 4-16

24" min.
straight curb

48" min.

48" min.

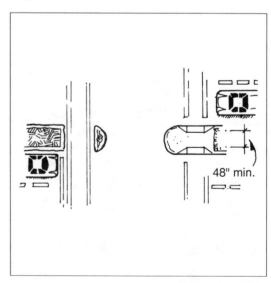

Figure 4-17

48" min.

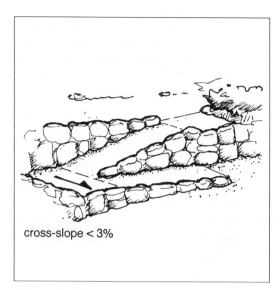

cross-slope < 3%

Figure 4-18

4.6   Maximum Grade

To provide access between different levels in outdoor recreation settings, some segments of outdoor recreation access routes will need to exceed the running slope standards presented in section 4.4. In the built environment, these path segments would be designed to meet the design standards for ramps (ADAAG 4.8). However, in the outdoor recreation environment where highly developed ramps are usually inappropriate, these path segments are termed "maximum grade" areas and should be designed according to the following requirements.

4.6.1   Clear Width
Maximum grade segments on outdoor recreation access routes must maintain a minimum clear width of at least 48 inches (1220 mm) in urban/rural settings and 36 inches (916 mm) in roaded natural and semi-primitive settings.

4.6.2   Slope and Rise (ADAAG 4.8.2)
All segments of outdoor recreation access routes must be designed with the least possible slope. The maximum allowable slope and rise varies by ROS setting:

	maximum grade allowed:	*for a maximum distance of:*
easy	8.3 percent	30 feet
moderate	10 percent	50 feet
difficult	10 percent	50 feet

4.6.3   Cross Slope (ADAAG 4.8.8)
Cross slope can make a maximum grade segment of a path nearly impossible to navigate for many people who use wheelchairs. The cross slope on maximum grade segments should never exceed 3 percent. When an outdoor recreation access route has a switchback or dogleg, any cross slope (not to exceed 3 percent) should be toward the change in direction (Figure 4-18).

IV

design guidelines

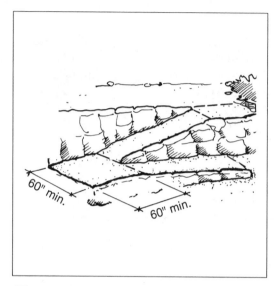

Figure 4-19

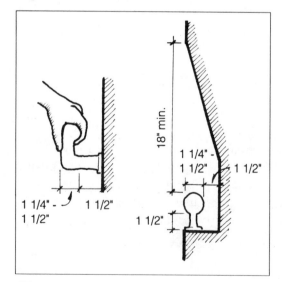

Figure 4-20

4.6.4   Surface of Maximum Grade Segments (ADAAG 4.8.6)
All segments of outdoor recreation access routes, including maximum grade segments, must meet the requirements for small level changes (4.4.6), gratings, (4.4.7) and surfacing materials (4.4.8).

4.6.5   Landings (ADAAG 4.8.4)
Landings provide important rest spaces and are required at the top and bottom of each maximum grade segment and at points where maximum grade segments change direction. Each landing must meet the following specifications:
(1) Standard Dimensions. The landing must be at least 60 inches (1525 mm) long, with no obstructions, and as wide as the path segment leading to it.
(2) Dimensions of Landings at Changes in Direction. If the path changes direction at the landing between two maximum grade segments, the landing must be at least 60 inches by 60 inches (1525 mm by 1525 mm) (Figure 4-19).

4.6.6   Handrails
The need for handrails must be determined by site designers and managers based upon the site's level of modification, customer expectations, and natural features (see "Integrating Universal Design in the Outdoor Environment," pages 53-56). Remember, handrails are provided to assist with balance and support in accordance with performance standards. In situations where safety is the primary concern, guardrails should be provided (see "Safety and Risk Management," pages 107-112). If only one handrail is provided, it should be placed on the downslope side.
(1) Location. If a maximum grade segment has a rise greater than 6 inches (150 mm) or a horizontal projection greater than 72 inches (1830 mm), it must have handrails on both sides. Handrails are not required on curb ramps or adjacent to seating in assembly areas. The inside handrail on maximum grade segments that switchback or dogleg must be continuous.
(2) Railing Size. Round handrails must have a diameter between 1-1/4 inches and 1-1/2 inches (Figure 4-20). Other shapes are allowed if they provide an equivalent gripping surface.
(3) Distance from Adjacent Surface. If handrails are mounted adjacent to a vertical surface such as a wall, there must be exactly 1-1/2 inches (38 mm) of clear

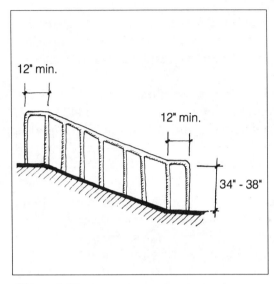

Figure 4-21

Figure 4-22

space between the surface and the handrail (Figure 4-20). Handrails may be located in a recess of a wall if the recess is a maximum of 3 inches (75 mm) deep and extends at least 18 inches (455 mm) above the top of the rail (Figure 4-20).

(4) Gripping Surface. The gripping surface of the handrail must be continuous.

(5) Handrail Materials. All handrails and adjacent surfaces must be free of sharp edges, burrs, and other abrasive elements. Edges must have a minimum radius of 1/8 inch (3.2 mm). While the materials used to construct handrails may vary, they should be commensurate with the site's ROS classification. All materials must comply with ASTM or other appropriate standards.

(6) Mounting Height. Handrails must be mounted so that the top of the handrail gripping surface is between 34 inches and 38 inches (865 mm and 965 mm) above the ramp surface.

(7) Extensions. Handrails must not end at the top and bottom of maximum grade segments. They must extend at least 12 inches (305 mm) beyond the top and bottom of the sloped segment, parallel with the ground surface (Figure 4-21).

(8) Handrail Ends. Handrails must not end abruptly. They must return to an adjacent vertical surface, a post, or the ground or they must be rounded. This will prevent the possibility of a person inadvertently injuring themselves on an exposed end.

(9) Rotation. Handrails must not rotate in their fittings.

(10) Structural Strength. Handrails and mounting devices must meet the following specifications:

(a) Bending stress in a handrail induced by the maximum bending moment from the application of 250 lbf (1112N) shall be less than the allowable stress for the material of the handrail.

(b) Shear stress induced in a handrail by the application of 250 lbf (1112 N) shall be less than the allowable shear stress for the handrail material. If the connection between the handrail and its mounting bracket or other support is considered to be fully stressed, then direct and torsional shear stresses shall be totaled for the combined shear stress, which shall not exceed the allowable shear stress.

IV

design guidelines

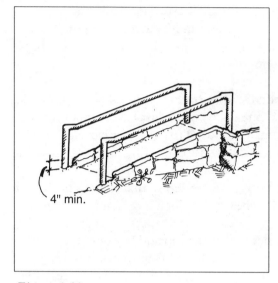

Figure 4-23

IV

Figure 4-24

(c) Shear force induced in a fastener or mounting device from the application of 250 lbf (1112N) shall be less than the allowable lateral load of either the fastener or mounting device or the supporting structure, whichever is the smaller allowable load.

(d) Tensile force induced in a fastener by a direct tension force of 250 lbf (1112N) plus the maximum moment from the application of 250 lbf (1112N) shall be less than the allowable withdrawal load between the fastener and the supporting structure.

4.6.7   Edge Protection (ADAAG 4.8.7)

All maximum grade path segments and landings must include protection from drop-offs at the path edges. This can be accomplished with walls, curbs, or railings that provide a suitable barrier at the edge of the path surface, such as a continuous rail immediately above the ground (Figure 4-22). Curbs must be 4 inches (102 mm) minimum high (Figure 4-23). Alternatively, the path surface may be widened to extend at least one foot past the handrails on each side (Figure 4-24).

Edge protection from drop-offs should be provided in urban/rural and roaded natural settings and in semi-primitive settings where safety is a concern. The materials used to construct edge protection should be commensurate with the setting's ROS classification. Concrete, asphalt, brick, cut stone, boulders, dimensional lumber, logs, and native earth may all be adequate and appropriate if constructed properly.

4.6.8   Drainage (ADAAG 4.8.8)

The surfaces of and approaches to maximum grade path segments must be designed so that water will not accumulate on them.

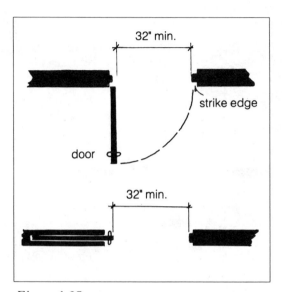

Figure 4-25

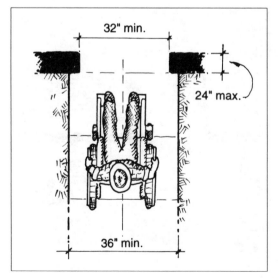

Figure 4-26

4.7   Gates, Doors, and Other Entryways (ADAAG 4.13)

All gates, doors, and similar entryways that are part of an outdoor recreation access route must meet the following specifications.

4.7.1   *Clear Width (ADAAG 4.13.5)*

Gates, doors, and other entryways must have a minimum clear opening of 32 inches (815 mm) when the gate or door is open 90 degrees. The clear width is measured from the face of the gate or door to the opposite stop (Figure 4-25). Openings that are more than 24 inches (610 mm) in depth may be 32 inches (815 mm) at a point, but must be at least 36 inches (915 mm) continuously (Figure 4-26). Gates and doors that do not require full passage, such as the doors to shallow closets, may have clear widths as small as 20 inches (510 mm) (Figure 4-27).

4.7.2   *Clear Area (ADAAG 4.13.6)*

Gates and doors that are not automatic or power-assisted must have maneuvering clearances that meet the minimum dimensions shown in Figures 4-28, 4-29, and 4-30. The floor area within the required clearances must be level and clear.

4.7.3   *Thresholds (ADAAG 4.13.8)*

Thresholds must not exceed 1/2 inch (13 mm) in height. Exterior sliding gates and doors may have thresholds of up to 3/4 inch (19 mm) in height. Raised thresholds and floor level changes at gates and doorways must be beveled with a slope no greater than 1:2.

4.7.4   *Gate and Door Hardware (ADAAG 4.13.9)*

Handles, pulls, latches, locks, and other operating devices on accessible gates and doors must be a shape that is easy to grasp with one hand and does not require tight grasping, tight pinching, or twisting of the wrist to operate. Lever-operated or push-type mechanisms and U-shaped handles are acceptable designs. When sliding gates and doors are fully open, operating hardware must be exposed and usable from both sides. Hardware that is required for accessible gate or door passage must be mounted no higher than 48 inches (1220 mm) above the floor.

IV

design guidelines

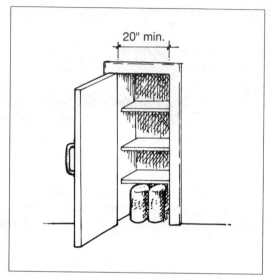

Figure 4-27

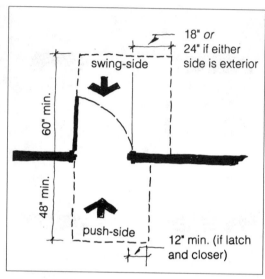

Figure 4-28

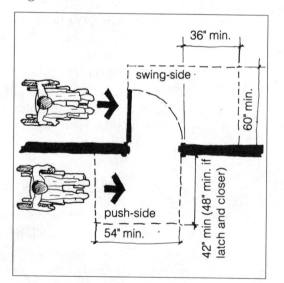

Figure 4-29

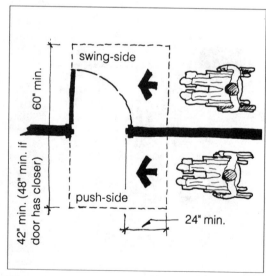

Figure 4-30

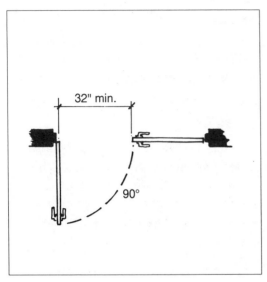

Figure 4-31

4.7.5   Closers (ADAAG 4.13.10)

If a gate or door has a closer, the sweep period of the closer must be adjusted so that the gate or door will take at least three seconds to move from an open position of 70 degrees to a point 3 inches (7.5 mm) from the latch, as measured to the leading edge of the gate or door.

4.7.6   Opening Force (ADAAG 4.13.11)

The force necessary to push or pull open a gate or door must not exceed the following standards. These standards do not apply to the force required to retract latch bolts or disengage other devices that may hold the gate or door in a closed position.

(1) Fire Doors. Standards for fire doors are set by local administrative authorities (typically, the local or state building code or the local fire department). Accessible fire doors must be operable by the minimum opening force allowable by the appropriate administrative authority.

(2) Interior Hinged Gates and Doors. The opening force for interior hinged gates and doors must not exceed 5 lbf (22.2N). No guidelines are currently available regarding the opening force for exterior hinged gates and doors.

(4) Sliding or Folding Gates and Doors. The opening force for sliding or folding gates and doors must not exceed 5 lbf (22.2N).

4.7.7   Double-leaf Gates and Doors (ADAAG 4.13.4)

If gates or doorways have two independently operated leaves, at least one leaf—which must be an active leaf—must have a clear opening of at least 32 inches (815 mm) when the gate or door is open 90 degrees, measured between the face of the gate or door and the opposite stop (Figure 4-31). In addition, these passages must have maneuvering clearances that meet the minimum dimensions shown in Figures 4-28, 4-29, and 4-30.

IV

design guidelines

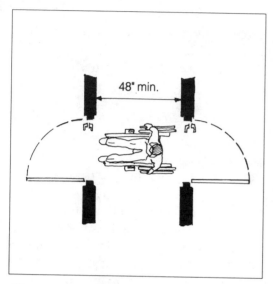

Figure 4-32

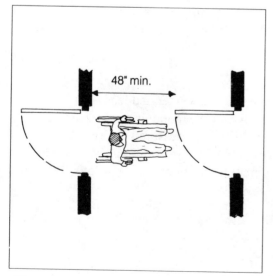

Figure 4-33

4.7.8   *Revolving Doors and Turnstiles (ADAAG 4.13.2)*

Revolving doors and turnstiles are not accessible. When such devices occur on an outdoor recreation access route, an adjacent door or gate that meets accessibility specifications must be provided and must be designed to facilitate the same use pattern.

4.7.9   *Doors or Gates in a Series (ADAAG 4.13.7)*

When two hinged or pivoted doors or gates occur in a series, there must be a clear, level space between them that is at least 48 inches (1220 mm) long. This space cannot include any area into which either door will swing. In addition, the doors or gates must either both swing away from the space between them or both swing in the same direction (i.e., only one door or gate may swing into the space) (Figures 4-32 and 4-33).

4.7.10   *Automatic and Power-Assisted Doors and Gates (ADAAG 4.13.12)*

Automatic doors and gates on outdoor recreation access routes must comply with ANSI/BHMA A156.10-1985. If the automatic door or gate is slow-opening and low-powered, it must comply with ANSI A156.19-1984. Such doors and gates must not open to back check faster than 3 seconds and must not require more than 15 lbf (66.6 N) to stop movement.

Power-assisted doors and gates must comply with the force requirements listed above as well as with the closing requirements in ANSI A 156.19-1984.

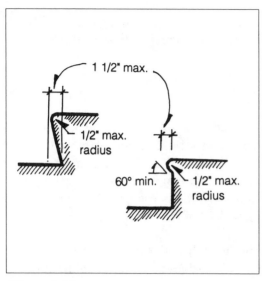

Figure 4-34

4.8   Stairs (ADAAG 4.9)

Stairs can be useful to many people. When provided in urban/rural settings, stairs in outdoor recreation settings must comply with the following standards.

4.8.1   Nosings (ADAAG 4.9.3)

Nosings must be designed so that a person with limited mobility can drag his or her foot up each riser without catching on the overhanging tread. Nosings may not project more than 1-1/2 inches (38 mm) over the riser below and must be rounded with a maximum radius of 1/2 inch (13 mm). Risers must be sloped or the underside of the nosing must be angled at least 60 degrees from the tread below (Figure 4-34).

4.8.2   Drainage (ADAAG 4.9.6)

Outdoor stairs and their approaches must be designed so that water will not accumulate on them.

4.8.3   Treads and Risers (ADAAG 4.9.2)

On any given flight of stairs, all steps must have uniform riser heights and uniform tread widths. Stair treads must be no less than 11 inches (280 mm) wide, measured from riser to riser.

4.8.4   Handrails (ADAAG 4.9.4)

In urban/rural settings, handrails should be provided on all stair segments in accordance with the following specifications. In roaded natural and semi-primitive settings, the need for handrails must be determined by site designers and managers based upon the site's level of modification, customer expectations, and natural features (see "Integrating Universal Design in the Outdoor Environment," pages 53-56). Remember, handrails are provided to assist with balance and support in accordance with performance standards. In situations where safety is the primary concern, guardrails should be provided (see "Safety and Risk Management," pages 107-112). If only one handrail is provided, it should be placed on the downslope side.

IV

design guidelines

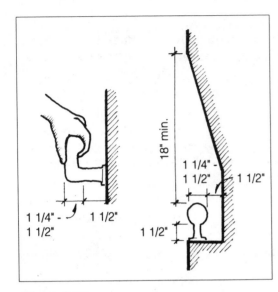

Figure 4-35

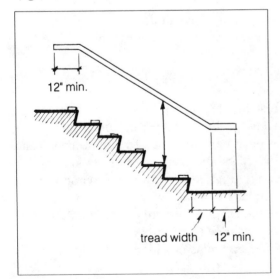

Figure 4-36

(1) Location. Handrails are not required adjacent to seating in assembly areas. The inside handrail on stair segments that change direction must be continuous around the turn.

(2) Railing Size. Round handrails must have a diameter between 1-1/4 inches and 1-1/2 inches (Figure 4-35). Other shapes are allowed if they provide an equivalent gripping surface.

(3) Distance from Adjacent Surface. If handrails are mounted adjacent to a vertical surface such as a wall, there must be exactly 1-1/2 inches (38 mm) of clear space between the surface and the handrail (Figure 4-35). Handrails may be located in a recess of a wall if the recess is a maximum of 3 inches (75 mm) deep and extends at least 18 inches (455 mm) above the top of the rail (Figure 4-35).

(4) Gripping Surface. The gripping surface of the handrail must be continuous.

(5) Handrail Materials. All handrails and adjacent surfaces must be free of sharp edges, burrs, and other abrasive elements. Edges must have a minimum radius of 1/8 inch (3.2 mm). While the materials used to construct handrails may vary, they should be commensurate with the site's ROS classification. All materials must comply with ASTM or other appropriate standards.

(6) Mounting Height. Handrails must be mounted so that the top of the handrail gripping surface is between 34 inches and 38 inches (865 mm and 965 mm) above the stair surface.

(7) Extensions. Handrails must not end at the top and bottom of stair segments. They must extend at least 12 inches (305 mm) beyond the top of the stair segment, parallel with the ground surface. At the bottom of stair segments, handrails must continue to slope for one tread width and extend 12 inches parallel with the ground surface (Figure 4-36).

(8) Handrail Ends. Handrails must not end abruptly. They must return to an adjacent vertical surface, a post, or the ground or they must be rounded. This will prevent the possibility of a person inadvertently injuring themselves on an exposed end.

(9) Rotation. Handrails must not rotate in their fittings.

(10) Structural Strength. Handrails and mounting devices must meet the following specifications:

(a) Bending stress in a handrail induced by the maximum bending moment from the application of 250 lbf (1112N) shall be less than the allowable stress for the material of the handrail.

(b) Shear stress induced in a handrail by the application of 250 lbf (1112 N) shall be less than the allowable shear stress for the handrail material. If the connection between the handrail and its mounting bracket or other support is considered to be fully stressed, then direct and torsional shear stresses shall be totaled for the combined shear stress, which shall not exceed the allowable shear stress.

(c) Shear force induced in a fastener or mounting device from the application of 250 lbf (1112N) shall be less than the allowable lateral load of either the fastener or mounting device or the supporting structure, whichever is the smaller allowable load.

(d) Tensile force induced in a fastener by a direct tension force of 250 lbf (1112N), plus the maximum moment from the application of 250 lbf (1112N), shall be less than the allowable withdrawal load between the fastener and the supporting structure.

IV

design guidelines

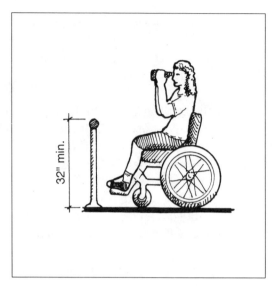

Figure 4-37

Figure 4-38

4.9   Guardrails, Fences, and Other Safety Barriers

Guardrails, fences, and other safety barriers are provided in hazardous areas to ensure the safety of visitors. They are not used to facilitate a particular function or activity, and should never be construed as substitutes for handrails, which are provided to assist users with balance and support. When balance and support are required, such as along maximum grades and stairs, the handrail guidelines in 4.6.6 should be applied (see "Safety and Risk Management," pages 107-112, for a more complete discussion of the distinctions between guardrails, handrails, and grab bars).

4.9.1   Location

Guardrails, fences, and other safety barriers must be provided where commensurate with safety and risk management objectives across the spectrum of recreation opportunity settings.

4.9.2   Height

When provided in urban/rural settings, the height of guardrails, fences, and other safety barriers should be determined by their function. In areas where safety is a primary concern, such as in congested areas near drop-offs, the top of the guardrail, fence, or safety barrier should be 42 inches (1066 mm) or higher above the ground. When such height might interfere with the recreation experience and is not necessitated by safety concerns, such as at a scenic overlook or fishing facility, the top of the guardrail, fence, or safety barrier may be lowered to 32 inches (813 mm) above the ground (Figure 4-37). (Wilson 1991)

4.9.3   Vertical Members

Vertical members should be provided on guardrails, fences, and other safety barriers in urban/rural settings and in other developed settings as warranted by safety considerations and the requirements of the recreation activity. Where safety is the primary concern, vertical members should be designed and spaced to prevent the free passage of a 4-inch (153 mm) sphere (Figure 4-38). (Wilson 1991)

4.9.4   Materials

All guardrails, fences, safety barriers, and any walls or other surfaces adjacent to them must be free of sharp edges, burrs, and other abrasive elements. Edges must have a minimum radius of 1/8 inch (3.2 mm). The materials used to construct guardrails, fences, and other safety barriers may vary considerably and should be commensurate with the recreation setting's ROS classification.

4.9.5   Structural Strength

Guardrails, fences, and other safety barriers and mounting devices must meet the structural strength requirements of the Uniform Building Code.

4.9.6   Rotation (ADAAG)

The bars of guardrails, fences, and other safety barriers must not rotate in their fittings.

Figure 4-39

4.10   Signs (ADAAG 4.30)

Signs are a critical part of an outdoor recreation access route, providing directions, identifying site features and facilities, and communicating important information to site visitors. This design guide provides guidelines for three types of signs, based on a similar breakdown of sign types applied by the ADA for the built environment: (1) signs that are required at site entrances; (2) signs that provide permanent identification of site elements and spaces; and (3) signs that provide directions or information. Temporary signs, directories, nameplates, and menus need not conform to these guidelines. Signs should always be provided in urban/rural and roaded natural settings. Signs are optional in semi-primitive settings.

4.10.1   Signs At Site Entrances (ADAAG 4.1.2(7)(c))

Signs must be provided at site entrances to help people locate accessible entrances.

(1) Directional Signs at Site Entrances. Signs must be provided that direct people arriving at the site to the accessible site entrance. However, these signs are not required if all site entrances are accessible.

(2) Signs at Accessible Entrances. Accessible entrances must be identified by the International Symbol of Accessibility (see 4.10.4(1) below). These signs are not required if all entries are accessible.

4.10.2   Signs for Permanent Identification of Elements and Spaces

Signs that identify the names or permanent uses of elements and spaces and signs that designate features such as site exits must meet the following guidelines.

(1) Mounting Location (ADAAG 4.30.6). Signs that provide permanent identification for elements and spaces must be installed on the wall adjacent to the latch side of entry doors (Figure 4-39). Where there is no wall space next to the latch side of the door, including double-leaf doors, signs must be placed on the nearest wall.

(2) Mounting Height (ADAAG 4.30.6). Signs that provide permanent identification must be mounted 60 inches (1525 mm) above the ground floor, measured to the centerline of the sign (Figure 4-39).

Figure 4-40

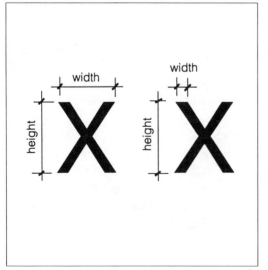

Figure 4-41

(3) Approach to Sign (ADAAG 4.30.6). Signs must be mounted so that a person may approach to within 3 inches (76 mm) of the sign without encountering protruding objects or standing within the swing of a door.

(4) Finish and Contrast (ADAAG 4.30.5). The characters and background of signs must have an eggshell, matte, or other non-glare finish. In addition, characters and symbols must contrast with their background—either light characters on a dark background or dark characters on a light background.

(5) Lettering Design (ADAAG 4.30.4). Signs that provide permanent identification of rooms and spaces must have raised characters and numbers. All sign text must be raised 1/32 inch, upper case, sans serif or simple serif type (Figure 4-40). In urban/rural settings, all sign text must also be presented in Grade 2 Braille.

(6) Character Height (ADAAG 4.30.4). The raised characters on signs that provide permanent identification of elements and spaces must be at least 5/8-inch (16 mm) high, but no higher than 2 inches (50 mm) (Figure 4-40).

(7) Pictograms (ADAAG 4.30.4). Pictograms must be accompanied by an equivalent text description placed directly below the pictogram. The border height of the pictogram must be at least 6 inches (152 mm).

4.10.3 Signs for Direction or Information

Signs that provide directions to or information on site features and facilities must meet the following guidelines.

(1) Character Height (ADAAG 4.30.3). Characters and numbers on signs must be sized according to the viewing distance from which they are to be read. A capital "X" is used as the standard character to measure height. The minimum heights for signs that provide directions or information are listed in the chart below. Lower case characters are permitted on these signs (signs that provide permanent identification may only use upper case characters).

Type of Sign	*Letter Height*
Directional signs mounted higher than 66 inches above the floor:	3 inches min.
Directional signs mounted within 66 inches of the floor:	1 inch min.

IV

design guidelines

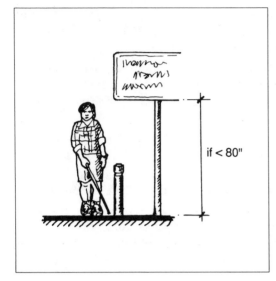

Figure 4-42

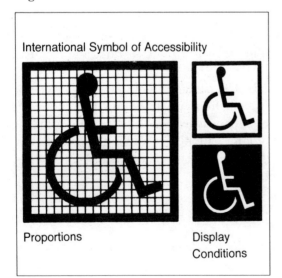

Figure 4-43

(2) Character Proportion (ADAAG 4.30.2). Letters and numbers on signs must have a width-to-height ratio between 3:5 and 1:1 (Figure 4-41).

(3) Line Weight (ADAAG 4.30.2). Letters and numbers on signs must have a stroke-width-to-height ratio between 1:5 and 1:10 (Figure 4-41).

(4) Finish and Contrast (ADAAG 4.30.5). The characters and background of signs must have an eggshell, matte, or other non-glare finish. In addition, characters and symbols must contrast with their background—either light characters on a dark background or dark characters on a light background.

(5) Vertical Clearance (ADAAG 4.4.2). Directional and informational signs that are suspended or projected overhead must have at least 80 inches (2030 mm) of clear head room between the bottom of the sign and the finished floor surface. If the vertical clearance on an accessible route is reduced to less than 80 inches, a barrier to warn blind or visually impaired persons must be provided (Figure 4-42).

4.10.4   Symbols of Accessibility (ADAAG 4.30.7)

The following symbols must be posted as required to identify accessible site elements:

(1) International Symbol of Accessibility. This symbol must be posted at accessible parking spaces, accessible loading zones, accessible site and facility entrances that are not the primary entrance, and accessible restrooms. The symbol shall be displayed as shown in Figure 4-43. The color, materials, and overall size of the sign and symbol should be selected to blend with the site's natural setting, as long as the selection does not conflict with the other design standards presented in this section.

(2) Universal Design Symbols. The level of accessibility for each outdoor recreation access route should be identified using the Universal Design Symbols shown in Figure 4-44. Signs should also provide adequate information and detail on site-specific features and design dimensions such that individuals can determine whether or not the route or element is accessible to them and that it meets their recreation expectations. Universal Design Symbols do not replace the International Symbol of Accessibility in the four areas where it is required to be posted.

(3) Volume Control Telephones. Telephones that are required to have a volume control must be identified by a sign containing a depiction of a telephone handset with radiating sound waves (see Figure 3-13, page 142).

(4) International TTY Symbol (TDD). This symbol must be used to identify text telephones (Figure 4-45). In addition, if a facility has a public text telephone, directional signs indicating the location of the nearest text telephone must be provided adjacent to all banks of telephones that do not contain a text telephone. These directional signs must also include the International TTY Symbol (TDD). If a facility has no banks of telephones, directional signs to the nearest text telephone must be provided at the entrance (e.g., in a building directory).

(5) International Symbol of Access for Hearing Loss. This symbol must be used to identify the availability of permanent assistive listening systems in assembly areas (Figure 4-46).

4.10.5   *Levels of Illumination (ADAAG 4.30.8)*

ADAAG does not yet provide recommendations for the illumination of signs at night. Likewise, no guidelines have yet been set forth for the illumination of signs in outdoor recreation environments.

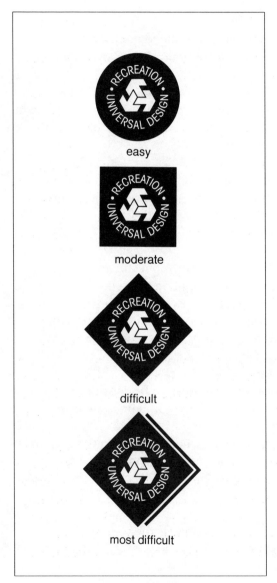

easy

moderate

difficult

most difficult

Figure 4-44

International TTY Symbol (TDD)

Figure 4-45

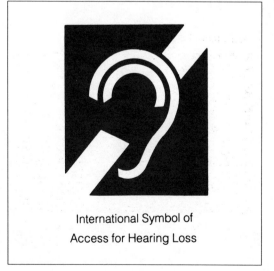

International Symbol of
Access for Hearing Loss

Figure 4-46

IV

design guidelines

5

access to other recreation elements and spaces (recreation trails)

Paths in outdoor recreation sites fall into two categories:

(1) Paths that provide access to the site's primary developed recreation elements and spaces, called *Outdoor Recreation Access Routes*, which are typically less than 1/4-mile in length; and

(2) Paths that provide access to the site's other, lesser-developed recreation elements and spaces, called *Recreation Trails*. These trails are typically 1/4-mile or more in length, connecting the lesser developed recreation activities with the site's access points and serving as part of the recreation experience itself.

Universal Access to Outdoor Recreation provides accessibility guidelines for both outdoor recreation access routes (presented in the previous section) and recreation trails (presented in this section). These guidelines differ because of the different levels of accessibility that visitors will expect for each type of path.

The guidelines for outdoor recreation access routes are applicable in urban/rural settings, roaded natural settings, and semi-primitive settings where visitors will expect the basic support services and primary activities of the site to be accessible at an easy or moderate level of accessibility. Access to major structures, such as visitor centers and office complexes, should be provided by access routes that meet ADAAG requirements (ADAAG 4.3).

The accessibility guidelines for recreation trails should also be considered in urban/rural, roaded natural, and semi-primitive settings. These guidelines are less stringent than the guidelines for outdoor recreation access routes because recreation trails typically provide access to lesser-developed areas of a site, where natural features are to be emphasized along with customer expectations and the level of development when determining accessibility modifications (see "Integrating Universal Design in the Outdoor Environment," pages 53-56).

Designers and managers must carefully identify the needs for both outdoor recreation access routes and accessible recreation trails in every site.

5.1   Identifying Accessible Recreation Trails

Essentially, all developed paths in a recreation site that are not outdoor recreation access routes are recreation trails.

Recreation trails are generally longer in distance than outdoor recreation access routes, typically 1/4-mile or longer. They provide access to recreation activities that are not among the site's primary elements and spaces. Often, recreation trails are considered a recreation activity in and of themselves (i.e., a hiking trail). Recreation activities served by a recreation trail might include scenic overlooks, interpretive sites, fishing platforms, or the out-of-doors. Recreation trails can be further subdivided, drawing a distinction between shorter, more developed trails—such as a trail connecting a trailhead, visitor center, or parking area with a recreation activity—and longer, less developed trails where hiking in the natural outdoors is the activity being sought. In the first group of trails, accessibility is a more important consideration—commensurate with the ROS setting. In the second group of trails, the recreation experience and natural environment are the most important considerations and modifications solely for accessibility would be inappropriate.

5.2   Number and Location of Accessible Recreation Trails

Whenever developed recreation trails are provided in urban/rural and roaded natural settings for use by the general public, at least one recreation trail connecting each of the site's developed recreation elements and spaces must be accessible.

To the maximum extent feasible, the accessible recreation trail must coincide with the route for the general public. At a minimum, accessible recreation trails must be designed to provide the expected level of accessibility given the site's ROS classification:

ROS Classification	Level of Accessibility
urban/rural	easy
roaded natural	moderate
semi-primitive	difficult
primitive	most difficult

IV

design guidelines

Recreation trails that are designed and managed exclusively for nonpedestrian use, such as routes for four-wheel drives and all terrain vehicles or equestrian-only trails, are exempt from accessibility requirements. However, such trails should be designed and constructed according to approved and accepted engineering standards in response to risk and safety considerations. In addition, if parking areas, restrooms, or similar facilities are associated with such recreation trails, they must be accessible.

Dual-purpose trails, such as a vehicular road that is also intended for pedestrian use, must—to the maximum extent feasible—provide the level of accessibility associated with the site's ROS classification.

5.3   Design of Accessible Recreation Trails

Summary of Design Standards for Accessible Recreation Trails

	Easy *(urban/rural)*	Moderate *(roaded natural)*	Difficult *(semi-primitive)*
clear width (minimum):	48 inches	36 inches	28 inches
sustained running slope (maximum):	5 percent	8.3 percent	12.5 percent
maximum grade allowed:	10 percent	14 percent	20 percent
—for a maximum distance of:	50 feet	50 feet	50 feet
cross slope (maximum):	3 percent	5 percent	8.3 percent
passing space interval (maximum):	200 feet	300 feet	400 feet
rest area interval (maximum):	400 feet	900 feet	1200 feet
small level changes (maximum):	1 inch	2 inches	3 inches

Note: There are no guidelines for accessible recreation trails in primitive recreation settings.

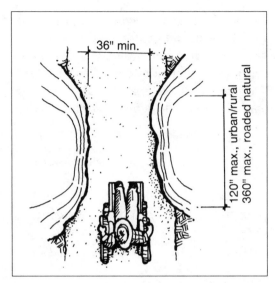

Figure 5-1

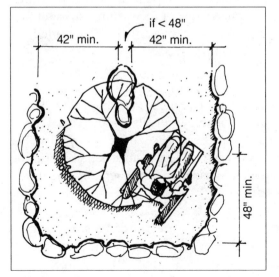

Figure 5-2

5.3.1   Clear Width

The required minimum clear width for an accessible recreation trail varies based on the expected level of access for each ROS setting:

Level of Accessibility	ROS	Required Minimum Clear Width
easy	urban/rural	48 inches (1220 mm)
moderate	roaded natural	36 inches (915 mm)
difficult	semi-primitive	28 inches (915 mm)
most difficult	primitive	not applicable

In urban/rural and roaded natural settings, the clear width may reduce to 32 inches (815 mm) for a reasonable distance, as listed below, if the trail must pass through significant geological features (e.g., rock formations) or between aesthetically important vegetation (e.g., large trees) (Figure 5-1).

	urban/rural	roaded natural
Max. distance allowed for 32 inch clear width:	10 feet	30 feet

If a person in a wheelchair must make a turn around an obstruction, the minimum clear width of the accessible recreation trail at that point shall be as shown in Figures 5-2 and 5-3.

In the rare situation in which an accessible recreation trail is required or provided at a primitive recreation setting, designers should apply the guidelines for semi-primitive settings.

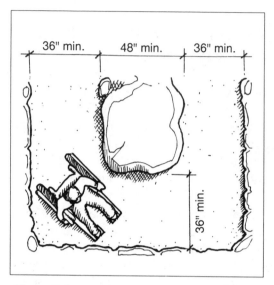

Figure 5-3

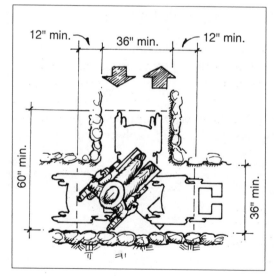

Figure 5-4

5.3.2   Sustained Running Slope

All accessible recreation trails should be designed to provide the most gentle slope possible within the constraints of the natural environment. The maximum sustained running slope allowed for accessible recreation trails in each ROS setting is shown in the following chart. If a segment of a recreation trail has a steeper slope than these allowed maximums, it must be designed according to the guidelines in section 5.4, *Maximum Grade*.

Level of Accessibility	ROS	Maximum Slope
easy	urban/rural	1:20 (5 percent)
moderate	roaded natural	1:12 (8.3 percent)
difficult	semi-primitive	1:8 (12.5 percent)
most difficult	primitive	not applicable

5.3.3   Cross Slope

Cross slope can make a pathway difficult to navigate for a person using a wheelchair or other mobility aid. Although some cross slope is desired to prevent water accumulation on the path surface, the cross slope of recreation trails should never exceed 3 percent (1:33) in urban/rural settings, 5 percent (1:20) in roaded natural settings, and 8.3 percent (1:12) in semi-primitive settings.

5.3.4   Passing Space

If an accessible recreation trail has less than 60 inches (1525 mm) of clear width, passing spaces must be provided at reasonable intervals not to exceed the distances shown below. Each passing space must be at least 60 inches by 60 inches (1525 mm by 1525 mm). A T-intersection of two trails is also an acceptable passing space (Figure 5-4). Designers are encouraged to use natural topographic features to provide passing spaces in recreation settings.

Level of Accessibility	ROS	Interval of Passing Spaces
easy	urban/rural	200 feet (61 m) max.
moderate	roaded natural	300 feet (91.5 m) max.
difficult	semi-primitive	400 feet (122 m) max.
most difficult	primitive	not generally applicable

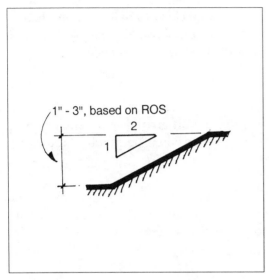

1" - 3", based on ROS

2

1

Figure 5-5

An accessible recreation trail with a clear width of 60 inches (1525 mm) allows the passage of two wheelchairs and eliminates the need for passing spaces. However, 60-inch (1525 mm) wide trails may not be appropriate in all recreation settings. The decision to construct a 60-inch (1525 mm) wide trail should be commensurate with ROS considerations and expectations of accessibility.

5.3.5   Rest Areas at Passing Spaces

Passing spaces can provide valuable rest areas for all people. In urban/rural and roaded natural settings, benches and other types of fixed seating should be provided adjacent to passing spaces as a matter of convenience and accommodation and should be accessible (see section 3-6). On accessible recreation trails, rest areas at passing spaces should be provided at passing spaces at reasonable intervals:

Level of Accessibility	ROS	Interval of Rest Areas
easy	urban/rural	min. every other passing space
moderate	roaded natural	min. every third passing space
difficult	semi-primitive	min. every third passing space
most difficult	primitive	not applicable

5.3.6   Small Level Changes

Accessible recreation trails may have small vertical changes in surface level if such changes do not create barriers to accessibility, given the expected level of accessibility associated with the setting. The following vertical changes in level are allowed in each ROS setting if beveled with a slope no greater than 1:2 (Figure 5-5).

Level of Accessibility	ROS	Max. Level Change (with bevel of 1:2)
easy	urban/rural	1 inch (13 mm)
moderate	roaded natural	2 inches (26 mm)
difficult	semi-primitive	3 inches (52 mm)
most difficult	primitive	not applicable

IV

design guidelines

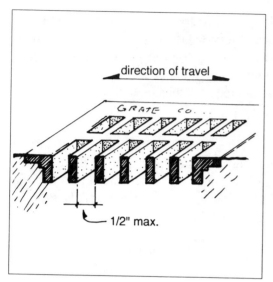

Figure 5-6

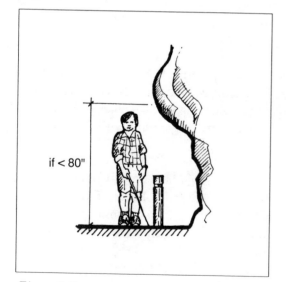

Figure 5-7

If the surface of an accessible recreation trail changes in level more than these allowed maximums, such change must be accomplished by means of a graded surface. An accessible recreation trail may not include stairs or steps.

5.3.7   Gratings

If gratings are located in the walking surface, they must have spaces no greater than 1/2-inch (13 mm) wide in one direction. If gratings have elongated openings, they shall be placed so that the long dimension is perpendicular to the dominant direction of travel (Figure 5-6).

5.3.8   Surfacing

The surfacing guidelines for accessible recreation trails are the same as the surfacing guidelines for accessible outdoor recreation access routes. Please refer to guideline 4.4.8.

5.3.9   Cattle Guards

Although accessibility guidelines are not yet available regarding the use of cattle guards in outdoor recreation settings, designers and managers of recreation settings are encouraged to use their best judgement in ensuring that the use of cattle guards does not create an undue barrier to accessibility on recreation trails.

5.3.10   Cross-drains and Water Bars

Like cattle guards, accessibility guidelines are not yet available regarding the use of cross-drains and water bars in outdoor recreation settings. Designers and managers of recreation settings are encouraged to use their best judgement in ensuring that the use of cross-drains or water bars does not create an undue barrier to accessibility on recreation trails.

5.3.11   Vertical Clearance

All accessible recreation trails must have clear head room of at least 80 inches (2030 mm). If vertical clearance of an area adjoining an accessible recreation trail is reduced to less than 80 inches (2030 mm), a barrier must be provided to warn people with limited vision (Figure 5-7).

5.3.12 Protruding Objects

Guidelines for protruding objects on accessible recreation trails are the same as the guidelines for protruding objects on outdoor recreation access routes. See guideline 4.4.10.

5.4   Maximum Grade

To provide access between different levels in outdoor recreation settings, some segments of accessible recreation trails will need to exceed the running slope standards presented in section 5.3. In the built environment, these path segments would be designed to meet the design standards for ramps (ADAAG 4.8). However, in the outdoor recreation environment where highly developed ramps are usually inappropriate, these path segments are termed "maximum grade" areas and should be designed according to the following guidelines.

5.4.1   Clear Width

Maximum grade segments on accessible recreation trails must maintain a clear width of at least 48 inches (1220 mm) in urban/rural settings, 36 inches (916 mm) in roaded natural settings, and 28 inches (710 mm) in semi-primitive settings.

5.4.2   Slope and Rise (ADAAG 4.8.2)

All segments of accessible recreation trails must be designed with the least possible slope. The maximum slope and rise of maximum grade segments depends on the expected level of accessibility:

Level of Accessibility	Max. Slope	For Distance Not to Exceed
easy	10 percent	50 feet
moderate	14 percent	50 feet
difficult	20 percent	50 feet
most-difficult	not applicable	

5.4.3   Cross Slope (ADAAG 4.8.8)

Cross slope can make a maximum grade segment of a path nearly impossible to navigate for many people who use wheelchairs. The cross slope on maximum grade segments must not exceed the following guidelines:

Level of Accessibility	Maximum Cross Slope
easy	3 percent
moderate	5 percent
difficult	8.3 percent
most-difficult	not applicable

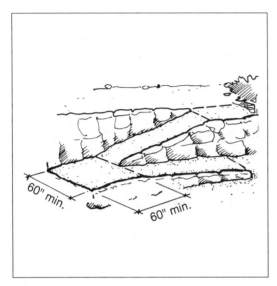

Figure 5-8

5.4.4   Landings (ADAAG 4.8.4)

Landings provide important rest spaces and are required at the top and bottom of each maximum grade segment and at points where maximum grade segments change direction. Each landing must meet the following specifications:

(1) Standard Dimensions. The landing must be at least 60 inches (1525 mm) long, with no obstructions, and as wide as the path segment leading to it.

(2) Dimensions of Landings at Changes in Direction. If the path changes direction at the landing between two maximum grade segments, the landing must be at least 60 inches by 60 inches (1525 mm by 1525 mm) (Figure 5-8).

5.4.5   Edge Protection/Safety Rails (ADAAG 4.8.7)

Protection from drop-offs at the edges of maximum grade segments should be provided commensurate with safety concerns and site conditions. This can be accomplished with walls, curbs, or safety rails that provide a suitable barrier at the edge of the path surface, such as a continuous rail immediately above the ground. Curbs must be 4 inches (102 mm) minimum high. Alternatively, the path surface may be widened to extend at least one foot past the handrails on each side (see Figures 4-22, 4-23, and 4-24 on pages 183 and 184).

Edge protection from drop-offs should be provided in developed settings. The materials used to construct edge protection should be commensurate with the setting's ROS classification. Concrete, asphalt, brick, cut stone, boulders, dimensional lumber, logs, and native earth may all be adequate and appropriate if constructed properly.

5.4.6   Drainage (ADAAG 4.8.8)

The surfaces of and approaches to maximum grade path segments must be designed so that water will not accumulate on them.

IV

design guidelines

Figure 5-9

5.5   Gates and Entry Points

Guidelines for gates and entry points on accessible recreation trails are the same as the applicable guidelines for doors and gates on accessible outdoor recreation access routes. See guideline 4.7, *Gates, Doors, and Other Entryways*.

Two design challenges that may be encountered when designing recreation trails are animal guard entrances and tank traps or similar vehicle barriers. Accessibility guidelines are not yet available to provide guidance in addressing these elements. Designers and managers of recreation settings are encouraged to use their best judgement in ensuring that animal guard entrances and tank traps or other vehicle barriers do not create undue barriers to accessibility on recreation trails.

5.6   Signs

Guidelines for signs on accessible recreation trails are the same as the guidelines for signs on outdoor recreation access routes (see section 4.10), with the following addition regarding trailhead information. Guidelines for the design of interpretive signs on recreation trails are being developed but are not yet available.

5.6.1   Trailhead Information

Data on trail attributes and features should be posted at information areas and trailheads to assist all trail users in determining the extent to which the trail is within their range of ability and interest. At a minimum, posted data should include the trail's average and maximum slope, cross slope, and width (Figure 5-9). When possible, a route map and grade profile should also be provided. Trailhead information signs can also be useful in lesser developed settings where the trails are not designed to the guidelines presented in this section. See the discussion of the "Trail Difficulty Rating System" on pages 89-90.

how to measure slopes

(adapted from Beneficial Designs 1993)

The actual slope experienced by a wheelchair when traversing a path is determined by both the surface of the path and the "footprint" of the wheelchair. The wheelchair footprint is measured by the wheelbase length (distance from the contact point of the trailing front caster to the contact point of the main rear wheel) and the wheelbase width (distance between the contact points of the two main rear wheels). The average wheelbase length and width are approximately 17 inches and 22 inches, respectively.

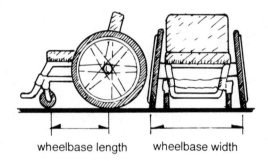

wheelbase length   wheelbase width

When a wheelchair encounters a change in the level of a pathway surface (e.g., a root projecting 1 inch above the pathway surface), the percent incline experienced by the wheelchair user will be determined by both the height of the level change and the size of the wheelchair's wheelbase. If the wheelchair has a 16-inch wheelbase length, a 1-inch change in level will result in a 6.3 percent incline for the wheelchair user. If this level change occurs on a maximum grade path segment that has an overall slope of 10 percent, then the slope experienced by the wheelchair at this point is 16.3 percent, well over the allowable maximum grade for an accessible outdoor recreation access route.

To help ensure that the actual slopes and cross slopes experienced by wheelchairs do not exceed the allowed maximums, slope and cross slope measurements should be made based on the footprint of an average wheelchair. Slopes should be measured across a distance of 16 inches and cross slopes should be measured across a distance of 22 inches.

slope conversion table

Rise:Run	% Grade	Angle Degrees
1:100	1.0 %	0.6°
1:90	1.1%	0.6°
1:80	1.3%	0.7°
1:70	1.4%	0.8°
1:60	1.7%	1.0°
1:50	2.0%	1.1°
1:45	2.2%	1.3°
1:40	2.5%	1.4°
1:35	2.9%	1.6°
1:30	3.3%	1.9°
1:25	4.0%	2.3°
1:20	5.0%	2.9°
1:19	5.3%	3.0°
1:18	5.6%	3.2°
1:17	5.9%	3.4°
1:16	6.3%	3.6°
1:15	6.7%	3.8°
1:14	7.1%	4.1°
1:13	7.7%	4.4°
1:12	8.3%	4.8°
1:11	9.1%	5.2°
1:10	10.0%	5.7°
1:9	11.1%	6.3°
1:8	12.5%	7.1°
1:7	14.3%	8.1°
1:6	16.7%	9.5°
1:5	20.0%	11.3°
1:4	25.0%	14.0°
1:3	33.3%	18.4°
1:2	50.0%	26.6°
1:1	100.0%	45.0°

ADA comparison table

The table on the following pages provides a comparative summary of the guidelines that appear in this design guide and the guidelines promulgated by the Americans with Disabilities Act.

■ The first two columns list the section number and title of the guidelines that appear in Chapter IV of this design guide (DG).

■ The third column lists the corresponding section number in the Americans with Disabilities Act Accessibility Guidelines for Buildings and Facilities (ADAAG), as published in the *Federal Register* (Vol. 56, No. 144; Friday, July 26, 1991). An entry of "--" signifies that there is no applicable ADAAG reference.

■ The final column provides a brief narrative description of the differences between the guideline presented in this design guide and the guideline presented in ADAAG.

This information is provided for comparitive purposes only. It should not be used as a substitute for the actual guidelines in either this design guide or ADAAG.

The following abbreviations are found in some descriptions: "U/R" for urban/rural; "RN" for roaded natural; and "SP" for semi-primitive. Other abbreviations and acronyms are defined in the glossary.

DG Section	DG Section Title	ADAAG No.	Differences
1.0	**Space Allowances and Reach Ranges**		
1.1	**Space Allowances**		
1.1.1	General Dimensions	--	--
1.1.2	Clear Width	4.2.1	Same
1.1.3	Clear Width at Door and Gate Openings	4.2.1	Same
1.1.4	Passing Width	4.2.2	Same
1.1.5	Turning Space	4.2.3	Same
1.1.6	Clear Ground or Floor Space	4.2.4	Same
1.2	**Reach Ranges**		
1.2.1	Forward Reach	4.2.5	Same
1.2.2	Side Reach	4.2.6	Same
2.0	**Parking Areas and Loading Zones**		
2.1	**Number of Accessible Parking Spaces**	4.1.2(5)(a)	Same
2.2	**Location of Accessible Parking Spaces**	4.6.2	Same
2.3	**Parking Space Design**		
2.3.1	Car Accessible Spaces	4.6.3	Same
2.3.2	Van and RV Accessible Spaces	4.1.2(5)(b) & 4.6.4	Same
2.3.3	Universal Design Spaces	A4.6.3	Same
2.3.4	Access Aisle Design	4.6.3	Same
2.3.5	Campsite Parking Spaces	--	--
2.3.6	Parking at Scenic Overlooks	--	--
2.4	**Vertical Clearance**	4.6.5	Same
2.5	**Passenger Loading Zones**	4.6.6	Same

DG Section	DG Section Title	ADAAG No.	Differences
2.0	**Parking Areas and Loading Zones (cont.)**		
2.6	**Bus Parking and Loading Zones**	--	--
2.7	**Parking Area Surfacing**	--	--
2.8	**Parking Area Slope**	4.6.3	ADA sets 1:50 max. in parking spaces; DG sets 1:20 max. overall, 1:50 in U/R parking spaces, 1:33 in RN and SP parking spaces.
2.9	**Signs**		
2.9.1	All Accessible Parking Spaces	4.9.1	Same
2.9.2	Van and RV Accessible Spaces	4.6.4	ADA says sign must read "Van Accessible"; DG says "Van and RV Accessible."
2.9.3	Location and Mounting Height	4.6.4	Same
2.9.4	Pavement Markings	--	--
2.9.5	Directional Signs	--	--
2.9.6	Colors and Materials	4.30.7	Same
2.10	**Tactile Warnings**	4.29.5	ADA requires a 36" strip of truncated domes next to vehicle areas; DG encourages tactile warning, but does not specify treatment.
2.11	**Lighting**	--	--
3.0	**Elements and Spaces in the Recreation Environment**		
3.1	**Toilet Rooms**		
3.1.1	Location and Minimum Number	4.22.1	ADA doesn't mention portable toilets.
3.1.2	Doors	4.13	Same
3.1.3	Clear Floor Space	4.22.3	Same
3.1.4	Stalls	4.17	Same
3.1.5	Water Closets	4.16	Same
3.1.6	Urinals	4.18	Same
3.1.7	Lavatories and Mirrors	5.1.7	Same
3.1.8	Controls and Dispensers	4.27	Same

DG Section	DG Section Title	ADAAG No.	Differences
3.0	**Elements and Spaces in the Recreation Environment**		
3.2	**Telephones**		
3.2.1	Number of Accessible Telephones	4.1.3(17)(a)	Same
3.2.2	Number of Accessible Text Telephones	4.1.3(17)(c)	Same
3.2.3	Volume Controls	4.1.3(17)(b)	Same
3.2.4	Hearing Aid and Volume Control Phones	4.31.5	Same
3.2.5	Clear Ground or Floor Space	4.31.2	Same
3.2.6	Mounting Height	4.31.3	Same
3.2.7	Protruding Objects	4.4	Same
3.2.8	Controls	4.31.6	Same
3.2.9	Telephone Books	4.31.7	Same
3.2.10	Cord Length	4.31.8	Same
3.2.11	Text Telephones	4.31.9	Same
3.3	**Trash Receptacles**		
3.3.1	Number	--	--
3.3.2	Location	--	--
3.3.3	Height	--	--
3.3.4	Operating Mechanisms	--	--
3.3.5	Exposed Surfaces	--	--
3.3.6	Clear Ground or Floor Space	--	--
3.3.7	Dumpsters	--	--

DG Section	DG Section Title	ADAAG No.	Differences
3.0	**Elements and Spaces in the Recreation Environment (cont.)**		
3.4	**Drinking Fountains**		
3.4.1	Location and Number	4.1.3(10)	ADA requires that 50%, but at least one, be accessible when one or more provided; DG requires one accessible when provided.
3.4.2	Spout Height	4.15.3	Same
3.4.3	Spout Location	4.15.4	Same
3.4.4	Controls and Operating Mechanisms	4.15.5	Same
3.4.5	Clear Ground or Floor Space	4.15.5	Same
3.4.6	Knee Space	4.15.5	Same
3.5	**Hand Pumps and Hydrants**		
3.5.1	Location and Number	--	--
3.5.2	Spout Height	--	--
3.5.3	Spout Location and Pad	--	--
3.5.4	Controls and Operating Mechanisms	--	--
3.5.5	Gratings	--	--
3.6	**Benches**		
3.6.1	Backs and Armrests	--	--
3.6.2	Clear Ground or Floor Space	4.32.2	Same
3.7	**Picnic Tables**		
3.7.1	Number	4.1.3(18)	ADA requires at least 5%, but not less than 1, of fixed and built-in tables be accessible; DG requires for all new picnic tables.
3.7.2	Location	--	--
3.7.3	Seating for People Using Wheelchairs	4.32.2	Same
3.7.4	Table Height	4.32.4	ADA allows a 28"-32" height; DG sets height at 32" max.

DG Section	DG Section Title	ADAAG No.	Differences
3.0	**Elements and Spaces in the Recreation Environment (cont.)**		
3.7.5	Knee Clearances	4.32.3	ADA requires 27" min. height, 19" depth; DG requires 28" min. height, 19" or 24" depth depending on toe clearance.
3.7.6	Clear Area Around Picnic Tables	--	--
3.7.7	Surface and Slope	4.5	Same
3.8	**Fire Rings and Grills**		
3.8.1	Number	--	--
3.8.2	Location	--	--
3.8.3	Clear Ground Space	--	--
3.8.4	Heights	--	--
3.8.5	Operating Mechanisms	4.27.4	Same
3.9	**Tent Pads**		
3.9.1	Number	--	--
3.9.2	Location	--	--
3.9.3	Clear Ground Space	--	--
3.9.4	Surface and Slope	--	--
3.9.5	Transfer Accommodations	--	--
3.10	**Terraces**		
3.10.1	Terrace Width	--	--
3.10.2	Edge Protection	--	--
3.10.3	Surface and Slope	--	--
3.10.4	Access to Terraces	--	--

DG Section	DG Section Title	ADAAG No.	Differences
3.0	**Elements and Spaces in the Recreation Environment (cont.)**		
3.11	**Assembly Areas**		
3.11.1	Number of Wheelchair Seating Positions	4.1.3(19)	Same
3.11.2	Aisle Seats	4.1.3(19)	Same
3.11.3	Location of Accessible Spaces	4.33.3	Same
3.11.4	Position of Accessible Spaces	4.33.3	Same
3.11.5	Design of Wheelchair Spaces	4.33.2	Same
3.11.6	Removable Seats	4.33.3	Same
3.11.7	Companion Seats	4.33.3	Same
3.11.8	Continental Seating	--	--
3.11.9	Access to Seating	4.33.3	Same
3.11.10	Edge Protection	--	--
3.11.11	Surfacing and Slope	4.33.4	Same
3.11.12	Access to Performing Areas	4.33.5	Same
3.11.13	Assistive Listening Systems	4.1.3(19)(b); 4.33.7	ADA specifies when required.
3.12	**Boat Launching Ramps and Boarding Docks**		
3.12.1	Boat Launching Ramps	--	--
3.12.2	Boarding Docks and Gangways	--	--
3.13	**Swimming Areas**		
3.13.1	Ramps into Water	--	--
3.13.2	Stairs into Water	--	--

DG Section	DG Section Title	ADAAG No.	Differences
3.0	**Elements and Spaces in the Recreation Environment (cont.)**		
3.14	**Fishing Facilities**		
3.14.1	Urban/Rural Fishing Stations	--	--
3.14.2	Roaded Natural Fishing Stations	--	--
3.15	**Equestrian Facilities**		
3.15.1	Accessible Transfer Platform	--	--
4.0	**Access to Primary Elements and Spaces (Outdoor Recreation Access Routes)**		
4.1	**Identifying Outdoor Rec. Access Routes**	--	--
4.2	**Number and Location of Outdoor Recreation Access Routes**	4.3.2	Same
4.3	**Alternative Routes**	--	ADA doesn't typically allow alternative routes.
4.4	**Design of Outdoor Recreation Access Routes**		
4.4.1	Width	4.3.3	ADA req.s 36" min.; DG sets min. from 48" to 36" based on ROS.
4.4.2	Sustained Running Slope	4.3.7	ADA sets 1:20 max.; DG sets max. 1:20 to 1:12 based on ROS.
4.4.3	Cross Slope	4.3.7	ADA sets 2% max.; DG allows 3% max.
4.4.4	Passing Spaces	4.3.4	ADA says 200' max. interval; DG sets max. interval based on ROS.
4.4.5	Rest Areas at Passing Spaces	--	--
4.4.6	Small Level Changes	4.5.2	ADA allows 1/4" vertical change, 1/2" with 1:2 bevel; DG varies requirement by ROS setting.
4.4.7	Gratings	4.5.4	Same
4.4.8	Surfacing	4.5.1	Same
4.4.9	Vertical Clearance	4.4.2	Same
4.4.10	Protruding Objects	4.4.1	Same

DG Section	DG Section Title	ADAAG No.	Differences
4.0	**Access to Primary Elements and Spaces (cont.)**		
4.5	**Curb Ramps**		
4.5.1	Location	4.7.1	Same
4.5.2	Clear Width	4.7.3	Same
4.5.3	Slope	4.7.2	Same
4.5.4	Surfacing	4.7.4	Same
4.5.5	Sides of Recessed Curb Ramps	4.7.5	Same
4.5.6	Built-up Curb Ramps	4.7.6	Same
4.5.7	Protection from Obstruction	4.7.8	Same
4.5.8	Curb Ramps at Marked Crossings	4.7.9	Same
4.5.9	Diagonal Curb Ramps	4.7.10	Same
4.5.10	Raised Islands in Crossings	4.7.11	Same
4.6	**Maximum Grade**		"Maximum Grade" in DG is equivalent of "Ramps" in ADA.
4.6.1	Clear Width	4.8.3	ADA req.s 36" min.; DG sets 48" min. in U/R, 36" min. in other.
4.6.2	Slope and Rise	4.8.2	ADA sets 1:12 max. slope (up to 1:8 in retrofits), 30" max. rise; DG sets max. slope 1:12 for 30' (U/R) or 1:10 for 50' (RN & SP).
4.6.3	Cross Slope	4.8.8	ADA sets 2% max.; DG sets 3% max.
4.6.4	Surfacing	4.8.6	Same
4.6.5	Landings	4.8.4	Same
4.6.6	Handrails	4.8.5	ADA requires handrails; DG leaves to discretion of designer.
4.6.7	Edge Protection	4.8.7	ADA requires 2" min. curbs; DG requires curbs to be 4" min.
4.6.8	Drainage	4.8.8	Same

DG Section	DG Section Title	ADAAG No.	Differences
4.0	**Access to Primary Elements and Spaces (cont.)**		
4.7	**Gates, Doors, and Other Entryways**		
4.7.1	Clear Width	4.13.5	Same
4.7.2	Clear Area	4.13.6	Same
4.7.3	Thresholds	4.13.8	Same
4.7.4	Gate and Door Hardware	4.13.9	Same
4.7.5	Closers	4.13.10	Same
4.7.6	Opening Force	4.13.11	Same
4.7.7	Double-leaf Gates and Doors	4.13.4	Same
4.7.8	Revolving Doors and Turnstiles	4.13.2	Same
4.7.9	Doors or Gates in a Series	4.13.7	Same
4.7.10	Automatic and Power-Assisted Doors/Gates	4.13.12	Same
4.8	**Stairs**		
4.8.1	Nosings	4.9.3	Same
4.8.2	Drainage	4.9.6	Same
4.8.3	Treads and Risers	4.9.2	ADA prohibits open risers; DG allows open risers.
4.8.4	Handrails	4.9.4	ADA requires handrails; DG leaves to discretion of designers.
4.9	**Guardrails, Fences, and Other Safety Barriers**		
4.9.1	Location	--	--
4.9.2	Height	--	--
4.9.3	Vertical Members	--	--
4.9.4	Materials	--	--
4.9.5	Structural Strength	--	--
4.9.6	Rotation	--	--

DG Section	DG Section Title	ADAAG No.	Differences
4.0	**Access to Primary Elements and Spaces (cont.)**		
4.10	**Signs**		
4.10.1	Signs at Site Entrances	4.1.2(7)	Same
4.10.2	Signs for Permanent Identification	4.30.1 - 4.30.6	Same
4.10.3	Signs for Direction or Information	4.30.1 - 4.30.6	Same
4.10.4	Symbols of Accessibility	4.30.7	Same, except DG recommends use of Universal Design Symbols to identify level of accessibility on outdoor rec. access routes.
4.10.5	Levels of Illumination	4.30.8	Same
5.0	**Access to Other Recreation Elements and Spaces (Recreation Trails)**		
5.1	**Identifying Accessible Recreation Trails**	--	--
5.2	**Number and Location of Accessible Recreation Trails**	4.3.2	Same; DG addresses issues particular to "recreation trails."
5.3	**Design of Accessible Recreation Trails**		
5.3.1	Clear Width	4.3.3	ADA req.s 36" min.; DG sets min. from 48" to 28" based on ROS.
5.3.2	Sustained Running Slope	4.3.7	ADA req.s 1:20 max.; DG sets max. 1:20 to 1:8 based on ROS.
5.3.3	Cross Slope	4.3.7	ADA sets 1:50 max.; DG sets max. 1:33 to 1:12 based on ROS.
5.3.4	Passing Space	4.3.4	ADA sets 200' max. interval; DG sets max. interval based on ROS.
5.3.5	Rest Areas at Passing Spaces	--	--
5.3.6	Small Level Changes	4.5.2	ADA allows 1/4" vertical change, 1/2" with 1:2 bevel; DG varies requirement by ROS setting.
5.3.7	Gratings	4.5.4	Same
5.3.8	Surfacing	4.5.1	Same
5.3.9	Cattle Guards	--	--
5.3.10	Cross-drains and Water Bars	--	--
5.3.11	Vertical Clearance	4.4.2	Same
5.3.12	Protruding Objects	4.4.1	Same

DG Section	DG Section Title	ADAAG No.	Differences
5.0	Access to Other Recreation Elements and Spaces (cont.)		
5.4	Maximum Grade		"Maximum Grade" in DG is equivalent of "Ramps" in ADA.
5.4.1	Clear Width	4.8.3	ADA req.s 36" min.; DG sets min. from 48" to 28" based on ROS.
5.4.2	Slope and Rise	4.8.2	ADA sets 1:12 max. slope (up to 1:8 in retrofits), 30" max rise; DG sets max. slope 1:10 to 1:5 (based on ROS) for max. of 50 ft.
5.4.3	Cross Slope	4.8.8	ADA sets 1:50 max.; DG sets max. 1:33 to 1:12 based on ROS.
5.4.4	Landings	4.8.4	Same
5.4.5	Edge Protection / Safety Rails	4.8.7	ADA requires 2" min. curbs; DG requires curbs to be 4" min.
5.4.6	Drainage	4.8.8	Same
5.5	Gates and Entry Points	See DG 4.7	--
5.6	Signs	See DG 4.10	--
5.6.1	Trailhead Information	--	--

glossary

Access Aisle. An accessible pedestrian space between elements, such as parking spaces or picnic tables, that provides clearances appropriate for use of the elements.

Accessible. According to ADAAG, the term "accessible" is used to describe a site, building, facility, or portion thereof that complies with the ADA guidelines. According to UFAS, the term "accessible" describes a site, building, facility, or portion thereof that "complies with these standards [UFAS] and . . . can be approached, entered, and used by physically disabled people." In this book, extrapolations have been made to integrate accessibility in outdoor recreation environments. In relation to this effort, the term "accessible" describes a site, building, facility, or portion thereof that (1) complies with the guidelines presented herein and (2) can be approached, entered, and used by people with physical disabilities in accordance with the expectations of accessibility evoked by the setting's location on the Recreation Opportunity Spectrum (ROS).

Accessible Element. An element that complies with the guidelines presented in this book (for example, a sign, bench, or telephone).

Accessible Route. According to ADAAG, an "accessible route" is a continuous unobstructed path connecting accessible elements and spaces. This route must meet the accessibility guidelines for the built environment presented in ADAAG. Due to the complexities of outdoor recreation environments, this book distinguishes between two types of paths that provide "accessible routes" in outdoor recreation settings—*outdoor recreation access routes* and *recreation trails*, both of which are defined in this glossary.

Accessible Space. A space that complies with the guidelines presented in this book (for example, a fishing facility, assembly area, or restroom).

ADAAG. Acronym for the Americans with Disabilities Act Accessibility Guidelines for Buildings and Facilities, published in the Federal Register (vol. 56, no. 144, July 26, 1991).

ANSI. Acronym for American National Standards Institute, a national nongovernmental organization that publishes a wide variety of voluntary standards, including ANSI A117.7, which provided the technical basis for the first accessibility standards adopted by the Federal government and most state governments (*see The First National Standard, page 11*).

ATBCB. Acronym for the Architectural and Transportation Barriers Compliance Board, also known as the Access Board, an independent regulatory agency with authority to enforce Federal accessibility standards, including MGRAD, UFAS, and ADAAG (*see pages 13-16*).

Automatic Door. A door equipped with a power-operated mechanism and controls that open and close the door automatically upon receipt of a momentary actuating signal. The switch that begins the automatic cycle may be a photoelectric device, floor mat, or manual switch (*see power-assisted door*).

Circulation Path. A way of passage from one place to another for pedestrians, including, but not limited to, paths, hallways, courtyards, crosswalks, stairs, and stair landings.

Clear. Unobstructed.

Clear Ground or Floor Space. The minimum unobstructed ground or floor space required to accommodate a single, stationary wheelchair and occupant.

Common Use Area. Refers to those rooms, spaces, or elements that are made available for the use of a restricted group of people (for example, the office area of a ranger station).

Cross Slope. The slope that is perpendicular to the direction of travel (*see running slope*).

Curb Ramp. A short ramp cutting through a curb or built up to it.

Detectable Warning. A standardized surface feature built in or applied to walking surfaces or other elements to warn visually impaired people of hazards on a circulation path.

Difficult Level of Accessibility. The general level of expected access to elements and spaces integrated into lesser developed recreation sites or portions of sites. These are typically in: semi-primitive settings; at sites managed to provide semi-primitive recreation experiences; or at sites managed to provide a difficult level of accessibility as defined by these guidelines.

Easy Level of Accessibility. The general level of expected access to elements and spaces integrated into developed recreation sites or portions of sites. These are typically in: urban/rural settings; at sites managed to provide urban/rural recreation experiences; or at sites managed to provide an easy level of accessibility as defined by these guidelines.

Egress, Means of. A continuous and unobstructed way of exit travel from any point in a building or facility to a public way. A means of egress comprises vertical and horizontal travel and may include intervening room spaces, doorways, corridors, passageways, balconies, ramps, stairs, enclosures, lobbies, horizontal exits, courts, and yards. An accessible means of egress is one that complies with these guidelines and does not include stairs, steps, or escalators.

Element. An architectural or mechanical component of a space or site, e.g., telephone, curb ramp, door, drinking fountain, picnic table, or fire ring.

Entrance. Any access point to a site or building used for the purpose of entering. An entrance includes the approach path, any vertical access leading to an entrance platform and the entrance platform itself if provided, the entry gate or door if provided, and the hardware of the entry gate or door.

Facility. All or any portion of buildings, structures, site improvements, complexes, equipment, roads, walks, passageways, parking lots, or other real or personal property located on a site.

Marked Crossing. A crosswalk or other identified path intended for pedestrian use in crossing a vehicular way.

MGRAD. Acronym for Minimum Guidelines and Requirements for Accessible Design (*see pages 13-14*).

Moderate Level of Accessibility. The general level of expected access to elements and spaces integrated into moderately developed recreation sites or portions of sites. These are typically in: roaded natural settings; at sites managed to provide roaded natural recreation experiences; or at sites managed to provide a moderate level of accessibility as defined by these guidelines.

Most Difficult Level of Accessibility. The general level of expected access to elements and spaces integrated into undeveloped recreation sites or portions of sites. These are typically in: primitive settings; at sites managed to provide primitive recreation experiences; or at sites managed to provide the most difficult level of accessibility as defined by these guidelines.

Operable Part. A part of a piece of equipment or appliance used to insert or withdraw objects, or to activate, deactivate, or adjust the equipment or appliance (for example, coin slot, pushbutton, handle).

Outdoor Recreation Access Route. A path that connects the primary accessible elements and spaces of a recreation site, including accessible parking spaces and site entrances. Such paths are typically less than 1/4-mile in (see recreation trails). Paths that provide access to major structures, such as visitor centers and office complexes, should be provided by access routes that meet ADAAG requirements (ADAAG 4.3).

Power-Assisted Door. A door used for human passage with a mechanism that helps to open the door, or relieves the opening resistance of a door, upon the activation of a switch or a continued force applied to the door itself.

Primitive Recreation Setting. An undeveloped recreation area in which structural modifications are rare, preservation of the natural environment is paramount, and visitors expect the most difficult level of accessibility (see Chapter II, *The Recreation Opportunity Spectrum*).

Public Use Area. Describes interior or exterior rooms or spaces that are made available to the general public (for example, the visitor area of a ranger station). Public use may be provided at a site or facility that is privately or publicly owned.

Ramp. A walking surface in a developed setting that has a running slope greater than 1:20. In the less developed environment of outdoor recreation sites, ramp functions are typically accomplished via the maximum grade segments of outdoor recreation access routes and recreation trails.

Recreation Opportunity Spectrum (ROS). Land use management taxonomy based on a development scale and used by the USDA Forest Service as outlined in the *ROS Primer Field Guide* (USDA Forest Service 1990) and Chapter II of this guide.

Recreation Trail. A path that connects the entrances and/or developed areas of a recreation site with the site's lesser-developed elements and spaces. Such paths are typically 1/4-mile or more in length and serve as part of the recreation experience itself (see outdoor recreation access routes). Paths that provide access to major structures, such as visitor centers and office complexes, should be provided by access routes that meet ADAAG requirements (ADAAG 4.3).

Roaded Natural Recreation Setting. A moderately developed recreation area in which structural modifications have been made but are not extensive, and such modifications emphasize the use of natural materials and preservation of natural features. Visitors expect a moderate level of accessibility (see Chapter II, *The Recreation Opportunity Spectrum*).

Running Slope. The slope that is parallel to the direction of travel (see cross slope).

Semi–Primitive Recreation Setting. A mostly undeveloped recreation area in which structural modifications are few, preservation of the natural environment is of high priority, and visitors expect a difficult level of accessibility (see Chapter II, *The Recreation Opportunity Spectrum*).

Signage. Displayed verbal, symbolic, tactile, and pictorial information.

Site. A parcel of land bounded by a property line or a designated portion of a public right-of-way.

Space. A definable area, e.g., a restroom, assembly area, campsite, or swimming area.

Tactile. Describes an object that can be perceived using the sense of touch.

Text Telephone. Machinery or equipment that employs interactive graphic (i.e., typed) communications through the transmission of coded signals across the standard telephone network. Text telephones can include, for example, computers or devices known as TTY's (text teletypes, also referred to as TDD's, telecommunication display devices or telecommunication devices for deaf persons).

UFAS. Acronym for the Uniform Federal Accessibility Standards (*see pages 13-16*).

Urban/Rural Recreation Setting. A developed recreation area in which there are significant structural modifications and accessibility to recreation elements and spaces is of high priority. Visitors expect an easy level of accessibility (see Chapter II, *The Recreation Opportunity Spectrum*).

USDA. Acronym for the United States Department of Agriculture.

Vehicular Way. A route intended for vehicular traffic, such as a street, driveway, or parking lot.

references

American National Standards Institute (ANSI) A117.a–1980. Specifications for Making Buildings and Facilities Accessible to and Usable by Physically Handicapped People. New York: ANSI.

American Society for Testing and Materials (ASTM). F1292. *Standard Specification for Impact-Attenuation of Surface Systems Under and Around Playground Equipment.* Philadelphia: ASTM.

Architectural and Transportation Barriers Compliance Board (ATBCB). 1988a. *Uniform Federal Accessibility Standards (UFAS).* Washington, DC: U.S. Architectural and Transportation Barriers Compliance Board.

———. 1988b. *Access to Outdoor Recreation Planning and Design: A Technical Paper of the Architectural and Transportation Barriers Compliance Board.* Prepared by the Federal Government Working Group on Access to Recreation, David C. Park, Chairman. Unpublished draft. Washington, DC.

———. 1991. *Americans with Disabilities Act: Accessibility Guidelines for Buildings and Facilities (ADAAG).* Washington, D.C.: U.S. Architectural and Transportation Barriers Compliance Board.

Ballantyne, Duncan S. 1983. *Accommodation of Disabled Visitors at Historic Sites in the National Park Service.* Washington, DC: USDI National Park Service, Cultural Resources Management Division, Park Historic Architecture Division.

Barrier Free Environments, Inc. 1991. *UFAS Retrofit Manual.* Washington DC: U.S. Architectural and Transportation Barriers Compliance Board.

Beneficial Designs, Inc. 1993. "Problems with Existing Accessibility Guidelines." Memo dated October 22, 1993. Santa Cruz, CA.

Bunin, N., Jasperse, D. and Cooper, S. 1980. *A Guide to Designing Accessible Outdoor Recreation Facilities.* Washington, DC: USDI Heritage Conservation and Recreation Service (Lake Central Regional Office, Ann Arbor, MI).

Bureau of Reclamation (BOR). No date. *Planning for Accessibility: Handbook*. Boise, ID: USDI Bureau of Reclamation, Pacific Northwest Regional Office.

Center for Accessible Housing (CAH). 1992. *Accessibility Standards for Children's Environments*. Final Technical Report to the Architectural and Transportation Barriers Compliance Board (Contract #QA90003001). Washington, DC.

Clark R. N., and Stankey G. H. 1979. *The Recreation Opportunity Spectrum: A Framework for Planning, Management, and Research*. Portland, OR: USDA Forest Service, Pacific Northwest Forest and Range Experiment Station.

Compton, D. M. 1985. The status of recreation participation by disabled persons in America. In *International Forum: Leisure, Sports, Cultural Arts, and Employment for Persons with Disabilities*, edited by Kelley, J. D. Geneva: World Health Organization.

Consumer Product Safety Commission (CPSC). 1991. *Handbook for Public Playground Safety*. Washington, DC: U.S. Government Printing Office.

Driver, B. L., and Brown P. J. 1978. *The Opportunity Spectrum Concept and Behavior Information in Outdoor Recreation Resource Supply Inventories: A Rationale*. Fort Collins, CO: USDA Forest Service, Rocky Mountain Forest and Range Experiment Station.

Gentle E. A., and Taylor J. K. 1977. *Images, Words, and Identity*. East Lansing, MI: Michigan State University.

Goldsmith, S. 1967. *Designing for the Disabled*. New York: McGraw-Hill.

Goltsman, S., Gilbert, T. and Wohlford, S. 1993. *The Accessibility Checklist: An Evaluation System for Buildings and Outdoor Settings*. Second Edition. Berkeley, CA: MIG Communications.

Harris, C. W., and Fishbeck, G. M. No date. Outdoor Access Standards. In Sasaki, H., Harris, C. W., and Dines, N.T. *Time Saver Standards for Landscape Architecture: Design and Construction Data*. New York: McGraw Hill.

Institute of Medicine. 1991. *Disability in America: Toward a National Agenda for Prevention; Summary and Recommendations*. Andrew Pope and Alvin Tarlov, editors. Washington, DC: National Academy Press.

Jones, D. K. 1992. The ambiguities of the ADA. In Identity: *The International Magazine of Signs & Corporate Graphics*, Spring 1992. Cincinnati, OH: ST Publications Inc.

Kerpen, S. M.; et al. 1980. Barrier free communities: guides for planning and design. Washington, DC: United States Department of Housing and Urban Development.

Kidd, B. J., and Clark R. 1982. *Outdoor Access for All: A Guide to Designing Accessible Outdoor Recreation Facilities*. Melbourne: Department of Youth, Sport and Recreation.

Kraus, L. E, and Stoddard, S. 1989. *Chartbook on Disability in the United States*. Washington, DC: National Institute on Disability and Rehabilitation Research.

Lais, McAvoy, and Fredrickson. 1992. *Wilderness Accessibility for People with Disabilities: A Report to the President and the Congress of the U.S. on Section 507(a) of the ADA*. Washington, DC: National Council on Disability.

LaPlante, M. P. 1988. *Data on Disability from the National Health Interview Survey, 1983-1985: An InfoUse Report*. Washington, DC: U.S. National Institute on Disability and Rehabilitation Research.

Lusher, R. H. 1989. A historical overview of the development of accessibility standards and laws. In *Design*, Winter 1989. Washington, DC: USDI National Park Service and National Recreation and Park Association.

Marshall, R. 1933. The Forest for Recreation. In *A National Plan for American Forestry: A Report Prepared by the Forest Service in Response to Senate Resolution 175 (72nd Congress)*. Washington, DC: U.S. Government Printing Office.

Moore, R., Goltsman, S. and Iacofano, D. (eds.). 1992. *Play For All Guidelines: Planning, Design and Management of Outdoor Play Settings for All Children*. Second Edition. Berkeley, CA: MIG Communications.

Mullins, G. W., and Wright, P. A. 1991. Public area recreation visitor survey: recreation participation by special populations. Unpublished draft. Ohio State University (Columbus, Ohio) and USDI National Park Service.

National Center on Accessibility. Unpublished. *Handbook on Universal Interpretation* (unpublished manuscript). Bloomington, IN.

Nordhaus, R. S., Kantrowitz, M., and Siembieda, W. J. 1984. *Accessible Fishing: A Planning Handbook*. Albuquerque, NM: New Mexico Natural Resources Department, Development Division.

Panero J., and Zelnik M. 1979. *Human Dimension and Interior Space: A Source Book of Design Defense Standards*. New York: Whitney Library of Design.

Park, D. C. 1989. What is accessibility? In *Design*, Spring 1989. Washington, DC: USDI National Park Service and National Recreation and Park Association.

Reis, Michael L. 1991. *Design Standards to Accommodate People with Disabilities in Park and Open Space Design*. University of Wisconsin–Extension.

Stankey, G. H. 1977. Some Social Concepts for Outdoor Recreation Planning. In *Outdoor Recreation: Advances in Application of Economics*. Washington DC: USDA Forest Service

Steinfeld, Edward et al. 1978. *Access to the Built Environment: A Review of Literature*. Washington, DC: United States Department of Housing and Urban Development.

USDA Forest Service. 1982. *ROS Users Guide.* Washington, DC: USDA Forest Service.

———. 1990. *ROS Primer Field Guide.* R6-REC-021-90. Portland, OR: USDA Forest Service.

———. 1991 (amended). *Trails Management Handbook* (FSH 2309.18). Washington, DC.

USDI National Park Service. 1990. *Standards for Rehabilitation of Historic Properties.* Developed by the National Park Service Preservation Assistance Division. Washington, DC: Secretary of the Interior.

———. 1992. *Preserving the Past and Making It Accessible for People with Disabilities.* A pamphlet published by the National Park Service, Cultural Resources Preservation Assistance Division. Washington, DC.

U.S. Department of Justice, Civil Rights Division. 1992a. *The Americans with Disabilities Act: Title II Technical Assistance Manual.* Washington, DC.

———. 1992b. *The Americans with Disabilities Act: Title III Technical Assistance Manual.* Washington, DC.

Wagner, J. Alan. 1966. *Campgrounds for Many Tastes.* USDA Forest Service paper. Ogden, UT: Intermountain Forest and Range Experiments Station.

Wilson, Keith. 1991. *Handbook for the Design of Barrier-Free Recreational Boating and Fishing Facilities.* Washington, DC: States Organization for Boating Access.

Wisconsin 1991. *See* Reis, Michael L.

Wolf, P. M. and Lajoie, L. No date. *Access to Parks: Guidelines.* Unpublished manuscript. State of California Department of Parks and Recreation.

World Health Organization. 1980. International Classification of Impairments, Disabilities, and Handicaps. Geneva.

index